DATE DUE

NOV 27 1993		
DEC 0 8 1995		
NOV 27 2003		
DISCARDED		

Internati
the

DAN

D0225173

Princeton Studies on the Near East

L. CARL BROWN

———— ✻ ————

International Politics and the Middle East

OLD RULES,
DANGEROUS GAME

Princeton University Press

Copyright © 1984 by Princeton University Press
Published by Princeton University Press, 41 William Street,
Princeton, New Jersey 08540

All Rights Reserved
Library of Congress Cataloging in Publication Data will
be found on the last printed page of this book

ISBN 0-691-05410-X

ISBN 0-691-10159-0 (Pbk.)

This book has been composed in Linotron Galliard

Printed in the United States of America by
Princeton University Press
Princeton, New Jersey

9 8 7 6 5 4

PREFACE

THE IDEA for this book was born on 6 October 1973 with the outbreak of the Ramadan or Yom Kippur War. At that time I had been with my family in Cairo for less than a month, intent on spending a sabbatical year engaged in research on topics of nineteenth-century Egyptian history. The stirring events beginning on 6 October quickly provoked a new research interest.

Or perhaps more accurately, my involvement in that war resolved an intellectual conflict that I had been unconsciously wrestling with ever since 1953, when I began a career devoted to the study of the modern Middle East. Like most of my generation of academicians specializing in Middle Eastern studies, I rejected the old scholarly and diplomatic tradition that regarded the Middle East as an arena of great power confrontation. The Middle East, I insisted, deserves attention in itself and for its own distinctive characteristics. Accordingly, I turned my back on anything smacking of Middle Eastern diplomatic history or international relations lest I, too, help keep alive the Western tendency to depict the Middle East as a stage on which all the really important actors are outsiders.

Of course, I did not completely ignore the fateful intertwining of East and West in my earlier studies, but I did attempt to keep the diplomatic dimension muted by concentrating on other themes. When, however, I witnessed a major Middle Eastern political leader start a risky war against a militarily stronger opponent, not so much in hope of victory but to provoke international intervention that might result in eventual gains for his country, I came to accept explicitly what I had long sensed implicitly: Middle Eastern political leaders have been taking similar actions for almost two centuries. And the outside powers have been engaged for just as long in diplomatic dances similar to what ensued following 6 October.

Thereafter, I could no longer justify avoiding modern Middle Eastern international relations. For better or worse, as I

v

PREFACE

see it, international relations has been the matrix of modern
Middle Eastern history. The challenge was to provide the proper
mix of old-fashioned, Eastern Question history with new style
study of the modern Middle East as important in its own
right. This book is my suggested answer to that challenge.

I am pleased to acknowledge the support of many different
institutions and individuals over the past decade. The American University in Cairo graciously granted me housing, hos-
pitality, and the stimulation of contact with its faculty and
students during the academic year 1973-1974. I am especially
grateful for these many kindnesses. The John Simon Guggen-
heim Memorial Foundation granted me a fellowship on the
basis of an entirely different subject proposal. May the above
lines and the present book serve as explanation and thanks. As
with so many academicians in my field I, too, have been helped
by the U.S. Fulbright-Hays Program, which has been
throughout the years a boon to the development of non-Western area studies. The Hoover Institution on War, Revolution
and Peace provided two summer research grants. I am especially grateful to Peter Duignan, director of the Africa and
Middle Eastern Programs, for making this possible and for his
support and encouragement in many other ways as well.

Support from my own university has been generous, including a summer research grant from Princeton University's
Center of International Studies and several different forms of
assistance from both the Program in Near Eastern Studies and
the Department of Near Eastern Studies.

Fouad Ajami, William Cleveland, David Gordon, and Norman Itzkowitz all offered helpful comments on this book at
different stages.

The entire staff of Near Eastern Studies at Princeton's Jones
Hall has at one time or another been involved in helping see
this book to publication. I wish to acknowledge my thanks to
each of them: Mary Craparotta, Grace Edelman, Judy Gross,
and Dorothy Rothbard.

It has been a pleasure working with Miriam Brokaw and
Margaret Case of Princeton University Press.

L.C.B.

vi

TABLE OF CONTENTS

CONTENTS

CONTENTS

LIST OF ILLUSTRATIONS

TABLES

INTRODUCTION

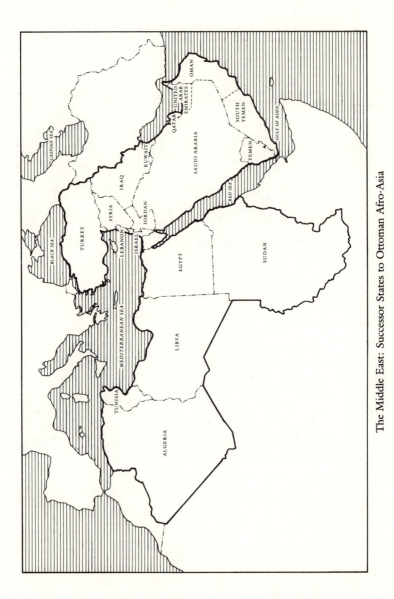

The Middle East: Successor States to Ottoman Afro-Asia

INTRODUCTION

INTERNATIONAL politics and diplomacy in the Middle East reveal a remarkable coherence and regularity. Such an argument would seem to challenge the received wisdom. The Middle Eastern diplomatic scene is usually summed up by words such as irrational, erratic, or chaotic. This book, however, seeks to show that the confused international politics of the Middle East can be reduced to a discernible pattern.

Of course, Middle Eastern international relations are labyrinthine in their complexity, just as they are dangerously volatile. The Middle East is so intimately intertwined with the wider world that the region's political problems are perilously likely to involve outsiders—as they have done over the past years. Some speak darkly of a Middle Eastern Sarajevo dragging all into a Third World War. Even the more sanguine accept the spillover potential of Middle Eastern politics.

It is decidedly *not* the thesis of this book to challenge these bleak appraisals. Present political trends in the Middle East bode ill for the people of the region and are threatening to the rest of the world. All the more reason, then, to study their underlying structure.

The key to understanding the international politics of the Middle East can be briefly stated: For roughly the last two centuries the Middle East has been more consistently and more thoroughly ensnarled in great power politics than any other part of the non-Western world. This distinctive political experience continuing from generation to generation has left its mark on Middle Eastern political attitudes and actions. Other parts of the world have been at one time or another more severely buffeted by an imperial power, but no area has remained so unremittingly caught up in multilateral great power politics.

The Indian subcontinent, for example, was long dominated

3

by a single great power, Britain, and to that extent India, while no doubt in the clutches of an outside force, was largely insulated from multilateral great power politics. The modern Middle East has never been controlled by a single great power.

China, like the Middle East, was long at the mercy of competing great powers, but China in this century regained its political unity. Ever since the Ottoman Empire became "the sick man of Europe," overall political unity, or even partial unity, has eluded the Middle East.

Most of Black Africa, like most of the Middle East, was gobbled up by different European imperial powers. Later, the states of the two regions achieved independence during roughly the same time period. The Western imperial period in Black Africa, however, created territorial boundaries and bureaucratic states where none had existed previously. In the Middle East the imperial powers operated generally within the framework of familiar territorial divisions and adapted an equally familiar tradition of centralized bureaucratic rule.

To a large extent Western imperialism in Africa created new political structures. In the Middle East, Western imperialism blended in with and built on existing political structures. In Black Africa the different imperial powers entered into intensive bilateral relations with their several colonies. The imperial powers came, destroyed, built, and left. In the Middle East the imperial period was (with rare exceptions, such as Algeria) more nearly a mutation of the earlier multilateral great power involvement in regional politics. In the Middle East the dominant West came earlier and has stayed later than in Black Africa.

The entire world has been shaken and shaped by the West in modern times, but nowhere has the political dimension of that fateful confrontation been more thorough and more consistent than in the Middle East. It is in this sense that the Middle East is the most penetrated international relations subsystem in today's world. The idea of a penetrated political system, as used in this book, is not simply a measure of the intensity of outside political or economic domination. Many countries and regions, for example, have experienced a longer, more violent, or more disruptive period of outside domination than the Middle East.

Some parts of the world, such as the Muslim areas of the Soviet Union, have been, or—more cautiously stated—are being absorbed into the conquering state's political system. In this case the process (barring the unlikely prospect of a future decolonization) is better described as absorption, not penetration.

In other areas the outside impact was at one time more intensive than what the Middle East endured, but such confrontation was not sustained. In these cases, the Western presence challenged and often largely destroyed the indigenous political systems, but later the West departed or at least slackened its pressure. This, too, is not the same as penetration.

A penetrated political system is one that is neither effectively absorbed by the outside challenger nor later released from the outsider's smothering embrace. A penetrated system exists in continuous confrontation with a dominant outside political system. The degree of penetration is perhaps best measured by the extent to which differences between local, national, regional, and international politics become blurred. That is, the politics of a thoroughly penetrated society is not adequately explained—even at the local level—without reference to the influence of the intrusive outside system.

The Middle Eastern political culture has not just been shaped by intrusive Western influences in modern times. That is a trivial truth since the same can be said about any part of the world. Rather, the Middle East has been so continuously interlocked politically with the West as to have become almost an appendage of the Western power system (which has always included Russia and now extends to the United States as well).

The Eastern Question Roots of Middle Eastern Politics. This distinctive, penetrated Middle Eastern political system has its roots in "the Eastern Question," the term given to that extended period from the late eighteenth century until just after the First World War, during which European powers slowly picked the Ottoman Empire to pieces.

A CONSULTATION ABOUT THE STATE OF TURKEY.

1. In the period of the Eastern Question, the once-feared enemy
had become the sick man of Europe (*Punch*, 1853).

The Eastern Question soon developed into an elaborate, multiplayer diplomatic game involving many different European states. Involved also on the other side were many different Middle Eastern "states" or veritable states or would-be states (these distinctions will be elaborated in due course).

Continuing for generation after generation the Eastern Question game itself created a particular attitude toward politics and diplomacy among the players, not just those from the Middle East but those representing the European state system involved in Eastern Question diplomacy as well. This produced the modern Middle Eastern pattern of politics.

This pattern of politics did not, however, come to an end with the final dismemberment of the Ottoman Empire after the First World War. The Eastern Question still exists.

That is to say, the Eastern Question in its conventional usage (Europe's slow sundering of the Ottoman Empire) provides the key to understanding a political culture that still characterizes the Middle East.

The Eastern Question at the same time may appropriately be used in a larger sense that embraces the conventional usage but goes beyond it—the Eastern Question as a two centuries old political game with its many elaborate rules. The game is still being played in the Middle East.

Such then, is the Eastern Question system as the term is to be used throughout this book.

Where is the Middle East? This idea of a distinctive Middle Eastern approach to politics and diplomacy growing out of the Eastern Question historical experience also serves to delimit the time and territory covered in this book.

The Middle East has always been defined in confusing and contradictory ways. Here one more definition is advanced, not with the claim that it resolves earlier confusions (it does not), but to give the subject of this book greater coherence. The Middle East in this book is composed of the Afro-Asian lands of the former Ottoman Empire.

In present-day terms the Middle East so defined embraces the entire Arab world (except Morocco and Mauritania), Israel and Turkey. Such a definition of the Middle East departs from many others by including most of North Africa and by excluding Iran. This offers certain advantages in more explicitly linking the land and peoples considered to the basic themes of the book.

For example, a Middle East so defined takes in the entire area of Afro-Asia that once formed part of the Ottoman political world, treating in a comparative framework all the lands of Ottoman Afro-Asia in all their variety and changeability:

1. Those directly administered from Istanbul
2. Those nominally part of the Empire but autonomous in fact (Algeria until 1830, Tripolitania until 1835, Tunisia until 1881, Egypt until 1882)
3. Those lost at different times to foreign control but not abandoned *de jure* (Algeria, Tunisia, Egypt, Anglo-Egyptian Sudan, Libya)
4. Those under a form of European stewardship (as Lebanon from the 1840s)
5. Those never effectively absorbed into the Empire but existing within the Ottoman political world (most of the Arabian peninsula)

By directing attention to these many different examples of varying size and juridical status we can more effectively test the notion of a pervasive Eastern Question. If a single international relations system can be shown to have characterized polities as different as the multinational central Ottoman Empire and tiny Tunisia, then the idea of an Eastern Question system has explanatory value.

Equally, treating the many different political actors in the Ottoman political world during the period of the conventional Eastern Question until the final collapse of the Ottoman Empire sets the stage for a comparative study of the many different Afro-Asian successor states to the Ottoman Empire.

To present the Middle East as the Afro-Asian lands of the former Ottoman Empire also gives the region an identity established not in terms of outsiders' interests but by an indigenous standard, that of having shared for centuries a common political culture.

This common bond of Ottoman political culture is emphasized because unconsciously held Western categories of thought tend to slight it. The West is accustomed to think in terms of nationalities as English, French or German. Thus Westerners consistently have referred to Ottomans as Turks.[1] Today, the West sees the Middle East as made up of Arabs, Turks, Persians, and Israelis.

Alternatively, recent events have for a time dusted off an even older Western proclivity to see the Middle East as the world of Islam.[2] This conceptual confusion between viewing the Middle East as made up of linguistic nationalities and classifying Middle Easterners according to religion can be avoided. One need only recall the Ottoman legacy. For centuries Middle Easterners received their political socialization within a multireligious, multinational, multilingual empire.

The Ottoman Empire, which survived into the third decade of this century, formed one of the most extensive and long-lived imperial systems ever organized. Its earliest beginnings go back to the last years of the thirteenth century. The capture of Constantinople in 1453 (almost a half-century before Columbus discovered America) from the truncated remnant of the Byzantine Empire symbolized the Ottoman arrival to full imperial status. By that time the Ottomans had inherited and built upon imperial traditions of the Byzantines, the Seljuks and the Abbasids.

Throughout the sixteenth century the Ottomans brought most of the Arab world within their orbit. Thereafter, the Ottoman sultans, with their impressive military machine and state bureaucracy, ruled over all northern Africa to the borders of Morocco, the Fertile Crescent, and parts of Arabia, Anatolia, the Crimea, and southeastern Europe as far north as the present states of Rumania and Hungary.

Significant losses of European portions of the vast Ottoman

---

[1] To a cultivated Ottoman the word "Turk" carried the connotation of "bumpkin." Eventually, as often happens in politics, the label applied demeaningly by one's enemies came to be warmly embraced. Turkish nationalism was the child not just of Ataturk's bold actions but also of inadvertent Western "turkification" since at least the beginning of the Eastern Question.

[2] In fact, only about one-fourth of the world's Muslims live in the Middle East as here defined.

Empire began, it is true, as early as 1699; and, as will be shown, after 1774 the steady dismemberment of the empire became the rule. Even so, all of the Afro-Asian lands that became part of the Ottoman Empire experienced Ottoman rule for at least three centuries, appreciable parts of the empire for more nearly four centuries, and the Anatolian heartland for over five centuries. During this long time span similar political institutions (army, bureaucracy, taxation system, judiciary, local governance, relations between imperial center and the different religious communities, management of tribes) shaped the political attitudes of all peoples involved, rulers and ruled.

For all these reasons to define the Middle East as the Afro-Asian lands of the former Ottoman Empire seems appropriate. This choice of the territory to be covered is not, however, totally satisfactory. For example, throughout the nineteenth century, the Ottoman Balkans figured prominently in Eastern Question diplomacy. To trace the evolution of the Eastern Question system without reference to the Balkans would be impossible. Yet, the workings of geography and history have—especially since the First World War—moved the former Ottoman lands of southeastern Europe more into a European international relations system.

For that reason it seems justified in this book to treat Balkan developments only to the extent that they clarify the growth and maturation of a distinctive Middle Eastern international relations system. This means that the Balkan countries are given less attention in general, usually leave the stage after achieving independence, and are not considered at all after the end of the Ottoman Empire.

Even this approach leaves several loose ends. For example, the Greek-Turkish dispute over Cyprus is not discussed, but this issue—and the passion it raises—can be fully understood only in the context of the Ottoman and Eastern Question legacy that Greece and Turkey share. Indeed, to assert, as this book does, that Turkish policy to this day can be illuminated by reference to that Ottoman and Eastern Question past, while implying that Greece's modern political legacy is different or that Greece belongs to a different international relations system, is misleading. The Cyprus dispute is a classic case of the continuing Eastern Question system.

Nor is the exclusion of Iran and Morocco from other than passing consideration above reproach. These two neighboring Muslim political systems would be especially appropriate cases for testing the relative importance of the Ottoman legacy (which they did not share) as opposed to the intrusive Western presence in modern times (which they all shared in roughly equal intensity) in creating a special attitude toward international politics.

To include Iran and Morocco or to give more attention to the Balkans would, however, stretch too far an already broadly conceived subject. Restricting attention to the Afro-Asian lands that experienced the Ottoman approach to politics seems to offer the most advantages with the fewest drawbacks.

This book is not a narrative account of Middle Eastern international relations over the past two centuries. Only enough historical background to explain the persistent Eastern Question system is given. The scope and quantity of historical background presented are governed by the goals of:

1. Tracing the rise and development of the Eastern Question system
2. Demonstrating the persistent pattern characteristic of this system
3. Explaining why the system survives in the face of many radical changes.

At the same time an effort has been made to include enough historical detail to enable the reader readily to situate the argument. If the book succeeds in its purpose, readers will be tempted to test the over-all explanatory theory advanced against specific Middle Eastern diplomatic issues—past or present. A bibliographical essay has been added with such interests in mind.

While not attempting a narrative diplomatic history from the earliest beginnings of the Eastern Question to the present day, this book does adhere in part to a chronological ap-

"I lost track . . . is it their turn to retaliate or ours?"

2. Reactive politics and a concern with short-term tactics have long
characterized Middle Eastern international relations (By permission of
Wayne Stayskal, *The Chicago Tribune*, 1981).

proach. Part One treats the conventional period of the Eastern
Question from the late eighteenth century to the fall of the
Ottoman Empire after the First World War, and Part Two
takes the story from immediately after the First World War to
the present. Both Parts One and Two offer a combined chronological and thematic treatment.

In both Parts One and Two many of the same issues are
studied from the different perspectives of different actors. For
example, Part One at times examines the unfolding Eastern
Question from the viewpoint of (1) the great powers, (2) old-
style regional contenders for power, (3) emerging national
liberation movements, (4) Muslim religio-political challenges,
and (5) the principal established Middle Eastern state systems—the central Ottoman Empire, Egypt and Tunisia.

In the same vein, Part Two, while addressing a number of
subjects, concentrates on two: (1) a demonstration that the
colonial period of Middle Eastern history represented less a
sharp break with the past than a continuation of Eastern
Question politics, with special attention to the Fertile Cres-

cent, and (2) a study of two different efforts to organize the Middle East in this century, Britain's Arab policy and pan-Arabism culminating in the ambitious drive to unity under Egypt's Nasser.

Many of these separate subjects in Parts One and Two are treated chronologically. For example, the early beginnings of the Eastern Question are traced in time. Much the same can be said for the evolution of Britain's Ottoman policy, Britain's later Arab policy, Nasserist Arabism, or the entry of the United States into Middle Eastern politics.

Treatment of other issues studied in Parts One and Two telescopes historical developments and concentrates on underlying patterns. An example of this approach is the brief discussion in Part One entitled "The Pattern of National Liberation Movements."

Part Three offers a different approach, that of more explicitly comparing nineteenth-century examples of Eastern Question diplomacy with those of the twentieth century in order to demonstrate the systemic continuity. One major theme— "The Myth of the Great Power Puppeteer and Regional Puppets"—is considered in detail. This is followed by several other examples of nineteenth- and twentieth-century Eastern Question systemic continuity presented in summary form.

The short conclusion asks what relevance the continued existence of a distinctive Eastern Question system has today. In these final pages an effort is made to be policy-relevant without becoming policy-oriented. The distinction is important. A policy-oriented conclusion would move toward suggesting what one or more players in the continuing Eastern Question game should do. A policy-relevant conclusion, as in this book, attempts to define the limits of the possible. The former suggests a strategy for one or more of the players. The latter is concerned only to explain the game and the standings of the players.

Playing the Game. The above lines evoke another point. Words such as system, pattern, political culture, strategy, game and players are used constantly throughout the book. Social scientists who employ such words usually take pains to give them precise definition. In this book they are used in a much more free-wheeling fashion.

Why then are such words adopted? Two reasons are suggested. One should already be obvious, the other less so. Since the organizing theme of this book is that a distinctive system of international politics began to emerge in the Middle East some two centuries ago and has proved to be strikingly durable, these words (pattern, system, game, and at times political culture,[3] or—a suggested neologism—diplomatic culture) are needed to remind the reader just what is being tested and interpreted. This is the obvious reason.

The less obvious reason is the author's belief that games theory terminology offers a way to greater objectivity in the study of diplomatic history and international relations. These are scholarly disciplines that deal with life-and-death issues, with war and peace. The fate of one's own nation or religion or way of life (if not all three) is seen as hanging in the balance. Even times long past are easily endowed with a certain gravity when the fortunes of states are considered. How easy it becomes, then, for a scholar to falter in objectively appraising all the parties.

If, however, the confrontation is presented in the metaphor of a poker game, with players holding different cards and having different stakes to bet, then value judgments cannot so easily slip into the discussion.

[3] "Political culture" was a term coined by Gabriel Almond. "Every political system," he asserted in his seminal article of 1956, "is embedded in a particular pattern of orientations to political actions. I have found it useful to refer to this as the political culture." See his "Comparative Political Systems," *The Journal of Politics* 18 (August 1956), reprinted in his *Political Development: Essays in Heuristic Theory* (Boston, 1970). A more elaborate statement of political culture is found in Gabriel Almond and Sidney Verba, *The Civic Culture* (Princeton University Press, 1963), especially Chapter One, "An Approach to Political Culture." The suggested neologism "diplomatic culture" is used to emphasize the international (indeed, inter-political culture) dimension. That is, the "pattern of orientations to political action" of those involved in Eastern Question politics are, of course, rooted in the Middle Eastern political culture, but they transcend that one political culture.

Likewise, the diplomatic historian's tendency to be lulled by the stately prose of diplomatic dispatches or the presumed majesty of high public office into presenting an overly prettied up account is neatly checked by breezy games theory jargon. An overly laudatory (or overly belittling) portrait of, say, Dulles or Nasser is difficult to sustain when the issues are restated in terms of games and players.

By way of apology to serious students of games theory, this use of their lexicon in no way pretends to be a contribution to games theory, as such. Who, for example, ever heard of games theory without mathematics? Perhaps the serendipitous argument will suffice: Many a good theory spawns quite unexpected results.

This book suggests that Middle Eastern international relations can be expressed in terms of a game that has developed its own rules. The game—like all such political games—was not simply created one fine day and played according to fixed rules thereafter. Rather, the game itself developed slowly over time, as will be explained in Part One. The game, like all games, has been subjected to certain changes of rules from time to time, as will be noted throughout the book.

Having said this, we must admit that the idea of a game is only a metaphor. Political games never have, in the eyes of participants or observers, the same explicitly recognized, consciously obeyed rules as would be found in, for example, a season of football games or the neighborhood weekly poker games. The games metaphor is useful only if—without violence to the facts—it explains recurring behavior on the part of otherwise disparate groups. The games metaphor is to be accepted only to the extent that it effectively organizes and interprets the complex political activity under study better than other metaphors, better than other explanatory patterns.

When in the analysis of international politics it is found that other important factors do change over time (e.g., political elites, economic organization, territorial boundaries), but that many basic rules of political interaction remain the same, then the games metaphor seems appropriate. That such has been

15

the case for Middle Eastern international relations over the past two centuries will be argued throughout this book.

In the process—keeping in mind the idea of political games as metaphors justified only by their explanatory value—the rules characterizing the Eastern Question game will be examined in the context of special diplomatic events. A brief statement of these rules—presented here as if from a rulebook without reference to origins and changes over time—may serve as a useful introduction.

The Rules of the Eastern Question Game. The durable international relations game played in the Middle East since at least the early nineteenth century is characterized by the following rules:

1. Many different regional and extra-regional political players combine and divide in shifting patterns of alliances.
2. The patterns of alliance making and breaking tend toward comprehensiveness. Outsiders are brought in until all are involved. Bilateralism evolves into multilateralism. As an Arab diplomat put it, "In the Middle East everything is related to everything else." The simile of the kaleidoscope serves to explain. Just as with a tilt of the kaleidoscope the many tiny pieces of colored glass *all* move to form a new configuration, so any diplomatic initiative in the Middle East sets in motion a realignment of all the players.
3. The diplomacy of the region is characterized by an exaggerated conflation of seemingly minor local issues and major international concerns. The boundaries dividing local, national, regional and international are blurred.
4. Political initiatives generated within the area are undertaken—more than in other parts of the world—with an eye to the reaction of the outside world. The Middle East is the most "internationalized" or—to use the term suggested earlier—"penetrated" diplomatic system in the world. This state of affairs has long been generally accepted by all concerned parties, intra-and extra-regional, haves and have-nots, radicals and reactionaries.

5. The Great Powers involve themselves in the Middle East more nearly as a function of their great power rivalries than to advance rationally conceived regional interests. From this tendency comes an inclination to see regional players in terms of extra-regional alignments. Country X is seen as "the best friend we have." Country Y as the "catspaw of our enemy."

6. The intensive interrelatedness of politics at all levels produces homeostasis. Diplomatic folk wisdom about the Middle East has it that "things are never so good nor so bad as they seem." Rarely does a single political actor—whether outside great power or regional power—have the ability to impose its will or even to set in motion major new orientations.

7. These special characteristics predispose Middle Eastern political actors (and, in most cases, outsiders dealing with the Middle East as well) to favor certain actions and political styles including:

   a. Politics of the limited fait accompli or the "quick grab." The obverse is a dogged unwillingness to accept, even as a preliminary bargaining position, changes in the status quo, however miniscule.

   b. A disinclination to divide conflict or bargaining situations into major issues and minor. Such issues, rather than being broken down conceptually into, say, roots and branches, tend to be perceived as a seamless web. Not only is everything interrelated, but there is a reluctance to establish priorities either of sequence or substance. Accordingly, there is a dearth of "petty change" points that can be conceded by a party to initiate bargaining or break a deadlock.

   c. A strong preference for reactive politics or diplomatic counterpunching. Limited initiatives—such as the "quick grab"—are countenanced and admired if successful, but the preferred long-term stance is that of maneuvering the other parties to take a position which can then be exploited. Even much of the fait accompli politics grows

17

out of carefully orchestrated diplomatic counterpunching.

d. A marked preference for conducting delicate political bargaining through use of mediators and third parties who, in the process, become intimately involved in and often guarantors of arrangements reached.

e. A great concentration on, and often considerable virtuosity in, tactics, but much less attention is given to strategy. The distinction between tactics and strategy is often not clearly drawn.

f. The mentality of zero-sum political games tends to prevail. A player's gain must necessarily come from commensurate loss by another player or players. The concept that in certain circumstances all might gain or all might lose (non zero-sum game) is seldom operative.

The above characteristics are not unique to the Middle East. Even so, the special combination of these elements—the intensity and persistence with which they are applied, and their neat interlocking—combine to make the Middle East in modern times a distinctive politico-diplomatic system. This is the justification for a new look at the Eastern Question. This is the thesis informing the present book.

The Eastern Question, according to Bismarck, was not worth the bones of a Pomeranian musketeer. If other Western statesmen before and after Bismarck had acted according to his axiom, there would be no need to write this book. Since they did not, and have not to this day, we study the bitter embrace between the Middle East and the West in modern times to find the key to understanding the distinctive Middle Eastern approach to international politics.

PART ONE

PART ONE

———— ✳ ————

The Classical Eastern Question:
1774-1923

UNLIKE most books on the Eastern Question, this one is primarily concerned with the very East which was in question. This interest determines the approach taken. The Eastern Question as a special topic in European diplomatic history is not given the usual full treatment. Only that part of the strictly European diplomatic history needed to explain the rise and flowering of a special Middle Eastern diplomatic culture is presented.

At the same time, little is gained in pointing out that most studies of the Eastern Question slight the East if one then proceeds to slight the West. The Eastern Question, properly understood, is a study in intense interrelationships between two unequal power systems. It is that tangled web of ties between East and West which forms the subject of this book, but within the organizing framework of tracing the evolution of the Middle Eastern—not the Western—diplomatic culture.

I. WHEN DID THE EASTERN
QUESTION BEGIN?

The Eastern Question began with the decline in Ottoman strength vis-à-vis Europe and the growing awareness by all parties concerned of this decline, a process usually held to have begun in 1774 at the earliest and by the 1820s at the latest.

Earlier dates have been suggested. As long ago as 1606,

when the Treaty of Sitvatorok was signed with Austria, the Ottomans sent plenipotentiaries to the frontier. Previously, they had been able to impose terms from Istanbul. They also, for the first time, accorded the imperial title to their Hapsburg rival. These symbolic concessions were consistent with a treaty of negotiated compromise ending a war that had produced no clear victor.

At the end of the same century, in 1699, the Ottomans for the first time signed a peace treaty as a defeated power obliged to concede territories. This was the Treaty of Carlowitz, coming 16 years after the second and last Ottoman siege of Vienna.

Yet, these setbacks of the seventeenth century were offset by several successes in the eighteenth. The Ottomans soundly defeated the army of Peter the Great at the Battle of the Pruth in 1711, recaptured the Peloponnesus (lost at Carlowitz) from Venice in 1715, and redressed the losses at the Treaty of Passarowitz (1718) with the Treaty of Belgrade (1739).

It is true that the Ottoman Empire had long ago lost its ghazi (frontier holy warrior) spirit, but then every major empire has necessarily moved from a heroic age of rapid expansion to one marked by consolidation, acceptance of territorial limits and normal relations with people beyond those limits.

Those who would opt for dates earlier than 1774, when the Treaty of Kuçuk Kaynarca ended the Ottoman Empire's disastrous war with Russia, can possibly present a case from the viewpoint of strictly internal Ottoman institutions. Even here, however, prudence is in order. Western historiography tends to draw up overly long periods of time for the decline of empires. (Is it the long shadow cast by Gibbon's *Decline and Fall of the Roman Empire?*) Surely, extended periods of time in which empires reveal ups and downs of political and military fortunes are best distinguished from those ages of almost monotonous regularity in either rise or decline.

From that stretch of time between the death of Sulayman the Magnificent in 1566 and the war with Russia ending in 1774—somewhat more than two centuries—it may well be that the successive leaders of the Ottoman Empire missed opportunities to maintain, if not increase, the strength of the state.

Even so, the capacity of the Ottoman Empire during that period to win some wars and at times to hold its own against its several European foes argues that successive generations of Ottoman leaders still had a working margin of error. Not so for the period after 1774. Thereafter, the Ottoman Empire was always at a power disadvantage against Europe.

The settlement reached in 1774 may be summarized as follows: Russia had reached the Black Sea and henceforth her ships had free navigation in what had previously been a closed Ottoman sea. Muslims living in the Crimean Khanate were granted an independence they had not sought. It was to be an "independence" in the darkening shadow of an expanding Russian state.

Russia also obtained ill-defined rights to make representations for the Orthodox Christian subjects of the Ottoman Empire. An equally vague implication concerning the Ottoman sultan's religious prerogatives over the Muslims of the Crimea—no longer Ottoman vassals—also found its way into the treaty of Kuçuk Kaynarca.

These were portentous ideas, later to be used and abused by all concerned throughout the next century and a half. Sectarian separatism was to merge with the new European ideology of nationalism to create an explosive force that would ultimately sunder the multireligious, multiethnic, multilingual Ottoman Empire into some two dozen little states. Those Russian and Ottoman representatives gathered at the modest Bulgarian village of Kuçuk Kaynarca had managed to plant durable and bitter grapes. The teeth of several generations of their descendants, and of countless others as well, were to be set on edge.

Yet, as with so many historical turning points that appear obvious in retrospect, the importance of Kuçuk Kaynarca in 1774 was not realized by either European or Ottoman statesmen in the years immediately following. In the years after

23

1774 the Ottomans actually pushed forward the claim (unsuccessfully) for the return of the Crimean Khanate. Those Ottoman statesmen who had signed the treaty of Kuçuk Kaynarca lost power at home, which suggests that the dismal terms of that treaty were not yet regarded in Istanbul as irreversible.

The Ottoman Empire even fought another long and inconclusive war with Russia (1787-1792), suffering only limited losses. Immediately following that war Sultan Selim III began efforts at military westernization, thus inaugurating a process of government-directed reforms (in effect, modernization by enlightened despotism—to yoke together two expressions born in different eras) that would continue with confusing ups and downs for more than a century. These were hardly the moves of statesmen and soldiers resigned to presiding over the liquidation of their empire.

The European appraisal of the Ottomans was not all that dissimilar. Nor, for that matter, were the European states bordering Ottoman territories paragons of centralized administrative and military efficiency. Russia, which under the whiplash of Catherine II achieved great gains at Ottoman expense and showed signs of seeking more, was a clumsy giant of massive potential but only sporadically effective real power.

The Austrian Empire, scarcely more efficient, was at that time rather unambitious in its foreign policy. France still clung to its traditional foreign policy of seeing the Ottoman Empire as a natural ally. Nor had Britain yet developed that intense concern about Middle Eastern affairs which was later to characterize her diplomacy. The fear of Russian encroachment southward—so marked a feature of British thinking in the nineteenth century—did not yet exist. Even so masterful a politician as William Pitt learned this to his grief in 1791 when he sent an ultimatum to Russia in an effort to limit Russian gains at the expense of the Ottoman Empire. The British public, seeing no Russian threat, would have none of it. Pitt was obliged to back down, saving face as best he could.

The age that was to bring Palmerston, the Crimean War, and the "great game" of Anglo-Russian rivalry from the Balkans to the Himalayas was not then too far away in chronological time. Yet, as late as the last decade of the eighteenth century Britons would have found such nineteenth-century passions inconceivable.

Another school of interpretation chooses 1798 as the date marking the beginning of modern times in the Middle East, and thus the beginning of that very modern problem, the Eastern Question. In 1798 Napoleon and some 40,000 French troops landed in Egypt in a daring military strike against Britain (intended to cut Britain off from India, perhaps establish a French imperium in the East—the prospects were limitless and, as events proved, fanciful). Lord Nelson and the British fleet assured that the out-flanker was out-flanked. Napoleon returned to France the following year, and by 1801 the remaining troops of the French expeditionary force (some 24,000) surrendered and were repatriated to France.

End of a bold scheme, but beginning of a new era. The French move, although abortive, revealed that thenceforth all Ottoman territories were vulnerable. The Ottoman Empire had long fought with Europe, but theretofore the struggle had been along shared borders in the Balkans and Central Asia. Napoleon had leapfrogged over the customary battle lines, striking boldly—and, for a time, successfully—against the Ottoman Arab heartland.

Although the French invasion eventually failed, and although the British who had moved troops into Egypt as allies of the sultan also left Egypt under duress by 1805, the incident marked the beginning of a game played with new rules. European plans to conquer interior portions of the Ottoman Empire, rather than being satisfied with nibbling away at the Eurasian edges, now became increasingly thinkable. Less than three decades after their check in Egypt the French began an occupation of Algeria (1830) destined to last for 132 years. Nine years later (1839) the British took Aden.

1798 also set in motion two additional factors of importance to the Eastern Question. After Napoleon's military venture to the Eastern Mediterranean, British statesmen never ceased worrying about the lifeline to India. From the British perspective, at least the Eastern Question began not with Kuçuk Kaynarca but with Napoleon's landing in Egypt. The specter that William Pitt had raised in vain only seven years earlier now appeared real enough to the British political establishment.

Second, the brief Bonapartist interlude in Egypt gave the opportunity for a dynamic political figure, Muhammad Ali, to seize power in Egypt. Muhammad Ali might well have ended his days in his native Kavalla buying and selling tobacco but for the Ottoman decision to raise an Albanian corps to fight Napoleon. Muhammad Ali, who came to Egypt with that Albanian corps, stayed, won out in the confused political battles following the French invasion, and founded a dynasty destined to survive until Nasser's Free Officers coup in July 1952.

Muhammad Ali provides another important ingredient to the Eastern Question. Ottoman weakness produced ambitious European claimants to the attractive spoils. That is well known. Equally important is the way in which that same weakness also produced claimants to the spoils from within the Ottoman sphere itself. The most spectacular and the most successful was Muhammad Ali, whose victorious armies twice brought the Ottoman Empire to the brink of destruction.

Muhammad Ali's rule in Egypt illustrates the wide gap between legal forms and political realities in the Eastern Question. Legally, Muhammad Ali was no more than the Ottoman provincial governor of Egypt. In fact, but for European intervention he would have set in motion the destruction of the Ottoman Empire almost a century before it occurred. Or, he just might have been able to go for the grand prize—replacing a dynasty that had ruled since the man who gave the dynasty its name, Uthman (whence the European form, Ottoman), came to power in 1280.

The Ottoman Empire had known rebels and provincial bids for power before Muhammad Ali, but previously, when the Ottomans could more than hold their own against outsiders, such occasional turbulence from the imperial periphery could be dealt with by the center in its own good time. Rebels before Muhammad Ali has also sought outside support from foreign enemies of the Ottoman state, but such allies, if engaged, were not crucial to the outcome of political battles.

Muhammad Ali signified the arrival of political leadership *within* the Ottoman framework, capable not only of flouting imperial authority but of threatening its very existence. Muhammad Ali demonstrated the new, two-tiered strategy that was thereafter to characterize the Eastern Question. This was the linking of regional military initiatives to a diplomatic campaign directed toward Europe.

Equally, Muhammad Ali, in being denied the fruits of his military victories, revealed the European state system as the ultimate arbiter in the Eastern Question. Muhammad Ali was an early example of a regional political leader's being not just stopped in his tracks but obliged to retreat—simply because the European state system so demanded. After Muhammad Ali any regional attempt (including those by the central Ottoman Empire, too) to bring about political change would be undertaken hand-in-glove with efforts to win over or at the very least neutralize Europe.

The Eastern Question, in its fully developed form, was thus a complex, diplomatic game. There were several independent or autonomous actors on the European side. This has always been well understood. There were also several independent or autonomous actors on the Middle Eastern side. This point, sometimes slighted when the Eastern Question is viewed through the narrow lens of European diplomatic history, deserves equal emphasis.

Yet, if Napoleon made possible the Muhammad Ali dynasty in Egypt (a curious coincidence—Napoleon and Muhammad Ali were born in the same year, 1769), Muhammad Ali's major contributions in shaping the Eastern Question came well after Napoleon's invasion of Egypt in 1798. Muhammad Ali began to loom large in Eastern Question diplomacy as late as the 1820s and even more in the 1830s. If Muhammad Ali's

3. Napoleon at Battle of the Pyramids, July 1778 (Mary Evans Picture Library, London).

innovations launched the Eastern Question, then the date must be advanced by twenty years or more beyond 1798.

This approach to periodization would pinpoint the Greek War of independence (in which Muhammad Ali was involved) and its attendant international complications covering the years 1821-1829.

The argument for beginning the Eastern Question in the 1820s is as follows: A persistent power imbalance to the disadvantage of the Ottomans in facing Europe was present by 1774. European maneuvers to strike well behind the conventional lines of Ottoman-European military confrontation were dramatically inaugurated by Napoleon in 1798. His action also brought Britain seriously onto the scene, making the Eastern Mediterranean an arena of multipolar great power confrontation.

The Greek War of independence added the remaining elements. For the first time the approach to international politics that was to set the tone for European diplomacy from the Congress of Vienna to the First World War was brought fully to bear on the Eastern Question (the very term, Eastern Question, came into use at this time).

Thereafter, any political shock from the Middle East would set in motion an intricate game of musical chairs. The several different European powers would move and maneuver in pursuit of their own interests while recognizing the legitimate role of the European state system as the final arbiter.

This is not to idealize the period from 1815 to 1914 as a golden age of internationalism when national self-interest deferred to the over-all interest of the larger group as arrived at by consensus. Rather, the reality of multipolar power in Europe (the balance of power system) and the acceptance of that reality as in the order of things combined to produce a stable, self-sustaining pattern of international relations. As regards the Eastern Question, the several different political units of the Middle East were brought into the game in a very special way—as pawns or as prizes.

The Greek War of independence also represented Western nationalism absorbed into the Middle East, an imported idea that perhaps more than any other doomed Ottoman efforts to keep alive its multinational empire. Moreover, the Greek War of independence brought the power of European public opinion into play on the Eastern Question for the first time. European nationalism, romanticism, and populism—fused in the fires of the French Revolutionary period—became thenceforth potent political restraints on European ministries.

A new form of interventionism—a new and secularized concept of crusade—was pouring out of Europe. The first and most consistent recipient of this inundation was the Middle East. This ideological component has remained very much a part of the Eastern Question.

Thus, there are three possible dates for the beginning of the Eastern Question—1774 or 1798 or the 1820s. Each records an important development. 1774 pinpointed the final turning of the power balance in Europe's favor at the expense of the Ottoman Empire. 1798 brought in all the principal European states, widened the arena of activity, and set in motion a new approach among political actors both within and outside the Middle East. The 1820s brought the delicate diplomatic dances of the post-Napoleonic European international system on the one hand and the wilder, almost uncontrollable impulses of nationalism and romanticism on the other.

Each date—1774, 1798, and the 1820s—adds an important component. There is much to be said for leaving that much temporal flexibility in the matter: The Eastern Question arose and reached its fully developed form in the years between 1774 and the 1820s.

II. THE TURBANNED HUMPTY DUMPTY

The pattern of Eastern Question history from the beginning period (1774-1820s) to the disappearance of the Ottoman Empire in 1923 is clear: The weakening Ottoman Empire was at the mercy of Europe. Only the checks and balances of intra-European rivalries gave the Ottomans some measure of maneuverability.

Even this modest potential asset that Istanbul might have used for reform and consolidation was offset by fissiparous tendencies within the area. These splintering tendencies were, of course, only strengthened by the very Ottoman weakness that could not be dissembled even in those brief periods when European pressure lessened. It was a vicious circle, or more accurately a long-term downward spiral. The kaleidoscopic configurations made by the combining and separating of many political actors both within and outside the region worked in a single, inexorable direction—toward the dismemberment of the Ottoman Empire into smaller political units.

These were troubled years for the Middle East, which lurched and stumbled from crisis to crisis. War or the threat of war

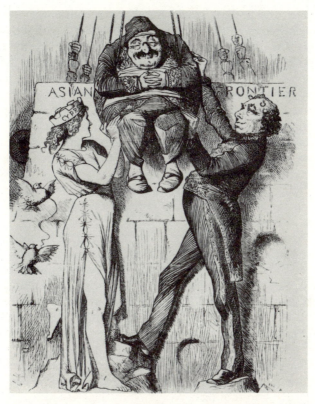

4. This cartoon from the time of the Eastern crisis conveys unwittingly an old theme, that of Europe steadily dismembering the Ottoman Empire while presuming to preserve it (*Punch*, 1878).

was the norm, peace and the effective settlement of differences the tantalizingly temporary exception.

If the period of European history from 1815 to 1914 was marked by the virtual absence of general war and only a limited number of local or two-party wars, no such happy conclusion may be made concerning the Middle East. Indeed, the only general European armed struggle between the years 1815-1914 grew out of the Eastern Question. This was the Crimean War.

The Middle East served Europe as a convenient arena in which European rivalries could be fought out with little risk. This is not to say that European statesmen accepted the Eastern Question in quite such starkly Machiavellian terms. Those in a position to dominate others usually find reasons to justify that domination. Often, the victims themselves are blamed. Thus, the Ottoman Empire was deemed at fault for being inefficient or unjust or out of step with the times.

Nor was Europe's harsh view of the beleagured Middle East consciously hypocritical. Europeans at the time genuinely believed in the values underlying the new world they were bringing into existence. They believed that the Middle East ought to move into the new world aborning. Any resistance was seen as at best benighted, at worst immoral.

In systemic terms, however, the Middle East has become a vast arena for sublimated, carefully regulated European conflict. The Middle East in these years was not just a power system in the unfortunate situation of facing a much stronger, and usually hostile, neighboring power system. It had, rather, been taken over by, but not actually absorbed into, Europe. The political integrity of the Middle East existed on European sufferance.

The Ottoman Empire steadily declined territorially from the beginning of the Eastern Question until the empire itself disappeared after the First World War. The Ottomans, in a few cases, did manage to get somewhat better terms by doggedly hanging on or by relying on European intervention to scale down the excessive gains of a single European power. In the context of the age, a settlement that secured a return to the status quo ante was a victory for the Ottomans.

This operating climate engendered among political leadership of the Middle East a diplomatic style of delay, dig in, play for time, raise peripheral points, and—in a word—refuse to grant the hectoring adversary the desired quick settlement. The Ottomans were schooled in just such tactics, generation after generation, during the age of the Eastern Question.

At the same time, the other political forces in the area—

whether independent in all but name, as the governments of Egypt or Tunisia, or parochial political leaders playing off the Ottoman central government with sundry European powers, as the Druze or Maronites of Lebanon or the many localized power groupings in the Balkans—were exposed to a similar schooling.

The only clear Ottoman victories during this extended period from 1774 to 1923 were won over lesser foes (either nominally still a part of the empire or former Ottoman provinces that had obtained independence). The Ottomans soundly defeated Greece, for example, in 1897 and came off well against Bulgaria in the Second Balkan War in 1913. In the first case, Great Power pressure saved the Greeks from severe losses. In the second, the mutually neutralizing interests of outside powers left the Ottomans free to exploit their gains won in the field. The two examples together illustrate the narrow confines of Ottoman maneuverability.

The pervasiveness of the pattern (a Middle Eastern regional sub-system integrated into the European state system in a way that tightly restricted independent Middle Eastern political activity) is further revealed by a seeming paradox: Ottoman military strength or weakness, Ottoman military victories or losses, had in many cases slight bearing on the outcome of events. Or, at times, they seemed to have perversely opposite results. The Ottoman armies were twice routed by Muhammad Ali's forces in the 1830s, but European diplomatic activity denied Muhammad Ali the fruits of his victories and left the militarily prostrate Ottoman Empire in a stronger position.

On the other hand, the Ottomans fought well in the Crimean War (relatively speaking, for no armies fought well in that classic example of diplomatic and military bungling), but emerged none the stronger for their efforts.

Or, in the Russo-Ottoman war of 1877-1878 the Ottomans fielded an efficient army, and at Plevna (now Pleven, in Bulgaria) the Ottoman commander, Osman Pasha, conducted a brilliant operation that held off the Russian army, throwing back three attacks, for a crucial half year. Yet, the heroic stand at Plevna may well not have helped the Ottomans. Russia probably did not dare arouse the European opposition that her marching into Constantinople would surely have provoked. And did Russia really seek to liquidate the Ottoman Empire at that time? Would a less effective Ottoman military defense during the months of July-December 1877 have stimulated a more effective European diplomatic riposte, sufficient to stay Russia's hand? The experience of the century before 1877 suggests the poignant irony that the Ottomans might have won more at the conference table by losing more on the ground.

The heroic efforts of Osman Pasha and his men left only a proud legend and the bitter dregs of a draconian peace settlement. The Ottoman Empire was "forced to give up two-fifths of its entire territory and one-fifth of its population, about 5.5 million people, of whom almost half were Muslims."[1]

No one in Europe (or even in the Middle East, except for the Ottoman ruling elite itself) had an interest in reconstituting the Ottoman Empire. If it fell, it would not be put back together. All parties acted on the assumption that the trend was irreversible. Ottoman losses would not be recovered, but Ottoman gains—if permitted at all—were not secure against later loss.

In this environment, the European great powers (as is the wont of great powers) shrank from taking decisive action. To set off the final, total dismemberment of the Ottoman Empire might create uncontrollable chaos. Better to pick away at the Ottoman spoils in less voracious but safer bites.

At the same time, the several European powers were always concerned that a rival might jump the gun. Then, the state which held back, refusing to take the initiative, might end up with less than its anticipated share. What was the answer? No power wanted the risks or the odium of single-handedly push-

---

[1] Stanford J. Shaw and Ezel Kural Shaw, *History of the Ottoman Empire and Modern Turkey*, Vol. II, *Reform, Revolution, and Republic: The Rise of Modern Turkey, 1808-1975* (Cambridge University Press paperback edition, 1977, p. 191).

ing the turbanned Humpty Dumpty off the wall, but neither did any power want to be caught napping in the shade of that wall when the inevitable fall came. A state needed to watch its rivals warily, be ready with contingency plans, and—just possibly—explore with others the idea of preparing for the eventual dismemberment. These countervailing pressures created an intricate pattern of intra-European diplomacy, including cautious soundings concerning possible preemptive actions, hedging of bets, exploratory diplomatic demarches, and elaborate multiparty contingency plans.

The fullest flowering of this distinctive diplomatic pattern emerged as grand designs for the partition of the Ottoman Empire. Such schemes were spawned regularly from the time of Kuçuk Kaynarca to Lausanne. Some were carefully thought out. Others were spur-of-the-moment affairs. Some were taken very seriously. Others were scornfully dismissed even in that age when statesmen were disinclined to dub outlandish anything that Europe might plan at Ottoman expense.

By way of illustration the following more important, or more fascinating, partition plans may be noted:

1781-1782	Catherine's approach to Austria, proposing an over-all partition and a reconstituted Greek Empire ruled from Constantinople by her grandson
1799-1801	Tsar Paul's overtures to France
1806	The Russian suggestion that Britain take Egypt while Russia would get the principalities of Moldavia and Wallachia
1807	Talks for a general Ottoman dismemberment between Napoleon and Tsar Alexander at the time of the treaty of Tilsit negotiations
1829-1830	French Premier Polignac's ambitious plan for a general realignment of boundaries in Europe (a veritable "waltz of territories" as one cynic put it) coupled with partition of the Ottoman Empire

1833	Munchengratz Agreement between Russia and Austria, more a contingency plan than a partition proposal
1844	Anglo-Russian Accord (Nesselrode Memorandum). Also a contingency plan (and a classic diplomatic misunderstanding concerning what had been agreed on)
1853	Tsar Nicholas's efforts to convince the British that the "contingency" had arrived and "the sick man of Europe" was dying
1876-1877	Austro-Russian planning for at least partial Ottoman dismemberment at the time of the "Eastern Crisis"
1876	Bismarck's plan to settle European disputes by way of Ottoman partition
1895-1896	The Salisbury partition initiatives with Germany. Whether only a "trial balloon" or serious probes (historians differ), they did mark another step in Britain's moving away from support of the Ottoman Empire
1915-1917	The confused cluster of British-French-Russian-Italian wartime discussions often referred to, incompletely, as the Sykes-Picot Agreement

None of these plans was completely realized. Too many states with too many conflicting claims had to be satisfied. Further, the role of spoiler was easily played. To initiate and then see to a successful conclusion an elaborate plan that would be accepted by all—or at least could not be effectively resisted by any—was much more demanding. Even the initiators of partition plans usually abandoned the effort.

Only the major powers could initiate—or at least sponsor—such schemes. The twelve schemes listed above were pushed by Russia, France, Germany, and Britain. The lesser powers—Sardinia (later Italy), Greece, or other formerly Ottoman territories—could suggest ideas or even provoke action, but this led to elaborate partition plans only when a great power patron became involved.

The exception that tests the above interpretation is Austria, surely to be numbered among the big four or big five powers throughout the period under consideration. Yet, there were no Austrian partition initiatives, and Austrian involvement in the partition plans spawned by others was always cautious and intended more to avoid being left out. This was perhaps because Austria itself was the European equivalent of the Ottoman Empire—a multinational, multilingual, multireligious empire that was itself beleagured by fissiparous forces and sought only to hold its own.

Russia was also a multinational and to a much lesser extent multilingual and multireligious empire, but the Russian Empire was expanding territorially and economically throughout the nineteenth century. It was a clumsy imperial giant that never realized its potential and fell victim to the Bolshevik Revolution. Nevertheless, it was a very different political entity from Austria during this period, and this difference was clearly perceived by the other powers in the game.

Austrian policy illustrates the extreme case of what was a common disposition. The partition plans and, even more, the response other powers gave to these plans were characterized by considerable circumspection. Most of these plans were defensive, more nearly designed to prevent unfortunate possibilities than to seize opportunities for aggrandizement.

It was small solace to Ottoman statesmen, but no European great power ever worked single-mindedly or consistently to destroy the Ottoman Empire. Its decline and final fall is best explained in terms of the prevailing system.

* * *

Concurrent with the European diplomatic and military activities that make up the better-known part of the Eastern Question were the Middle Eastern initiatives. The Middle Eastern responses to the new political rules created by the Eastern Question can be grouped as:

1. Those provoked by other than Ottoman, and often anti-Ottoman, political forces in the area, and
2. Those taken by existing ruling establishments within the larger Ottoman world.

The following three sections (III, IV, and V) review the different varieties of regional power bids directed against the Ottoman center. These many threats from within the region itself to Middle Eastern governments—all coming during a period of relentless European pressure—highlight the difficulties and the responses of the established regional political elites. This is the subject of Section VI.

III. MAJOR REGIONAL POWER BIDS IN THE GREATER OTTOMAN WORLD, 1774-1923

During the last years of the eighteenth and the first years of the nineteenth century the central Ottoman Empire was in danger of falling apart. Just as imperial China periodically faced threats from the periphery in the form of warlords, so the Ottoman Empire was stricken with an epidemic of warlordism.

In the Middle Eastern context these warlords might be called *ayan* (notables) or *derebeys* (literally, valley lords), but whatever the name they were individuals whose modest provincial power base suddenly grew in this time of Ottoman weakness. Throughout this period they asserted themselves in the Balkans, the Arab lands, and even in Anatolia, the Turkish-speaking heartland of the Ottoman Empire.

Posing an equally dangerous threat were the many duly appointed provincial governors who attained a control of their provinces that Istanbul could not challenge. In the Fertile Crescent, for example, such long-tenured rulers as Sulayman Pasha in Iraq (1780-1802) or Jazzar Pasha, ruling much of the Syro-Palestinian area from Acre (where he turned back

Napoleon's seige in 1799), or Amir Bashir Shihab II in Mount Lebanon made a mockery of central government control.

Then, there were the provinces of Ottoman Africa (Algiers, Tunis, Tripoli, and Egypt), long virtually autonomous but in this extended period of Ottoman weakness liable to slip away from central government control altogether.

It was this threat of disintegration from within that Sultan Mahmud II (1808-1839) would confront and eventually overcome (not without bitter losses). Thereafter, others ruling from Istanbul joined the battle to re-assert central government control. This enduring motif—the struggle to attain or retain control from the center—provides a continuity to Ottoman history from the death of Mahmud II to the death of the empire itself eighty years later. In conventional historical periodization the period is divided into three phases:

1. The age of the Tanzimat (1839-1876)
2. The period of Hamidian despotism (1876-1908)
3. The time of the Young Turks (1908-1919)

This three-part periodization of Ottoman history from 1839 to 1919 is useful, but it must not be permitted to obscure the continuity of efforts from Istanbul to overcome political fragmentation. This was a constant theme in Ottoman history from the beginning of the Eastern Question until the end of the empire.

Giving due attention to Ottoman history as seen from within provides a corrective to the narrowly Eurocentric perspective of classical Eastern Question diplomatic history. This is the way Ottoman history is now being written. Yet, neither the newer historical writing nor the older Eurocentric diplomatic history quite manages to capture the systemic change ushered in with the beginning of the Eastern Question.

That is, a useful distinction may be made between traditional challenges from the periphery in times of central weaknesses and Eastern Question era challenges. In the former the confrontation was essentially intra-Ottoman. Outsiders might intervene (e.g., Iran, Austria, or Russia) to support provincial rebels, but such intervention was sporadic and not usually decisive. In the Eastern Question era, however, the outside intervention was consistent, powerful, and anticipated by both Ottoman center and periphery.

Thus, one pattern of provincial revolt characterized the long period of Ottoman self-sufficiency. Another pattern emerged in the period of Ottoman weakness and subordination to the outside world. As with the issue of when the Eastern Question began, no change from one day to the next is to be sought. Clearly, however, the period after 1774 witnessed an increasing number of new-style provincial challenges (revolts against Istanbul keyed to anticipated European intervention).

ALI PASHA

Perhaps the first of the new style provincial challengers was Ali Pasha of Janina (1741-1822). Ali Pasha was from a family of mountain notables (or brigand chiefs, depending on one's perspective) in the area of what is now Albania and northwestern Greece. His long political career offers, at first sight, a seemingly incomprehensible maze of shifting alliances and warfare, but the broader contours of his life and times reveal a solid plan and performance.

Ali Pasha relied on his local roots and the secure power base this provided. He sought, and came very close to achieving, his own "state" in the area of Albania, Epirus, and Thessaly. Whether this was to be a genuinely independent state or nominally linked to the Ottoman Empire, like the beylik of Tunis or the deylik of Algiers, was a matter that the pragmatic Ali Pasha was willing to leave open. He kept his eye on the entire political spectrum, from the highly local problem of what the neighboring tribal chieftain had in mind to the larger concerns of relations with the Porte and of alliances with European powers. In 1798, for example, he offered to revolt against the sultan in return for French support, but when he saw the European powers in coalition against France and France unwilling to give him the established position he sought Ali Pasha reaffirmed his loyalty to the sultan.

For the last two decades of his life Ali Pasha maintained his autonomous position, always ready to seize any local or international issue to enhance his standing. His loyalty to the sultan was contingent until a better opportunity came along. The Porte, in turn, accepted him (neither Ali Pasha nor the ruling elite in Istanbul had any illusions) solely because of the prevailing power balance. The sultan "rewarded" him with provincial postings because Ali Pasha was too strong to be removed.

Three Ottoman appointments granted Ali Pasha outside his home area of Janina (in 1788, 1799, and 1801) can be interpreted as attempts to dilute his strength. In each case Ali Pasha, while accepting the new assignment, kept his political fences in good order at home. In the last two instances he simply remained in Janina, sending subordinates to rule over the remoter province. Such center-periphery games had long been played in the Ottoman Empire (as in other imperial systems). These games became more complex with the introduction of important European players.

Ali Pasha even had a French artillery commander (one Colonel Charbonnel) and French advisers for his military, yet another way in which he was a harbinger of things to come. He also became a romanticized cult figure in the West and was visited in his mountain bastion by such worthies as Lord Byron.

This man, dubbed the lion of Janina, was able to thrive for so long in a political climate reminiscent of Renaissance Italy through more than cleverness and pluck. For all his cruelty and deviousness Ali Pasha did provide a significantly higher level of public order and rough justice than his rivals. In such a political climate the leader who was harsh but at least predictable was likely to win the day.

MUHAMMAD ALI

Ali Pasha in many ways foreshadows the even more celebrated Muhammad Ali of Egypt. Muhammad Ali, "the founder of modern Egypt,"[2] figures often in this book, so dominant was his role during the first half of the nineteenth century. A master of political infighting, Muhammad Ali skillfully played off mamluks, ulama, and the Ottoman forces to win out as pasha in Egypt. From the beginning, he effectively integrated great power politics and local political concerns. In the years of his rise to power, the British were supporting one mamluk faction, the French another, while the Ottomans sought a winner who would also prove loyal. Not able to secure outside support in those crucial first years, Muhammad Ali carefully maintained the pretense of Ottoman loyalty.

Yet, the limits of Muhammad Ali's allegiance were apparent when Sultan Selim III attempted to remove him from the scene by appointing him pasha of Salonika (1805), a ploy similar to that tried with Ali Pasha of Janina, and just as unsuccessful. Muhammad Ali refused to leave, pleading that it was necessary for him to remain in Egypt to preserve order. In so doing he blithely overlooked the awkward reality that an Ottoman army had landed in Egypt to enforce the sultan's order. With adroit military action against his mamluk rivals, Muhammad Ali was able to convince the Ottomans that working with him would prove less costly than attempting to force him out of Egypt.

After consolidating his position in Egypt, Muhammad Ali looked for new worlds to conquer. At the behest of the sultan he intervened against the Wahhabis in Arabia and the insurgent Greeks. Later, he sent his armies in victory against the Ottomans twice and came within a whisker of overthrowing the dynasty. He negotiated with the French about an expedition against Algiers, and worked closely with France during the two Syrian crises of the 1830s. Throughout his long tenure in power Muhammad Ali also sent out feelers to his principal great power obstacle, Great Britain. A variant gambit, he began the Egyptian conquest of the Sudan without really

[2] Thus the title of an early and still useful study by Henry H. Dodwell (Cambridge University Press, 1931).

42

engaging Ottoman or great power diplomacy, probably sensing that this was an arena in which he could safely operate unilaterally.

Muhammad Ali was willing to work with the international system when this was necessary or convenient. He was also quite prepared to go it alone. He could negotiate elaborate schemes in advance of action. He could just as readily present the region and the world with a fait accompli.

Muhammad Ali was probably more responsible than any other individual for accelerating the pace of direct European involvement in the Middle East. He brought European military and technical advisers to Egypt. He sent Egyptian student missions to Europe. In these and countless other ways he set in motion the westernization of Egypt.

He also stimulated similar actions on the part of his nominal sovereign and great rival, Sultan Mahmud II, for with that very human tendency to imitate one's enemies, Sultan Mahmud was fortified in his own westernizing impulses by seeing the apparent success Muhammad Ali was enjoying.

In the process, Muhammad Ali became an individual about whom few European diplomats or opinion-molders had neutral views. The Albanian born in the Macedonian port city of Kavalla who came to rule Egypt like a pharaoh was portrayed in Europe without nuance. He either represented the Europeanized wave of the future—efficient, rational and modern— or he was a barbaric, meddlesome parvenu whose aggressive designs were causing needless trouble to all. Few Europeans seemed able to keep clearly in focus the possibility that a bit of both might be involved.

THE SERBS

If Ali Pasha and Muhammad Ali were examples of the dynamic man-on-the-make working within the framework of the Eastern Question, the Serbian leader, Kara George represented the proto-nationalist leader. Kara George (1760-1817) personified emerging Serbia. He had served for a time in the

Austrian army and was a pig merchant by trade. That Austrian connection was in accord with the increasing ties his compatriots had come to have with Austria throughout the eighteenth century (with a corresponding increase in hope for political succor). His trade put him in the mainstream of Serbian economic life, a society of independent-minded mountain fighters and small farmers concentrating on their pigs.

The rise of Serbian nationalism is linked, ironically, to an effort by Sultan Selim III to improve their lot. Selim wanted to break the power of the unruly Janissary auxiliaries (Yamaks) and restore central control over the province. A dynamic governor was appointed who had some military success against these Serbian-style feudal barons.

As a safeguard against future incursion by the Yamaks the governor worked out with the native Christian leadership a plan for Serbian military service. Since the protection needed would require increased taxes if provided by additional regular Ottoman troops, the native leadership embraced the governor's proposal that they play a role in their own defense. Thus began, as a practical response to an immediate problem, a revolutionary departure from standard Ottoman practice.[3]

This step toward "nationalizing" the military was destined to be repeated at different times throughout the Ottoman provinces, providing a major stimulus to those sentiments of nationalism that would ultimately destroy the Ottoman Empire.

The new plan of what might be called proto-national self-defense only got underway in the dying months of the eighteenth century. There was little time for training the native Serbian auxiliaries before regular Ottoman troops were being pulled out of the Balkans to fight the French in Egypt. This removal of regular troops was just the opportunity the Yamaks, plus sundry other adventurers, needed. A struggle for power, destined to last for the next several years, soon began.

---

[3] "Thus for the first time in centuries, rayas were allowed to bear arms in defense of their homes." Shaw, *Between Old and New, The Ottoman Empire under Sultan Selim III, 1789-1807* (Harvard University Press, 1971), p. 306.

Early in the contest the newly recruited Christian *ra'ayas* actually defended the Ottoman governor and pushed the Yamaks out of Belgrade and Serbia (which demonstrated the potential of "nationalized" self-defense).

Later developments saw the governor himself treacherously assassinated by a Janissary officer. In the resulting confusion the Yamaks regained control and, to make matters worse, the army sent in by Selim III succeeded only in keeping the fighting alive with increased atrocities on all sides.

The Serbs, feeling their new power and impatient with Istanbul, began moving toward a demand for national independence. The Eastern Question dimension of the Serbian revolt was roughly as follows: The Serbs under Kara George had fought the Yamaks to a stand-off by 1804. The Yamaks opened negotiations and offered generous terms. Kara George, however, wanted any settlement to be guaranteed by the foreign powers. Nothing came of these negotiations, but the insistence on internationalization—advanced by a non-Muslim subject—was portentous for the beleagured Ottoman Empire.

Throughout 1804 and after, the Ottoman government kept trying to arrange a settlement while working against the Yamaks and in favor of Kara George's forces. Then in 1805 the Ottoman government reversed itself and sent a military expedition against Kara George. One can speculate that the policy grew out of frustration (Ottoman inability to force a settlement on all sides) mixed with lingering misgivings (fear that Kara George's newly raised army was taking an anti-Ottoman tack and would, in any case, set a bad precedent for other disturbed areas). The new hard line failed dismally. The army sent from Istanbul was bested by Kara George's men. The die was then cast. The Serbs no longer had any reason to revolt in the name of a sultan who had sent troops against them, and in those encounters of 1805 they went a long way toward losing that centuries-old feeling of awe for Istanbul's political authority. The Serbian-inspired tentatives toward "internationalization" that had been in germ all along henceforth blossomed unhindered.

The story of Serbia's move to autonomy (1817) and then complete independence (1878) need not be reviewed here. From the perspective of the central Ottoman Empire this Serbian revolt beginning in the early years of the nineteenth century, with roots going back to the last years of the eighteenth, was only the first in a procession of "national" revolts that would cover the Balkans and then spread before the end of the century to the easternmost reaches of the empire to include the Armenians (theretofore seen as the "most loyal millet").

Eventually, this new virus brought in from Western Europe—nationalism—would even infect Muslim populations of the Empire, creating what earlier would have been quite unthinkable to a traditional Ottoman—Arab and Turkish nationalism.

THE GREEK REVOLT

The European powers at the time did not attach much importance to the Serbian revolt. That area of the Balkans was still too remote, and the stirring events of the Napoleonic years monopolized public attention. Europe was aroused, instead, by the Greek revolt that began in 1821. Thereafter, it became part of the European "received wisdom" that national liberation movements were the wave of the future and that the multinational Ottoman Empire was living on borrowed time. Not for the first time in history, a major political system that had been able to withstand either outside power or prejudice faltered and finally fell before the combined onslaught of both.

The Greek revolt evokes to this day connotations of victory won by freedom over tyranny, of naturalism over formalism and of radicalism over reaction. This is because the Greek revolt was caught up in romanticist, populist, and radical movements in arts, literature, and politics that had been brought to luxuriant bloom in the rich soil of the Enlightenment and the French Revolution. To many Westerners, the Greek revolt still

46

Eugene Delacroix, "Greece Expiring on the Ruins of Missolonghi"

5. Romanticism and the Eastern Question came of age together. And
diplomats began to be restrained by domestic public opinion
(By permission of Musée des Beaux-Arts, Bordeaux).

means Missolonghi and Byron, plus the empassioned artistry of Delacroix.

Here, we must leave aside the poetry and the pathos in order to concentrate on the power politics. The Greek Revolt (1821-1829) was the first nationalist movement fully entangled in the Eastern Question web. Its very confusions and contradictions offer a paradigm of things to come. It brought, for instance, an early example of emigré politics, of uprooted individuals imbued with radical ideas seizing the opportunity to create a revolutionary organization far beyond the borders of the state they sought to challenge.

This was the Hetairia Philike, founded in 1814 by Greeks living in Odessa. Why was a Greek society founded in the Russian city of Odessa on the northern shore of the Black Sea? Because in the years since the Treaty of Kuçuk Kaynarca (1774) opened the Black Sea to commerce the Russian grain trade had grown enormously. Most of the merchants and sailors involved in that lucrative trade were Greeks. These members of the Hetairia Philike represented a rising class of the upwardly mobile who had both strong ideological motives and the economic confidence to challenge the old order. Their task was not only to resist the Ottoman government but also to defy the old guard leadership within the large Greek community of the Ottoman Empire.

Dominating this latter group were the Phanariot Greeks, so named after the quarter (Phanar or Lighthouse) of Istanbul where they lived. The Phanariots virtually controlled the upper ranks of the Greek Orthodox church, were heavily represented in the Ottoman bureaucracy (even serving as governors—hospodar was the title—of Moldavia and Wallachia), and had their hands in trade, tax farming, and government monopolies. To add to the complicated picture, many of those thriving in the growing Russian grain trade were themselves of Phanariot background.

In what was to become a typical nationalist tactic in the context of the Eastern Question, the Hetairia Philike sought national liberation with the support of a foreign patron. The

48

natural choice was Russia, whose people shared with the Greeks an Orthodox Christian and Byzantine heritage. What could better indicate the Greek nationalists' courting of foreign support than their ideas about who should lead the movement? Their first choice was John Capodistrias (1776-1831), a Greek who had entered Russian service in 1809 and by 1815 was sharing the post of Russian foreign minister with Nesselrode.

Capodistrias, however, declined the offer. Some three years later, the Hetairia Philike turned to another Greek in Russian service, Alexander Ypsilantis (1792-1828). Belonging to an eminent Phanariot family that claimed descent from Byzantine emperors, Ypsilantis had served with distinction in the Russian army and had risen at an early age to the rank of general. He took over as head of the Hetairia Philike in 1820 while still in his twenties.

The relative youth of Ypsilantis points to yet another way in which the Greek revolt serves as a prototype. Revolutions are for the young, and revolutions coming to maturity in the heady days of European Romanticism especially so. Groups such as the Hetairia Philike and its many successors found themselves challenging not only the old order but the old generation.

To force Tsar Alexander's hand and to get Russia committed to the Greek cause, Ypsilantis led a small invasion party into the Ottoman Danubian principalities. This, it was hoped, would not only spark the revolt in the Peloponnesus and the Greek Islands that had been rather haphazardly planned but, more important, would bring in Russia. Ypsilantis naively thought his incursion into the principalities might stimulate support from the Rumanians, but to them the Greeks *were* the oppressive establishment. Phanariot hospodars had ruled there since 1711. Ypsilantis's own father had served as hospodar of Moldavia, his grandfather hospodar of Wallachia. The invasion set off no groundswell of support from Rumanians. It did, however, provoke the Ottoman government to abolish the practice of appointing Phanariot Greeks as hospodars.

This rash attempt to provoke great power intervention was

a humiliating failure. Tsar Alexander's passion for political legitimacy outweighed for the time his crusading Christian tendencies. The Ottomans easily defeated the motley Greek forces. Ypsilantis crossed the border to Austria, seeking asylum. He was, instead, thrown into prison, where he remained until his death in 1828.

Shortly after the Ypsilantis-led invasion had begun, but well before its ignominious end, revolt broke out in Greece itself. The ill-fated invasion of the principalities was probably a negligible factor in triggering revolt farther south. More important was the general feeling in Greece that the time was ripe. As with so many revolutionary situations, mutually reinforcing hopes and fears (hopes that forceful action might succeed, fears of being too far committed to find safety in inaction) served as precipitants.

In the previous year, 1820, the wily Ali Pasha of Janina was again at odds with the Ottoman government. He, as a traditional Ottoman-style warlord, made gestures to various Greek forces, including the emerging nationalists, in order to strengthen his local base of support.

Add to this initiative the general Greek awareness that the Ottoman Empire no longer had the strength of previous times—the genuine nationalism of the provincial clergy, the ready penchant of the celebrated mountain brigands (the klephts) to join a fight, and the rising fortunes, with concomitant rising expectations, of the peasantry[4]—and it is easy to see that only a spark was needed to ignite such seasoned tinder.

When the Ottoman authorities summoned local leaders in March 1821, these latter had to weigh the risk of possibly being arrested and held as hostages for good behavior of the

[4] It has been estimated that prices of Greek products rose over threefold from 1794 to 1815. Greek peasants also achieved gains, not nearly so much as Greek merchants in the Black Sea grain trade but perhaps enough to make what had for so long seemed tolerable now quite intolerable. For example, an estimated 40,000 Turks living in the Peleponnesus owned twice as much as the roughly 360,000 Greeks. See L. S. Stavrianos, *The Balkans Since 1453* (New York, 1958), pp. 276-280.

Greeks in their district against ignoring the summons and declaring a revolt. The second choice was taken, and the Greek revolt was underway. The Greeks made early gains which brought in their wake massacres of defenseless Turks. This provoked, in turn, Ottoman reprisals, including the hanging of the Greek patriarch of Constantinople (who had, in fact, taken a public position against the revolt).

This cycle of outrages also started the internationalization of the conflict that Ypsilantis had so singularly failed to achieve. As early as July 1821 the Russian government, provoked by the massacres and the execution of the patriarch, had issued an ultimatum, which the Ottomans rejected. For the moment, however, the skillful intervention of Metternich and Castlereagh kept Tsar Alexander on the side of legitimate government and against revolution.

It was only a limited respite. By 1822 the Ottoman government, having finally brought off the surrender, and the treacherous execution of Ali Pasha of Janina (January 1822), could devote more attention to the Greek revolt. Yet, the Sublime Porte was not able to finish the job. The Greek revolt in the north of the country was effectively suppressed, for this area was more vulnerable to Ottoman punitive expeditions posted from Istanbul. In the Peloponnesus and certain of the Greek islands, however, greater distance from Ottoman strength and superior seamanship gave the Greeks a strategic advantage.

The Greek nationalists were no more effective than the Ottoman government in exploiting opportunities that came their way. Instead of rallying together in a cohesive resistance movement, the Greeks dissipated much of their potential in internecine feuding. The issue seemed to be moving toward stalemate.

To break the deadlock Sultan Mahmud called in Muhammad Ali of Egypt, who had already put down the Wahhabi uprising in Arabia. It was a measure of the sultan's desperate military situation that he would risk enhancing even further the reputation of his most powerful vassal. Those at the pinnacle of power in Istanbul were accustomed to setting one unruly provincial leader against another, thereby weakening both while economizing on limited military power maintained at the center, but the trick in such divide-and-rule tactics was to avoid letting any leader beyond Istanbul's direct control go from strength to strength. Sultan Mahmud did not have the resources to play the imperial game safely. Within less than a decade he would regret his decision.

At first, Sultan Mahmud's plan to end the Greek revolt seemed to be working. Ibrahim Pasha, Muhammad Ali's competent son, was given command of operations in Crete and by 1824 had crushed the Greek insurrection there. In February of the following year Egyptian troops began landing in Greece itself. The impact of well-trained troops under a first-rate commander was immediately felt. By early 1826 the combined Egyptian and Ottoman forces dominated the Peloponnesus and seemed destined to snuff out the remaining revolutionary embers.

In the meantime, pressures for European intervention to save the Greeks continued. Unspeakable acts of cruelty and even massacres had been shamefully rife on both sides since the outbreak of hostilities, but it was the story from one side—that of Ottoman atrocities against Greeks—that reached and stirred Europe. Probably the Ottoman massacre of Greeks on the island of Chios in 1823, memorialized in Delacrox's painting, pushed European public opinion to the point of no return. That year Britian extended belligerent status to the Greek insurgents. The following year brought the first of a series of privately raised loans "which, in effect, made the City of London the financier of the revolution."[5]

It was at this time that Lord Byron, the personification of European Romanticism, joined the Greek rebellion. He arrived at Missolonghi in January 1824, where he was to die of a fever three months later. Two years later, in April 1826, the Missolonghi that Bryon had made a household word fell to

[5] Barbara Jelavich, *Century of Russian Foreign Policy, 1814-1914* (New York, 1964), p. 68.

the Ottoman-Egyptian siege. There was another casualty at Missolonghi. This was the spirit, championed by Metternich, of diplomacy as practiced before the French Revolution, in which the public was neither consulted nor considered. Thereafter, public opinion became part of the Eastern Question.

By the time the impact of Ibrahim Pasha's victories had been felt, the principal European powers were nudging each other toward some form of intervention, either under pressure of public opinion at home or from fear that a European rival might gain the advantage. A primary goal of the other European powers was to prevent unilateral Russian intervention.

Russia, in turn, could use the threat of unilateral action to pressure the other powers. A Russian ultimatum to the Ottomans in March 1826 helped to bring about an Anglo-Russian agreement in April. In this, the St. Petersburg protocol, Britain and Russia agreed to impose a settlement on the Ottomans and Greeks, should that become necessary. From the British side this agreement may also be seen as a stage in Canning's shrewd diplomacy of keeping Russia in check by means of cooperation rather than confrontation.

The hard-pressed Greeks, having suffered the fall of Missolonghi that very month of April 1826, requested mediation on the basis of the St. Petersburg protocol. Sultan Mahmud, already putting the final pieces in place for his plan to destroy and abolish the Janissary Corps (June 1826), played for time, accepted Russia's March ultimatum, and later agreed to the Russo-Ottoman Convention of Akkerman (October 1826) covering other points in contention between the two. Russia's very gains at Akkerman inclined Britain and, even more, Metternich's Austria to diplomatic foot-dragging which raised again the disturbing possibility that the Tsar's government might act alone. From this European tug-of-war emerged in July 1827 the Anglo-French-Russian Treaty of London, essentially the St. Petersburg protocol with teeth, providing joint pressure against whichever belligerent might refuse an armistice.

By this time John Capodistrias, who just ten years earlier had declined to lead the Hetairia Philike agreed to accept the presidency of a Greek government (April 1827). For a man of his distinguished background to have accepted the post then, given the domestic military and political situation, would seem to have been foolhardy. Capodistrias was no fool. A seasoned diplomat, he saw that the struggle for Greece was to be won in European chancelleries rather than in Greek villages. Before taking the position, Capodistrias obtained the approval of Tsar Nicholas I. A former Russian foreign minister had become president of the Greek Republic. The Greek war was internationalized indeed.

The fall of 1827 brought the famous battle of Navarino, a devastating defeat of the Ottoman-Egyptian forces by the combined Anglo-French-Russian fleets. In a three-hour engagement on 20 October the Ottoman and Egyptian forces lost some 57 ships and 8,000 men. Greek independence was assured in this brief battle of five foreign fleets. The irony is that the battle of Navarino was unintended. Only a show of force was expected, part of a carefully orchestrated European plan to bring the Ottomans and the Greeks to a negotiated settlement. The Russian government, intent on forcing the issue, was not displeased, but to Metternich Navarino was "a frightful catastrophe," and Wellington, who became foreign minister after Canning's death in August 1827, labelled it an "untoward event." The contradictory Western European, especially British, policy of settling the Greek problem at Ottoman expense while at the same time supporting the Ottoman Empire as a would-be bulwark against Russia was coming unstuck.

Muhammad Ali, ever the realist, was willing to evacuate his troops and await a more favorable opportunity to advance his expansionist plans. Sultan Mahmud, however, reacted differently. Instead of prudently cutting his losses by accepting that all Europe (including presumed friends such as Britain) was moving toward agreement on independence for Greece, Mahmud lashed out in bitter defiance. Denouncing Navarino as a "revolting outrage" he demanded compensation, refused to carry out the terms of the Akkerman convention with Russia, and in February 1828 closed the straits to foreign shipping. This gave Russia the *casus belli* it sought, and war was declared in April. Most scholars fault Wellington for inadvertently encouraging Ottoman resistance to Russia and thus bringing about the war that Britain sought to avoid and the Ottomans were destined to lose.

Had Canning lived, war might have been avoided and the Ottoman Empire, while still losing Greece, would have emerged somewhat stronger. Yet, a different thesis, complementary rather than contradictory, deserves attention. Sultan Mahmud was pressed by his principal advisers to hold firm. Public opinion does exist in all political systems, including traditional imperial autocracies. Mahmud had destroyed the Janissaries in 1826 and was imposing westernizing reforms upon his bureaucracy, army, and religious establishment. Reaction to these reforms was taking an increasingly religious coloration. To have appeared as always tough at home, but always supine abroad, would have branded Mahmud as the infidel sultan. The Greek revolt and the ensuing European support had raised to fever pitch on both sides atavistic Muslim-Christian antipathies.

Sultan Mahmud's long reign offers several examples of his sustained prudence in the face of provocation followed by dramatic, even impetuous, reaction. The destruction of the Janissaries, his response to Navarino, and then just over a decade later his military campaign against Muhammad Ali, all bespeak a ruler whose patience was limited and who preferred to go down fighting rather than be nibbled to death.

Sultan Mahmud's response prefigured what was to become a common, and understandable, reaction of Middle Eastern rulers caught in the net of Eastern Question politics. The tendency of beleaguered Middle Eastern rulers to give alien tormentors one last "run for their money" occurs too consistently to be explained away by the personal idiosyncrasy of this or that ruler. Do we not have, instead, a patterned reaction understandable in terms of recurring political, and psychological scenarios? There will be occasion to return to this theme.

The Ottomans, for all their disorganization following Mahmud's destruction of the Janissaries and the many disruptive westernizing reforms then being launched, fought tenaciously. It was only by 1829 that Russian strength prevailed. Adrianople fell in August, and Istanbul, whose inhabitants could hear the sound of Russian cannon, was to be saved by diplomacy, not by arms.

The denouement reveals the Greek war of independence as a fully elaborated model of multi-party Eastern Question diplomacy. After Adrianople fell, Tsar Nicholas convened a special governmental commission which reported in September that, on balance, it was in Russia's interest to keep the Ottoman Empire in existence. The decision (not, of course, announced publicly) moved Russia to offer the Ottomans moderate peace terms.

This accorded with the aims of the other European powers, who as always most feared that one of their number would benefit exclusively. The follow-up London conference, beginning in November 1829 and leading to the London protocol of February 1830, confirmed the joint European interests.

Two years passed before the European powers had agreed on a member of European royalty to serve as king of Greece, the Bavarian prince Otto. Before that time Capodistrias had been assassinated (October 1831) by rival Greek political forces, and the new kingdom was off to a shaky start. The more specifically Greek aspect of the story must be passed over here. In fact, the Greeks had played only a minor role in the unfolding story since Navarino.

Ominous for later developments, the settlement finally reached left a tiny kingdom of some 800,000 Greeks while well over 2,000,000 Greeks continued to live under Ottoman rule.[6] Phanariot predominance in the Ottoman Empire was now a memory. The modern logic of nationalism had triumphed, and it was to ride the wave of the future; but it left an untidy debris for later statesmen.

[6] Not to mention the Greeks living in the British-controlled Ionian Islands.

IV. THE PATTERN OF NATIONAL
LIBERATION MOVEMENTS

By the end of the Greek war of independence the pattern of national liberation movements within the special operating climate of the Eastern Question was fixed. Many other examples would follow in the decades to come. Each national liberation movement had its own distinctive characteristics and circumstances, but from the viewpoint of this book they may rightly be seen as variations on a familiar theme. This process of national liberation in time produced new states such as Rumania, Montenegro, Bulgaria and Albania.

Yet other parts of that once firmly held Ottoman estate would become bones of contention among varying combinations of the newly independent little states and the European powers. The roll call of these stirs dusty memories of bygone crises— Macedonia, Crete, Novi Bazar, Bosnia, and Herzegovina. Still other groups such as the Armenians and the Arabs, previously either reconciled to their political lot or never having thought in terms of "national" identity, were eventually carried along in the current.

To treat seriatim each of these national liberation movements, even in summary fashion, is perhaps not the best way to trace the rise and development of a distinctive Eastern Question system. Instead, what was foreshadowed in the Serbian revolt and fully developed in the years of the Greek struggle can be abstracted into a generalized model that covers the later examples during the years 1830-1914.

The model of classical Eastern Question national liberation movements presents the following characteristics:

1. The actual outbreak of hostilities was preceded by a period of cultural renaissance of decidedly nationalist or proto-nationalist orientation (e.g., language reform, interest in vernacular literature, new literature adapting

Romanticist themes, evoking a past "golden age" of the specific "national" group as the exemplar of what must be recaptured).

2. The revolt involved a challenge to both the Ottoman authorities and the native elites (political, economic, and religious) enjoying privileges under the Ottoman system.

3. Efforts were made by the resistance leaders to line up outside support in advance or, failing that, to use the timing and manner of taking up arms with an eye to provoking outside intervention.

4. The outside powers engaged in concurrent, but clearly separate and occasionally contradictory, efforts to (a) induce policy changes on the part of the Sublime Porte and (b) arrange for a common European policy to be imposed.

5. The Ottoman government, sensing the implicit European duplicity in the above and having limited options in any case, vacillated between acceptance of imposed conditions in principle while delaying implementation in fact and dogged refusal of all advice, whether proferred by friend or foe.

6. All sides attempted to present others concerned, friends or foes, with faits accomplis.

7. Positions won by force of arms on the spot were never so determining as the final consensus decision reached by the European powers.

8. The nationalist leaders exercised their maximum leverage in getting others involved. They had less control over the course of events once their struggle was under way. They were not able to keep international action confined to the issues that triggered hostilities.

Unlike the traditional Ottoman style "warlord," such as Ali Pasha of Janina or Muhammad Ali of Egypt, the national liberation leaders played by different rules. So, too, did the Ottoman authorities in dealing with them. The nationalists' appeal to self-determination would, if unchecked, sap the foundations of the Ottoman state. Theirs was a systemic challenge.

An Ali Pasha could rebel and return to play the game as a loyal Ottoman official without risking the loss of his own power base. He was not responsible to any political constituency for ideological consistency. His only concern, and the sole basis on which others judged him, was tactical political efficacy.

Not so the national liberation leaders. They might lose control over their own constituency by coming to terms too soon or too readily with the Ottomans. For the same reason, the Ottoman authorities could not really trust such leaders to honor an old-style personal political deal.

An Ali Pasha was mortal, and he might well be followed by a less imposing successor. The central government could bide its time with such men. It could, in extremis, even make major concessions under pressure of events (as with Muhammad Ali) buoyed by the not unreasonable hope that at some future time the situation could be restored. The national liberation leaders were also mortal, and as a matter of fact often made of much frailer stuff than the likes of Ali Pasha or Muhammad Ali, but the idea they represented showed virulent vitality.

Since compromise between national liberation rebels and the Ottoman government was considerably more difficult for both sides than equivalent arrangements between old style warlords and the central government, the national liberation movements tended to rely more on outside intervention. Also, if defeated by existing authority and unsuccessful in efforts to bring in the great powers, such movements tended to go underground rather than out of existence. They would quite likely then hit upon the use of guerrilla or terrorist activities—the last weapon of the weak.

Of course, a successful Ottoman-type warlord operating in the context of the Eastern Question could become the unplanned patron of nationalism. The way in which our history books refer to the Albanian from Kavalla as Muhammad Ali of Egypt reveals the metamorphosis.

It is interesting to speculate what might have happened if

Muhammad Ali and his successors had been able to hold on to Crete, Greece, Syria, or Arabia, instead of being confined to the Nile Valley after 1840 (with loss even of Sudan in the 1880s). Would his dynasty have survived until 1952 if Muhammad Ali had been able to found the multinational empire that he sought? Certainly, the bleak history of the Ottoman Empire (and the Austrian) in that age of rising nationalism suggests that the Muhammad Ali dynasty lasted almost a century and a half only because the diplomatic defeats suffered by the founder left his successors presiding over a people that history and geography had combined to make a nation-state even before the term was coined.

Unless the Ottoman-style warlord was able to recruit a nationalist following, his successes and even more his successors were likely to be few in number. Even in failure, however, such leaders could and often did have a major role in the development of other nationalist movements. Muhammad Ali, again, provides the most notable example. His domination of Syria for less than a decade in the 1830s gave a great impetus both to what became Lebanese as well as Arab nationalism.

The dynamic warlord who did embrace a nationalist movement (even if his motives were purely tactical) could provide that movement the effective political leadership so often missing. This suggests another speculative point: What if Ali Pasha of Janina and the Hetairia Philike had joined forces? Would Greek independence have been achieved more easily, and would the new state have begun its political life endowed with somewhat more unity and authority? Quite possibly. If Ali Pasha, who understood power, had been impressed by the Hetairia Philike, then the fate of the two could have become increasingly intertwined, perhaps to the advantage of both.

Both warlordism and national liberation movements challenged Ottoman rule, but with regional variations. Although warlordism existed throughout the empire, national liberation movements came first and were most numerous in Ottoman Europe. The reason is simple.

Ottoman Europe was an area not just of great religious,

ethnic, and linguistic diversity (the Ottoman-controlled Fertile Crescent was all this as well). It was also an area of Christian not Muslim, majorities, and these Christians had religious and linguistic ties with the adjacent European powers. They could appeal to powerful correligionists and identify with European ideologies religious or secular. Moreover, geographical proximity permitted them to use sanctuaries beyond Ottoman control and play off neighboring great powers (e.g., Austria and Russia). The national liberation movements of Ottoman Europe had greater motivation, greater opportunity and greater chance of success than their equivalents throughout the rest of the empire.

Things were not so simple in the Ottoman lands of Muslim majorities. It was a long time before Arabic speakers and Turkish speakers began to think of themselves as Arabs and Turks. Not that they had a modern, nation-state type of loyalty to the Ottoman Empire. Even to present the issue in those terms is to expose the anachronism. The Ottoman Empire, a premodern bureaucratic imperial system ruling over diverse religious, linguistic, and ethnic groupings, made no such demands on its subjects. The overwhelming majority of the Ottoman Muslims did, however, identify with the Ottoman Empire. It was the last great Muslim state holding out against European encroachment.

The very idea of nationalism involved the Muslims of the Ottoman Empire in agonizing choices spared the Christians. Nationalism seemed opposed to Muslim unity. It could be presented as blasphemous or at the very least a foolhardy playing into the hands of the intrusive Europeans who wished nothing more than to divide the Muslim peoples as a step toward subjugating them.

Accordingly, that Western European import, nationalism, was not immediately accepted by Ottoman Muslims. Among the Ottoman Christians, diverse individuals from traditional clerics to starry-eyed liberals bedazzled by the French Revolution could work together, selectively emphasizing common religion or language or ethnicity, opposing what, in the nationalist jargon, was the infidel, incomprehensible, and alien Ottoman Empire.

No such easy lumping together was available to the Muslims. The Muslim path to nationalism was long and tortuous. The suggested model for national liberation movements in the context of the Eastern Question applies to Ottoman Muslims, but the change was decidedly slower and more traumatic. For the time covered in this chapter, Arab and Turkish nationalisms remained inchoate.

V. NON-NATIONALIST MUSLIM CHALLENGES TO THE OTTOMAN SYSTEM

The Ottoman areas of Muslim majorities offered a different kind of regional challenge—non-national Muslim religio-political movements. The three major examples were the Wahhabiyya, Sanusiyya, and the Sudanese Mahdiyya. All three were activist religious movements. To use the terms associated with the work of Max Weber, these movements were this-worldly rather than other-wordly, ascetic rather than mystical. All drew their inspiration from traditional Muslim sources and were not influenced by the West. Two (Wahhabiyya and Mahdiyya) were revolutionary in calling for a fundamental change in existing institutions and were sectarian in taking the position that those not with them were against them. The Sanusiyya was more meliorist and accommodationist.

All three, by challenging the existing Muslim religious leadership, started a process that eventually tore to shreds the carefully woven fabric of relationships between the Muslim religious establishment and the Ottoman state. All three, ironically, strengthened a major force totally alien to their own most cherished goals: By putting great strains on the weakened Ottoman Empire and, even more, by helping to undermine the legitimacy of the empire in the eyes of Muslims, they facilitated the sundering of that large portion of the Muslim *umma* held together by the Ottomans. This left the path open for secular nationalist movements that were to flourish in the twentieth century.

These three movements illustrate the need for a third category: To that of (1) Ottoman-style warlordism and (2) classical Eastern Question national liberation movements should be added (3) non-nationalist Muslim religio-political movements.

* * *

Such, then, were the many diverse challenges from within faced by established Middle Eastern political authority. Harried and bullied by the great powers, constantly facing threats from within the shrinking Ottoman world, what were these governments to do? This is the question addressed in the next section.

VI. ESTABLISHED MIDDLE EASTERN POLITICAL AUTHORITY FACING THE EASTERN QUESTION

The Ottoman Empire itself was the major example of established Middle Eastern political authority. It was the largest, most powerful, and also the most hard-pressed political entity within the Middle East, but there remain two other examples of veritable state systems to be set alongside that of the Sublime Porte. These were Egypt and Tunisia. Admittedly, both were juridically part of the Ottoman Empire, but they possessed a de facto independence with their own army, their own bureaucracy, and their own political traditions.

In the early decades of the nineteenth century two other Muslim polities nominally within the framework of the Ottoman Empire also enjoyed virtual independence. These were the deylik of Algiers and the beylik of Tripoli. Both then lost that independence. Algiers fell prey to French rule, beginning

63

in 1830, and Tripoli was restored to direct Ottoman rule in 1835.

That there were three separate, de facto independent Muslim states within the Ottoman Empire throughout the nineteenth century draws attention to the kaleidoscopic motif emphasized throughout this book—a situation of many different political actors both within and outside the Middle East converging in complicated interaction. Moreover, if it can be shown that all three responded in roughly the same manner to the new situation brought by the Eastern Question and that their separate actions led in all three cases to similar results, this strengthens the argument that a distinctive international relations system characterized the Middle East.

Such, indeed, was the case. In all three states the first to be aware of the new challenge coming from Europe were the existing political elites. Their perception of the problem came directly from contact with Europe. Unlike early modern Europe where developments initiated by non-governmental forces (e.g., a rising bourgeoisie, an intelligentsia) began the process of change that only later confronted the established political elites, in the Middle East those making up government were the first to be involved.

How did they respond? Seeing the European military threat, the political elites of the three separate polities came up with strikingly similar answers. They saw the challenge in narrowly technical terms. Europe had somehow managed to advance in military technology, giving it a decided power advantage. The balance would be righted if these political elites could graft that technology on to the existing state system. No more than this was planned by that first generation of modernizing Muslim monarchs—Selim III and Mahmud II of the Ottoman Empire, Muhammad Ali of Egypt, and Tunisia's Ahmad Bey.

It was not to be that simple. To borrow European military technology a state needed both European military advisers and native officers who could speak the appropriate European language. Thus, all three states recruited European military advisory teams and also sent student missions abroad, especially to France.[7] Those put in touch with a dynamic alien culture learned more than military drill. They and their successors would be heard from.

A newly westernized army was of little utility if materiel was to be obtained only beyond the borders of the state, and—even worse—from that very Europe which posed the threat. Thus, the felt need for military self-sufficiency got the three states involved in establishing industries to serve military needs.

Nor was this all. The new armies required more than new drill, new uniforms, and new weapons. They needed, or so the prevailing European doctrine insisted, greater numbers. Post-Revolutionary Europe had moved in the direction of the *levée en masse*, of the large citizen army. The modernizing Middle Eastern political establishments went along, sadly for them, with this thinking. All three adopted conscription. All three moved from the older pattern of small professional armies assisted as needed by irregulars who, while perhaps not efficient, were not costly.

These expensive innovations stirred up resistance both from within the political establishment and among the populace. Spearheading the resistance from within the government were the traditional military corps—the Janissaries of the Ottoman Empire, the Mamluks in Egypt, and the regular Turkish troops[8] of Tunisia. A Janissary revolt cost Selim III his throne and

[7] Both the Ottoman Empire and Egypt organized student missions abroad, beginning in the 1820s. The returning students became, in large measure, the founding fathers of the many diverse Westernizing and liberalizing movements that steadily grew in numbers and influence throughout the century. No formal student missions as such were sent from Tunisia, and the process of training members of the Tunisian political elite in European languages and European ways seems to have been rather more haphazard. Even so, essentially the same result was achieved: witness the later modernizing school of Tunisians that rallied around Khayr al-Din al-Tunisi.

[8] So designated in the Tunisian sources because they were recruited from outside Tunisia, largely but not exclusively from Turkish-speaking areas, and the language of command was Turkish. They were not Ottoman troops sent by the Porte and subject to transfer. Tunisia also had a small number of Mamluks who held the top military and political posts.

6. Muhammad Ali and the massacre of the Mumluks, 1811
(from a lithograph by H. Vernet).

ultimately his life. Muhammad Ali faced the challenge of
Mamluks and, even later, an insurrection of his own Albanian
corps. Immediate predecessors of Tunisia's Ahmad Bey barely
survived two separate coups by the Turkish troops.

All three reformist elites also concluded that no structural
change was possible until the power of the military old guard
was broken. The riposte in Egypt and the Ottoman Empire
took an especially dramatic form: Muhammad Ali's massacre
of the Mamluks in 1811 and Sultan Mahmud II's destruction
of the Janissaries in 1826. In Tunisia the result was achieved
more circumspectly, by earmarking the top positions in the
new westernized units for the leading Mamluk and Turkish
officers while phasing out the old regular infantry.

Popular resistance to conscription and the increased taxation these westernizing innovations required posed less of an

immediate threat to existing government, but proved more difficult to stifle in the long run. The flight of young men from rural villages, self-mutilation to avoid conscription, protests, efforts to get religious leaders (the traditional spokesmen for society) to intervene with government, and occasional outbreaks of violence, all kept government edgily aware that its bold plans for change might never get implemented in the countryside. This recalls the continuous problem of warlordism that Middle Eastern government faced. Having decided that the only way to face the *outside* challenge from Europe was to borrow Europe's military technology, how were the modernizing elites to master the multiple *domestic* resistances?

One overall strategy, adopted by all three—Egypt, Tunisia and the central Ottoman Empire—seemed to confront equally all the many obstacles, whether military old guard or warlordism or sullen subjects digging in their heels. This was nothing less than the strengthening and centralization of government. As with military reform, the model followed was Europe, although reformers in all three states tended to present these innovations in a more acceptable Islamic and Middle Eastern guise.

In the Ottoman Empire westernization was described as an effort to return to the tried-and-true practices to be found in the reign of Sulayman the Magnificent (1520-1566), the golden age of Ottoman strength. In fact, the programs represented a consolidation of power at the center such as had never existed previously. There is irony in this. As seen from St. Petersburg or London, the Ottoman Empire was the "sick man of Europe." Earlier pages documenting Ottoman difficulties throughout the century suggest that the sobriquet was on target.

Yet, that same sick state did manage to wipe out warlordism in Anatolia and the Fertile Crescent (admittedly, after getting greater Syria away from Muhammad Ali only as a consequence of European intervention), restore Tripolitania to direct Ottoman rule, make certain advances on the fringe of the

Arabian peninsula (as in Yemen), while continuing to field armies—occasionally with distinction—against foreign foes.

Muhammad Ali, for his part, brought under his control the people and resources of Egypt to such extent that a contemporary observer characterized the entire country as "one large tax farm." This was a far cry from the semi-feudal partition of political and economic power under the Mamluks in Ottoman Egypt.

The task of centralization was easier in Tunisia, a much smaller country with an accessible, sedentary core area radiating out from the capital city of Tunis. Moreover, those natural barriers to central government control—mountains and desert—were located on the western and southern extremes of the country, respectively.

Even so, much remained to be done by way of effective centralization; and Ahmad Bey, followed similar western-inspired ideas of administration with similar economic and social costs. For all three, what had begun as a limited plan to adapt western military technology expanded step-by-step into a broad program of Westernization—legal codes, schools, tax systems, representative councils, abolition of slavery, and, most revolutionary of all, the move toward western-style civil rights and duties. This latter point involved moving away from the notion of legal status determined largely by religious affiliation (the celebrated millet system) toward the idea of secular citizenship.

These ambitious goals were not achieved, and this was hardly surprising (although supercilious European contemporaries kept harping on the point as if they could have been accomplished with ease). What was significant—and largely overlooked by those same supercilious European contemporaries—was the steady chipping away at centuries-old Muslim concepts of state and society.

How did these westernizing developments relate to the Eastern Question? The Ottoman Empire, Egypt and Tunisia each wrestled with the threat posed by Europe. In all three states Muslim equivalents of the eighteenth-century enlightened despots attempted to effect radical, westernizing changes.

These Muslim enlightened despots, in the process, slowly recruited converts from within the existing political elite. They also aroused opposition both within the political elite and among the populace. As if this were not enough they were already saddled with the age-old problems of warlordism. They needed help from Europe to carry out their modernizing programs, but they also had to be on guard against overly close collaboration, lest their risky plan of using Europe to insure independence should lead instead to irreversible dependence.

Theirs was not just a two-front war. It was conducted on three fronts. The reformers within the established political elites faced simultaneously:

1. Intra-elite opposition
2. Domestic opposition from both the largely mute, foot-dragging subjects who preferred the traditional ways of limited government and the warlords (with the likelihood that the latter could work to exploit the grievances of the former)
3. The European power structure whose several states if united could work their will on the Middle East

In the intricate, multiplayer game that evolved, a major tactic of the Middle Eastern reformers facing Europe was "divide that ye may not be ruled."[9] Thus, the Ottoman reformers long relied on Britain as a support against Russia and other possible European foes, but when this relationship began to sour, the Ottomans moved toward Germany. Muhammad Ali tried to deal with Britain to no avail and found himself usually working closely with France.

Tunisia, fearful that the central Ottoman Empire intended to reestablish direct control just as it had done in Tripolitania

[9] The term used by Ernest Gellner to describe how tribes escape central government control is equally apt for the situation in which lesser governments seek to avoid great power control. See Ernest Gellner, *Saints of the Atlas* (University of Chicago Press, 1969), pp. 41 ff.

in 1835, worked closely with France, especially since Britain in the middle years of the nineteenth century strongly supported Ottoman claims in Tunisia. Yet, the Tunisian elite was not unaware of the French danger, seeing what had happened in neighboring Algeria.

The established Middle Eastern political elites also attempted to hedge their European bets by recruiting military advisers and granting governmental contracts to representatives from different European powers. The Middle Eastern reformists had to buy time and good will from Europe if their modernizing gamble was to succeed. Several public actions bound to please Europe were timed to escape an especially confining diplomatic bind. The best known examples are the three major constitutional acts of the nineteenth century Ottoman Empire:

1. The 1839 Hatt-ı Şerif of Gulhane was intended to attract European support for the Empire in danger of being overrun by Muhammad Ali.
2. The 1856 Hatt-ı Humayun (extending civil liberties especially to the non-Muslim minorities) was issued just a week before the plenipotentiaries gathered in Paris to negotiate the end of the Crimean War. It was designed to strengthen the Ottoman hand at the coming Congress of Paris.
3. The 1876 Ottoman Constitution cut the ground from under the Constantinople conference (of Great Power representatives—Ottoman representatives were even excluded from the earlier meeting!) plan to settle the Eastern crisis by imposing territorial adjustment and political reforms on the Ottomans.

Reformist political elites in Egypt and Tunisia responded similarly, buying time and good will from Europe when needed. For example, Said (1854-1863) ended Muhammad Ali's state monopolies and began the campaign against the slave trade in the Sudan, thereby getting on the right side of two issues championed by Britain—free trade and anti-slavery. His successor, Ismail (1863-1879), continued this approach. At the height of his financial woes in 1874, he appointed Charles Gordon as governor-general of the Sudan, with a mandate to abolish slavery. Earlier, in 1866 Ismail had established a representative assembly. Then, in 1878, he proclaimed a system of ministerial responsibility. All these moves, designed to give the appearance that Ismail was leading his country on the path of European-style progress, were part of the khedive's desperate efforts to frustrate European interference.

In Tunisia throughout the 1840s Ahmad Bey first stopped the slave trade and then abolished slavery completely. The Tunisian ruler was then at the height of his euphoric belief that his country could be accepted into the European club. Accordingly, he risked domestic opposition and got out well ahead of European (mainly British) pressure on this issue.

Tunisia's first basic civil liberties charter, the Fundamental Pact ('Ahd al-Aman) of 1857,[10] was a response to Europe's outrage with the summary execution of a Tunisian Jewish subject who had allegedly blasphemed the Prophet Muhammad. This basic charter was approved by the most reactionary of nineteenth-century Tunisian rulers, Muhammad Bey, so great was the concern of his ministers that European intervention was imminent unless drastic action could be taken at once.

Then, three years later in 1860 the westernizing Muhammad al-Sadiq Bey visited Napoleon III in Algiers, brought along the draft Tunisian constitution (destined to be the first in the Arab world), and obtained the emperor's approval. This act of "clearing" a country's constitution with a foreign ruler poignantly underlined the diplomatic dimension of domestic reform during these years.

Contemporary European statesmen and observers often responded cynically. The old European canard about the Tan-

[10] Patterned on the Ottoman Hatt-ı Şerif of Gulhane (1839), not the later and more comprehensive Ottoman Hatt-ı Humayun 1856.

zimat stopping at the doorstep of the Sublime Porte epitomized their attitude, and the historical record is filled with
similar European dismissals of other Ottoman, Egyptian, or
Tunisian efforts at westernization. Wily Oriental gentlemen
were tossing dust in the eyes of upright Europeans. The reality was more complex. The small but growing number of
westernizers among the established political elites genuinely
believed that such reforms could strengthen the state. They
also sought structural changes that would greatly increase their
own political power. These reformers were a vulnerable minority, likely to lose out in the international game of seeking
Great Power support, likely to lose out to rivals within the
political elite of their own state, and subject to a change of
fortunes following on some unanticipated domestic upheaval.
The safest way to win over, or silence, opposition to their
reforms was to argue that these steps were necessary to gain
European support or to frustrate European designs against
the state.

If one insists on a cynical interpretation it would be most
accurate to argue that the reformers were misleading everyone, not just Europe. In dealing with Europe they exaggerated domestic opposition in order to solicit more patience and
more support. In treating opposition at home they exaggerated the baleful possibilities of European intervention if reforms were not adopted. It was the tactic of those seeking to
implement daring new programs but possessing limited political power. One result was a thorough blending and confusion
of domestic and international politics. Here are to be found
the Eastern Question roots of a characteristic still distinguishing the Middle East.

Unfortunately for the reformers, any number could play the
game of divide-that-ye-may-not-be-ruled. And quite a number
did. Even the most traditionalist members of the established
political elite—who if consistent with their ideology would
eschew any trafficking with Europe—sought support from
whatever European power opposed the European power that
the reformers happened to be working with. The warlords

7. Europe tended to see the frenetic westernizing efforts of
Middle Eastern governments as at best idle play, at worst
intentional deceit (*Punch*, 1877).

and, especially, national liberation movements were even more
inclined to seek outside patrons. With good reason the great
Tanzimat statesman Fuad Pasha could point out to a European diplomat: "Our state is the strongest state. For you are
trying to cause its collapse from the outside, and we from the
inside, but still it does not collapse."[11]

[11] Cited in Roderic H. Davison, *Reform in the Ottoman Empire, 1856-1876*
(Princeton University Press, 1963), p. 9.

The game of playing off European powers and domestic rivals might have continued indefinitely, so balanced were the many forces involved, but for one stubborn factor that totally resisted the virtuosities of diplomatic maneuver: government finances. The move toward stronger government, larger armies, and vastly increased governmental operations put an unbearable strain on the traditional tax structure. Vastly increased government expenditures were even more intolerable because, except for a brief time in Egypt during the cotton boom (that peaked in the years of the American Civil War, which disrupted the normal flow of cotton from the American South to the mills of Manchester), there was no economic development commensurate with rising government expenditure. Even Egypt's temporary good fortune proved a mixed blessing. With the end of the American war cotton prices dropped sharply, and Khedive Ismail was caught short. By 1876 Egypt was bankrupt.

Egypt's fiscal adventures were the most dramatic, but all three states fell into the same trap. Efforts to squeeze more taxes out of the peasantry were attempted with, here and there, some short-term success, but at a cost that made the long-term goal of creating self-sufficient, modern states even more distant. By harsh tax policies (especially in Egypt and Tunisia) these governments confirmed the peasantry in their distrust of government and of landlords, thereby destroying any possibility of stimulating an expansive, entrepreneurial spirit in the countryside. In Tunisia, the oppressive governmental tax policy provoked a full-scale revolt in 1864 that almost toppled the Husaynid dynasty.

All three governments sought loans abroad. There was no lack of European consuls, bankers, and middlemen to facilitate such a move. Since the loans, raised at exorbitant rates of interest, covered current expenses, rather than development projects which might have paid for themselves, the end was predictable. State bankruptcy came to Tunisia in 1869, the Ottoman Empire in 1875 and Egypt in 1876. The European powers, who had shown little concern while the debts were piling up, now moved in to insure that these improvident Middle Eastern states paid for their folly. European-directed debt liquidation commissions were imposed upon all three countries. For two of the three—Tunisia and Egypt—these debt commissions proved to be the last stage before outright western control.

The several obvious ways in which Egypt, the Ottoman Empire, and Tunisia were not at all similar throughout the nineteenth century highlight the strong pull of the Eastern Question pattern. The Egypt of Muhammad Ali and his successors was an expansionist political system, conquering the Sudan, intervening for a time in the Arabian peninsula, Greece, Syria, and even Ethiopia, until state brankruptcy during Khedive Ismail's reign ended such ambitions. The Ottoman Empire was just that—an empire. Moreover, it was a beleagured empire seeking frantically to keep what it already possessed. Tunisia was a tiny state surrounded by larger neighbors. The Tunisian strategy was completely defensive—a careful balancing of powerful and threatening neighbors.

Egypt and Tunisia possessed a geographic and demographic consistency that would facilitate the emergence of a nation-state. Egypt was the "gift of the Nile." Tunisia was a small, contiguous sedentary area with the barriers of mountains and deserts located on its borders. Both countries had populations that were overwhelmingly Sunni Muslim and Arabic-speaking.

The Ottoman Empire was at the other extreme of the spectrum, attempting to hold together peoples of different languages, religions, and races who were juxtaposed in mountains, plains, deserts, seashores, remote hinterlands, along rivers fit for irrigated agriculture, and in semi-arid zones destined according to the moods of man and the seasons to swing between a precarious dry-farming and pastoralism.

Tunisia, unlike Egypt, was a tiny state having a population of probably 1,000,000 to at most 1,500,000 and boasting no significant natural resources that could be exploited for forced-draft economic development (such as Egypt's long staple, cot-

75

ton, not to mention the general agricultural potential of the rich Nile valley).

Yet, these many imposing differences distinguishing Egypt, the Ottoman Empire, and Tunisia did not significantly modify the basic international relations pattern linked to the Eastern Question—options chosen by the regional political elites, policies of the outside powers, responses from within the different Middle Eastern societies, the intra-elite struggles between westernizers and reactionaries, and (most of all) the seemingly inexorable manner in which all these elements combined in all three states to give strikingly similar results—from military modernization to state bankruptcy.

Two other points support the argument of Eastern Question systemic continuity. First, the three different Middle Eastern states directly dealt with Europe while carefully linking their actions to what was taking place in the region. The result was a complete blending of domestic, regional, and international politics. For example, Sultan Mahmud II emulated his arch-rival, Muhammad Ali. Sultan Mahmud II, within the space of a few years, followed the steps of Muhammad Ali in (a) opening a western-style medical school, (b) sending student missions to Europe, and (c) establishing an official gazette.

All three state systems used the term *nizami*, first introduced by Selim III, in describing their military innovation, just as all felt even more justified in taking such westernizing steps by the knowledge that the other regional states were doing the same.

Moreover, Ahmad Bey's drawing closer to France after the Ottoman Empire re-established direct administration over Tripoli and his successor's drawing closer to Britain and the Ottoman Empire to counter an Italian threat may be compared, *grosso modo*, to Sultan Mahmud II's rashly provoking war[12] with Muhammad Ali in 1839 and Sultan Abdul

[12] Or was Mahmud's action so rash? Although soundly defeated in the field, the sultan provoked European intervention and got Muhammad Ali out

Hamid's willingness to act on British and French urging and dismiss Khedive Ismail in 1879.

The regional political elites viewed regional and international politics as an unbroken continuum. They still do. At times the major threat was from within the region (Muhammad Ali against Sultan Mahmud II or Ottoman designs on Tunisian autonomy in the 1830s). On other occasions (and more often, given the general power distribution) the major threat was from Europe. Then a Tunisia would move closer to the Ottoman Empire, an Abdul Hamid would consider pan-Islam as a unifying doctrine, or an Ismail would proffer bribes and subsidies in Istanbul to get his title of khedive (for the very act of soliciting the new title underscored Egypt's link as a province of the Ottoman Empire—an Ismail less threatened by Europe might have chosen to move toward independence).

Second, the regional political elite operated from a very narrow power base, and they realized this bleak fact. Muhammad Ali might well for a brief time have had the exhilarating feeling of going from strength to strength, but if so his being cut down to size in 1840, so soon after his son's smashing defeat of the Ottoman forces, was a sobering lesson to him and to others—whether sultans, pashas, or warlords—who might aspire to a dominant role in the region. Knowing that they had limited power and equally limited maneuverability, the established elites chose prudence and paranoia. Better to go for the small gain or to await what little advantage the mistakes of others might bring.

Better to act on the assumption (which accorded so well with experience) that the apparently solid support of an outside power might dissolve from one day to the next, that the defeated enemy could quickly be restored to power by outside

---

of Syria. A comparison with President Sadat's starting the October 1973 war comes to mind. The military cards were stacked against success; the Egyptian forces, although they fought with distinction, did not win, but the great powers were provoked to take actions that favored Egyptian interests.

forces, that today's ally in the bureaucracy might join one's enemy tomorrow, and that policies favoring certain peoples within the state offered no guarantee that those so favored would refrain from supporting opponents.

The bitter sense among the political elites of their relative powerlessness in a kaleidoscopic, Hobbesian world created in them a cynicism and a manipulative spirit which, in turn, helped to sustain the very system that oppressed them.

VII. CONCLUSION: STABILITY AND FLUX

By the time the post-World War One settlements had been worked out (the 1923 Lausanne Treaty offers a precise terminal point), the Middle East was a radically different place from what it had been when Catherine imposed the harsh Treaty of Kuçuk Kaynarca on the defeated Ottoman Empire.

The Ottoman Empire was no more, sundered into some two dozen different political entities, either already independent as small to middle-sized states or under different forms of Western tutelage and destined to become, in their turn, independent later in the twentieth century.

The ideology of nationalism, imported from Europe had challenged, and throughout much of the area defeated, the centuries-old idea of bureaucratic empire presiding from afar over peoples compartmentalized into self-contained social units by religion, race, language, and ecological life style, but most of all by religion.

A view of politics that envisaged a political world of imperial despotism mitigated by benign neglect in all but security and taxation was giving way to the idea of government as responsible for setting and implementing society's goals. (This new outlook was already well advanced on the level of prevailing ideology. It was much less well established as operating reality.) The notion of a remote government ruling over

78

subjects was fading before the idea of a government working for, but also making extensive demands upon, citizens.

In 1923 most of the former Ottoman Middle East was either under direct Western colonial rule or various forms of indirect Western tutelage. The only real exception was the Republic of Turkey, created by Kemal Ataturk out of the Turkish-speaking Anatolian core of the Ottoman Empire, for the nominally independent political entities of Arabia were beholden to Western advice and subsidies (Ibn Saud and Sharif Husayn) or holding on to a tenuous Tibet-like independence (Yemen).

With such massive change, how can one talk of continuity? Quite simply, by carefully separating out the limited aspects of continuity: The pattern of international politics which has been examined from different perspectives in Part I did not die with the Ottoman Empire. As a distinctive, identifiable system of political interaction it continued after 1923 and continues to this day. This is the argument treated in Part II.

One more word on this point may help to avoid misunderstanding. For some perverse reason, arguments for the existence of a long-lived *system* risk being interpreted as denying that any fundamental change has taken place. Yet, to assert that a pattern of human interaction survives for generations is not to argue that no significant change occurs either within the framwork of, or alongside, that pattern.

This stable international relations system characterizing the Middle East of the Eastern Question era demonstrated impressive fluctuations in the pecking order of states and in such matters as which states were seeking to expand and which were satisfied to hold what they had, which states were perceived by others as rising powers and which as declining. The stable system was, in short, dynamic. Part I concludes with Table I, presenting the broad lines of this process in simplified form. Part II will conclude with a similar table for the later period.

TABLE I
EASTERN QUESTION TEAM STANDINGS AND STRATEGIES,
1774-1923

1768-1796   Period of persistent Russian advances against weakening Ottoman Empire. Limited response by other European powers.

1798-1801   Napoleon's bold but unsuccessful move against Egypt. In response, beginning of active British involvement in Middle East.

1798-1815   Napoleon's initiatives dominating great power actions in the Middle East.

1815-1822   Creation and development of Congress system, formalizing idea that changes in the Middle East subject to European concurrence, with appropriate compensations to maintain European balance of power.

1821-1845   Heyday of regional initiatives with powers tending to respond to actions begun in the Middle East, e.g.:
—Greek war of independence (1821-1829)
—1st and 2nd Syrian crises pitting Muhammad Ali against the Ottoman Empire (1830s)
—Lebanese disturbances (1840s)
—Ottoman restoration of direct rule in Tripolitania (1835)
—Tunisian push for strengthened autonomy under Ahmad Bey (1837 until financial stringency in late 1840s)

1856-1870   Era of Crimean System. Russia in temporary eclipse. Italian and German unification changing European power balance to detriment of, among others, Austria.

1870-1891   France struggling back from defeat in Franco-Prussian War
Bismark as "honest broker"

80

	British Middle Eastern strategy moves southward with Egypt as linchpin, with concomitant cooling of British support for Ottoman Empire.
1891-1914	Post-Bismarck Germany joins the European "club," actively seeking interests in the Middle East.
	Baroque period of classical Eastern Question with four major powers (Britian, France, Germany, and Russia) plus one declining power (Austro-Hungarian Empire) and one aspiring power (Italy), all reconsidering long-held strategies and jockeying for new positions.
	Pan-Islam of Abdul Hamid gives way to Turkism of Young Turks.
	Early stirrings of Arabism.

This review of the "classical" age of the Eastern Question has argued that the peculiar combination of kaleidoscopic relations characterizing Middle Eastern diplomacy produced a distinctive international relations system.

It remains now to present the argument that the Eastern Question system did not die with the Ottoman Empire but continues to this day. Such is the task of Part II.

PART TWO

PART TWO

———— ✳ ————

New Wine, Old Bottles

AT THE end of the First World War the Ottoman Empire was destined, at long last, for destruction. The coup de grâce was not, however, delivered by the victorious allies. They were willing to keep a tiny Ottoman remnant in existence after all else had been parcelled out.

Instead, five years later, in 1923, a prestigious member of the Ottoman ruling class and the most eminent Ottoman military officer during the First World War, Mustafa Kemal (who later assumed the title, Ataturk, or father of the Turks), abolished the empire, replacing it with the Republic of Turkey. It was poetic justice that a member of the immediate family should finally, in an act of euthanasia, dispatch the sick man of Europe.

In the same year Ataturk moved the capital to Ankara, a hitherto modest interior city that had the advantage of being in the heart of his new Turkish nation state. Thus ended for Istanbul a sixteen-century mission as imperial capital (first for the Byzantines and then the Ottomans).[1] Ended as well was the role of Istanbul as the capital of any sovereign state whatsoever.

Following the First World War, the Middle East as it is defined today was taking shape. The "East" no longer in-

---

[1] To be precise, 1593 years, dating from 330, when Constantine made it his capital. There were two brief periods breaking this impressive chain—the period of Crusader domination from 1204 to 1261 and the four-year interval between 1453, when the Ottomans took the city, and 1457, when they made it their capital.

85

cluded the southeastern corner of Europe, where Ottoman institutions had for so long held sway. This region was absorbed into the European political world. The results of the Greco-Turkish War of 1920-1922 dramatized this parting of the ways. In 1919 the Greeks as one of the victorious Allies landed in Smyrna and the following year began an ambitious military campaign to extend Greek territorial holdings into those portions of Western Anatolia having significant numbers of Greeks (or, more precisely, Christians, for many had become Turkish-speaking). This invasion gave Ataturk the cause needed to rally the Anatolian masses and undermine the legitimacy of the beleagured Ottoman government in Istanbul, still hoping to save what it could by diplomatic rather than military means.

By the spring of 1922 Ataturk had routed the Greeks. The settlement that followed provided for a compulsory exchange of Greek and Turkish populations. Some 1.3 million Greeks were moved from Turkey to Greece and 500,000 Turks from Greece to Turkey. It would be cruelly inaccurate to speak of repatriation. "A Western observer, accustomed to a different system of social and national classification, might even conclude that this was no repatriation at all, but two deportations into exile—of Christian Turks to Greece, and of Muslim Greeks to Turkey."[2] The resulting step in the direction of de-Christianizing Anatolia and deIslamizing Greece left each side free (if that is the proper word) to pursue its nation-state aims in different political worlds.

From this time on the Middle East under consideration here is the Afro-Asian area of the former Ottoman world, overwhelmingly Muslim in religion, overwhelmingly Arabic or Turkish in language. The Ottoman Empire was no more, the Middle East had become more narrowly defined, and by 1923 most Middle Easterners were under Western colonial rule.

[2] Bernard Lewis, *The Emergence of Modern Turkey* (Oxford University Press, 1961), p. 349.

I. THE OLD/NEW EASTERN
QUESTION

With such radical changes in the contours of Middle Eastern international politics after the First World War, how could the old Nineteenth-Century Eastern Question pattern of international relations survive? This is what must now be examined.

Eastern Question style international relations had emerged from the interaction of two factors, both of which endured for a long time:

1. A vulnerable regional political system (the Ottoman Middle East) was exposed to a threatening, expanding neighboring system (Europe). Both sides reacted to the resulting opportunities and threats.
2. Both political systems were characterized by multiplicity of autonomous political entities—a number of distinct states on the European side matched in the Middle East by what might be dubbed states, de facto states, and would-be states. They differed in size and strength from great powers to non-state ethnic or religious groupings (as the Armenians, Druze, or Maronites), but all interacted in a kaleidoscopic, multilateral fashion.

It might appear that the Middle East following the First World War ceased to be a vulnerable regional system exposed to a threatening neighboring system, becoming instead parcelled out by different states from the dominant system. Accordingly, it would seem that virtually all the Middle East (with Turkey the major exception) moved from Eastern Question multilateralism to colonizer/colonized bilateralism.

No such systemic change in Middle Eastern international relations developed after the First World War. The Middle East was not absorbed into the European state system following the demise of the Ottoman Empire. The parcelling out of

87

Middle Eastern territories among a few European great powers—that seemed so irreversible in the twenties—proved short-
lived. The Middle East remained a vulnerable region, thoroughly penetrated by the Western state system but never
definitively absorbed into that system. The systemic characteristic of kaleidoscopic multilateralism never died out. It was at
most dormant in the years between the two world wars.
Thereafter luxuriant multilateralism has become more than ever
the dominant motif of Middle Eastern international politics.

In the nineteenth century the players (European and Middle Eastern) were never able either to change the existing system or to proceed to a definite division of the spoils. This is
what kept the game alive. The more-or-less orderly division
of the spoils appeared to have been realized after the First
World War, but in fact the players involved soon perceived
that the old rules pertained because the old game was being
played. No new regional system of international politics
emerged. No single state, either from within the area or from
outside, was able to establish effective hegemony and thus to
organize the Middle East. Instead, within less than a generation after the Treaty of Lausanne marking the end of the
Ottoman Empire, the Middle East was yet again an arena in
which the complex blending of regional and great power rivalries could be plotted in terms of the Eastern Question system.

The period of direct Western imperial rule over the Middle
East did not destroy the older kaleidoscopic style of Middle
Eastern international politics. One speaks of Western imperialism in the Middle East, and these words evoke the image of
a consistent pattern of alien rule, rather like the Roman Empire or the early Arabo-Muslim empire or the British Raj in
India. Nothing of the sort happened in the Middle East. There
was, not a single Western imperial power, but three. Britain
and France divided up the lion's share. Italy had to be satisfied
with Libya.

France in North Africa and Britain in the Nile Valley as
well as the southern and eastern portions of the Fertile Cres-

cent each had impressive clusters of contiguous territories. Even this partial move toward uniformity was offset by different imperial regimes. Algeria, for example, was juridically absorbed into France, while Tunisia was a protectorate.

Both Britain and France were hampered by the newly evolving ideas of imperial stewardship that informed the mandates system. The mandate system provided in principle for a temporary trusteeship, justified only to the extent that the mandatory guided the mandated territory on the road to independent statehood.

It is all very well to insist that much of this League of Nations rhetoric was old Europe's hypocritical turning of Wilson's principles to its imperial purposes. This was partially true, but the mandate system also represented a European change of heart. Europe was no longer unreservedly imperialist in good conscience.[3] The new orientation was not lost on the peoples of the mandated territories in the Fertile Crescent.

In duration Western imperial rule in the Middle East breaks down into such extremes as an Algerie Française lasting 132 years, contrasted with only 11 years of the British mandate in Iraq.

A look at important individual cases of Western imperial rule in the Middle East further disrupts the image of enduring systemic change. What might appear to have been a sustained period of colonizer/colonized bilateralism does not hold up under examination. For example, from one perspective the British exercised imperial hegemony over Egypt from 1882 until 1954 or even 1956. Yet, until the 1904 Anglo-French Entente, Egyptians opposing the British occupation sought and received support from France. Immediately after the First World War Egyptian nationalists pinned their hopes on Wilson and American support. Then, less than twenty years later

[3] The telling phrase used by Henri Brunschwig to describe the general mentality of European imperialism before the First World War. See his *Mythes et Realities de l'Imperialisme Colonial Français 1871-1914* (Paris, 1960).

TABLE II. WESTERN COLONIAL RULE IN THE MIDDLE EAST

Colonized Country	Colonial Power	Beginning Date	Independence Achieved	Duration (Years)	Legal Status	"Pacification" Completed
Algeria	France	1830	1962	132	Annexed to France	1847
Aden	Britain	1839	1967	128	Linked to British India, after 1925 crown colony	1857
Cyprus	Britain	1878	1960	82	British controlled, Ottoman sovereignty 1878-1914, Crown colony from 1925	1878
Tunisia	France	1881	1956	75	Protectorate	1882
Egypt	Britain	1882	1936[1]	54	Military occupation 1882-1914 Protectorate 1914-1922 Limited independence 1922-1936 Nominal independence from 1936. Admitted to League of Nations 1937	1882

Sudan	Anglo-Egyptian	1898[2]	1956	58	Condominium	1898
Libya	Italy	1911	1951	40	Annexation made de jure 1924. Limited autonomy for Sanusi amir, Idris 1920-1923	1931
Iraq	Britain	1919[3]	1930	11	Mandate	1920
Lebanon	France	1919[3]	1944[4]	25	Mandate	1919
Palestine	Britain	1919[3]	1948	29	Mandate	1919
Syria	France	1919[3]	1944[4]	25	Mandate	1926
Transjordan	Britain	1919[3]	1946[5]	27	Mandate	1919

The British control in Kuwait, Bahrain, the Trucial Coast and Oman, while substantively equivalent to protectorates, involved such informal, and often imprecise, arrangements that these cases do not accurately fit into the above table.

[1] It could be argued that Egypt received substantive independence only in 1954, with the signing of the Anglo-Egyptian treaty providing for British evacuation of Suez military base.

[2] End of the reconquest. The Condominium agreement between Britain and Egypt was signed in 1899.

[3] Taking the date of effective military presence with intent to remain, rather than the de jure transfer of sovereignty in the Lausanne treaty (1923).

[4] French troops departed under local and Anglo-American pressures only two years later, in 1946.

[5] British troops left only in 1957. Given the intimate military and political presence of Britain until that date the period of substantive British colonial rule in Jordan might more appropriately be given as lasting 38 years, until 1957. (Transjordan became Jordan in 1949.)

certain Egyptian politicians looked for assistance from Fascist Italy and Nazi Germany. This being of no avail, Egyptians turned to the possibility of working with Britain's principal ally, the United States, in order to loosen the British grip on Egypt. At the same time, Egyptians began to realize the possible utility of organizing an Arab bloc as a way of enhancing Egypt's diplomatic potential.

This is not to belittle the strong, bilateral confrontation linking Britain and Egypt in the seventy-four year period from 1882 to 1956. No study of modern Egyptian political history can do other than place the Anglo-Egyptian imperial connection in the center of the picture.

The very intensity of Egyptian concern to escape Britain's imperial grasp does, at the same time, offer a clue to the systemic dimension. Unlike many other colonial situations—as, say, British India or French Algeria—there never was a political generation of Egyptians during the period of British domination who did not see a glimmer of hope for getting Britain out of Egypt. This sense that succor from some outside source could be expected kept alive the political habits developed during the classical period of the Eastern Question.

Or, in Libya what would appear to be a forty-year period of intensive Italian presence is shown to be a very disjunctive imperial encounter. "Pacification," that colonial euphemism, was achieved only in 1931. There followed the phase of Mussolini's ambitious "demographic colonization." Given more time, perhaps settling thousands of Italians in such a thinly populated country might have changed the course of Libyan history, but a decade later Libya became a World War II battlefield. Cyrenaica, the site of Mussolini's major agricultural colonization, changed hands three times. When by 1943 the British Eighth Army had driven the Axis forces out of Libya little remained of Italy's colonizing efforts.

The irony of Libyan independence in 1951 also bears an Eastern Question stamp. That country did not receive its formal independence earlier than most of its Arab neighbors because it was more economically advanced. Libya was then a woefully underdeveloped country. Nor did independence come as a result of an organized and adamant nationalist movement whose demands wore down imperialist resistance. Libya achieved independence as early as it did because the great powers could not agree on any other course.

THE FERTILE CRESCENT: BALKANS OF THE TWENTIETH CENTURY

No better example of persistent kaleidoscopic, multilateral international politics is to be found than the Fertile Crescent after the First World War. In international politics the twentieth-century Fertile Crescent is playing the role of the nineteenth-century Balkans. This significant development calls out for special study. This can best be done by reviewing Fertile Crescent diplomacy since the beginning of the Eastern Question.

Direct Great Power relations with the Fertile Crescent in the nineteenth century, aside from Lebanon, were relatively limited. Nor was the Fertile Crescent made up of autonomous political entities, again except for Lebanon after 1861.[4] The rest of the Fertile Crescent remained under direct Ottoman rule, except during the 1830s, when greater Syria came under Egyptian control. Most of the diplomatic demarches were directed at existing political centers such as Istanbul or Cairo. Moreover, the Fertile Crescent, unlike the constantly shrinking Ottoman territories of the Balkans, shared no common border with the European great powers. Nor were there, as in the Balkans, majority communities of Christians who could realistically aspire to a national existence and look to coreligionists in Europe for support.

Lebanon again offers a partial exception, for by the early nineteenth century the Maronites outnumbered the Druze in

---

[4] By looking to *de facto* rather than juridical standing one can see a much older autonomy for Mount Lebanon, going back to the time of Amir Bashir II (1788-1840). Moreover, the period of what might be called great-power imposed autonomy begins not in the 1860s but the 1840s.

Mount Lebanon. The rest of the area as a provincial hinterland was spared the fate of the Balkans or of Egypt, blessed and cursed by its strategic position and the Suez Canal, or of Tunisia, too close to Europe and to French Algeria.

In retrospect, the Fertile Crescent, Lebanon aside, probably remained free of direct European control until after the First World War because a short route to India via Aleppo to the Euphrates and thence down to the Persian Gulf was never developed. Instead, the Suez Canal was dug.

In the Fertile Crescent the nineteenth-century Eastern Question game was played for smaller stakes by lesser players. France championed native Catholics; Russia supported the Orthodox; and Britain—finding no native Protestants[5]—settled for the Druze. As the Crimean War showed, Eastern Question crises might start in the Holy Land, but they were either settled or spilled over into war as a result of actions taken in political capitals.

The Protestant-Catholic-Orthodox rivalries of missionaries, backed in varying degrees by one or another of the great powers, had an enormous impact on the educational and cultural development of the Fertile Crescent throughout the nineteenth century, and in general history of the Middle East these activities would loom large. In the study of diplomatic history, however, such efforts are to be seen in a different light.

These missionary activities did provide training in multifaceted Eastern Question politics to a newly emerging native elite. Those educated in foreign Protestant or Catholic or Orthodox schools tended to regard the western power from which their missionary mentors came as "their" patron. The new elite also learned to link cultural activities to politics; to confuse domestic, regional, and international issues; and to view the political world as peopled by many different actors, native and foreign. It was an education in Eastern Question politics. Even

---

[5] Although British and American missionary efforts did manage to bring into existence tiny groups of Middle Eastern Protestants, thus adding to the long roster of Middle Eastern religious communities.

so, throughout the nineteenth century the Fertile Crescent leadership had limited opportunity to put these western-inspired political orientations to work, again except for Lebanon. That most of those educated in missionary schools were Christians, a small minority of the entire Fertile Crescent population, also slowed down the process of acting on these new ideas.

The nineteenth-century Fertile Crescent did provide the arena for two "Syrian crises" (1832-1833 and 1839-1840) which were really tests of strength between Muhammad Ali and the Ottoman Sultan, triggered developments that later brought on the Crimean War, and occasioned intensive European involvement in the affairs of Lebanon from the 1840s onward. There was, however, nothing like the consistent, intense involvement with regional and great power politics that plagued statesmen ruling in Istanbul, Cairo, and Tunis. Political actors in the Fertile Crescent were like understudies awaiting the opportunity to play a major role. In the meantime, they continued their training.

Perhaps the best starting point for this new phase of Fertile Crescent history would be 1908, the year of the Young Turk revolt. Thereafter, the Ottoman leaders were increasingly bent on a policy of Turkification. In reaction Arab political leaders turned to Arabism. With the fall of Sultan Abdul Hamid, who had emphasized Muslim solidarity, Arab nationalism could be presented in terms palatable to the Muslim majority.[6]

This introduces from the Fertile Crescent perspective World War I diplomacy in the Middle East and the fate of these

[6] This is not to suggest that the majority of politically conscious Arabs in the Fertile Crescent were anti-Ottoman and embraced Arabism after 1908, or even by 1918. The work of such scholars as Dawn, Haim, Kedourie, and Zeine clearly demonstrates that the earlier, exaggerated interpretations of Arab antipathies to Ottoman rule must be rejected. See, for example, Sylvia G. Haim (ed.), *Arab Nationalism: An Anthology* (University of California Press Paperback, 1964) or C. Ernest Dawn, *From Ottomanism to Arabism* (University of Illinois Press, 1973). The breakthrough to what *eventually* became the prevailing political ideology—Arab nationalism in all its confusing varieties—starts, however, with the Young Turk Revolt.

negotiations during the post-war settlement. To the casual observer the British negotiations with Arab leaders during the First World War bring to mind the Byronic "Revolt in the Desert" and the saga of T. E. Lawrence. The reality—consistent with Eastern Question politics—was more complicated and less romantic. Sharif Husayn, who with his sons Faisal and Abdullah conducted the negotiations, was scarcely an Arab nationalist. He was a traditional leader whose power base in the Hijaz derived from custom, family standing and his sharifian (i.e., descendant of the Prophet Muhammad) origins. His was the world-view of a conservative Muslim and provincial leader thoroughly at home with Ottoman center-periphery politics. He was not a secular nationalist.

Those Arabs of the Fertile Crescent playing the dangerous wartime game of trying either to get an enhanced political status within the Ottoman Empire or to negotiate with European enemies of the Ottomans for support in a bid for independence (i.e., toying with treason) were more in the secular nationalist stream. Several leading members of the early Arab secret societies were, themselves, Ottoman officers. They were, thus, political heirs of the tanzimat, the centralizing efforts of Abdul Hamid, and the ethno-linguistic nationalist tendencies advanced by the Young Turks. They, and the inhabitants of the Fertile Crescent they claimed to represent, thought of themselves as politically and culturally far in advance of the Arabian peninsula Arabs. As conspirators must, they worked with whom they could. Sharif Husayn had established contact with the British, and remote Mecca was a safer place to conduct such delicate negotiations. The Arab nationalists of the Fertile Crescent went along with these plans while intending that they—not Sharif Husayn and his family—would emerge as leaders of the Arab nationalist movement.

Others, especially Christian Arabs, were in contact with France, a development that might have had greater historical impact if French troops, rather than British, had conducted the military operations in Palestine, Syria, and Mesopotamia.

Still other Arab leaders of the Fertile Crescent remained

loyal to the Ottoman Empire, and the great majority stayed prudently on the sidelines. By the end of the First World War Middle Easterners were aware of Allied agreements concerning the dismantling of the defeated Ottoman Empire. They knew of the Balfour Declaration, with its support of a Jewish national home in Palestine. They realized that Russia, the counterweight to Britain from the Levant to India, was *hors de combat* for a time. They watched with keen interest the death throes of the Ottoman Empire and the surprising emergence of what was soon to become a strong Turkish nation-state under Kemal Ataturk. They embraced the ideas contained in President Wilson's Fourteen Points and welcomed the arrival of an anti-imperialist United States as a major great power participant in Middle Eastern politics.

These criss-crossing strands produced an intricate pattern of multilateral international relations. The early nineteenth-century training in kaleidoscopic politics learned from missionaries and foreign consuls, plus the older Ottoman-style provincial politics played out among local warlords, notables, and religious leaders, had conditioned the new elites to act as they did. The Arab nationalists lost the first round of Eastern Question politics. Britian and France divided up the Fertile Crescent. The more Westernized Fertile Crescent had no independent states at all. That distinction fell only to the more "backward" Arabian peninsula, where Ibn Saud was creating Saudi Arabia and Imam Yahya maintained a precarious independence in Yemen.

Yet, even the mandate period brought little stimulus for the Fertile Crescent political leadership to move toward bilateral patterns in foreign relations. The Iraqi mandate was terminated by 1930, and an ostensibly independent Iraq, while clearly in the British camp, kept hopes alive for similar goal in neighboring Syria.

The Arab-Zionist problem in Palestine was throughout the period an inter-regional issue, one that fostered Arabism as an ideology both in the Fertile Crescent and, eventually to the ends of the Arab world. Even in the twenties the Palestine problem had an international, as well as regional, dimension. From the Zionist side such was ineluctably the case. This unique religio-cultural nationalist movement involved an ambitious effort to bring peoples from diverse and distant countries back to a homeland where Jews had not lived as a "nation" for over seventeen centuries.

The Arabs, also, realized that the international arena was of critical importance. Arab knowledge that mandatory policy was subject to the scrutiny of the Permanent Mandates Commission of the League of Nations (although this offered little solace to the Arab side), and the realization that important bodies such as the Catholic Church had strong views on Zionism and the Holy Land, nurtured a keen awareness that Palestine could never be just a local problem.

The contending Palestinian Arabs and Zionists soon learned that the mandatory authority itself was divided in a way not to be found in normal colonial situations. The recurring pattern of local disturbances followed by investigating commissions from which then emerged governmental White Papers demonstrated that the Palestinian Arab case was more likely to be favorably received by those officials on-the-spot in Palestine, while the Zionist case consistently got a better hearing in London. Both the Palestinian Arabs and the Zionists learned to play the diplomatic game with these circumstances in mind.

In addition, the British decision in 1921 to make Transjordan a separate entity, removed from the Jewish National Home stipulations of the Palestine mandate, gave Abdullah, the ambitious son of Sharif Husayn, a neighboring political base from which he could play an important role in Palestinian affairs. This added one more player to Palestinian politics even in the time of the Mandate.

Syria and France during their brief colonial encounter never really experienced a time when either side had the feeling that the mandate would last. Bitter in the defeat of their independence hopes, encouraged by neighboring Iraq's rapid emergence from colonialism, concerned more than other Arabs with the Palestine problem, and goaded into resistance by crude

French divide-and-rule tactics, the Syrian political elite never accepted the idea that their politics was in the hands of France. In, say, Sudan, Tunisia, Algeria, or Morocco, periods of time can be discerned during which the colonized political elites accepted that, like it or not, colonial rule was likely to survive for an indefinite term, and they might as well make the best of it. This never happended in Syria.

Even Lebanon did not become a tiny enclave state satisfied with close bilateral ties to France and limited links to the surrounding area. France, itself, foreclosed such a possibility by adding to the areas of traditional Mount Lebanon to give Lebanon its present borders. Enlarging the state dominated by pro-French Maronites failed to advance long term French goals. Lebanon no longer contained a clear Maronite majority. Indeed, before the end of the Mandate, it was obvious that the enlarged Lebanon no longer contained a Christian majority (Maronite plus others) at all.[7]

The move polarized Lebanese politics, with the Christians seeking to assure the political integrity of their country in its existing borders (and keeping close to France for that purpose) and the non-Christians supporting political union with Syria or at the very least a firm commitment that Lebanon was part of the Arab world.

The measure of France's loss in this diplomatic game was seen with the celebrated "National Pact" of 1943 between the principal Maronite leader, Bishara al-Khuri, and the Sunni Muslim Riyad al-Solh. This provided a quid quo pro between Christians and Muslims, the former accepting in good faith that Lebanon was part of the Arab world and the latter agreeing to the political integrity of Lebanon within its existing borders. Then, after the defeat of France in 1940, Syria and Lebanon were administered by a weakened Vichy government that was hard put to maintain even a semblance of authority

---

[7] The last census was in 1932, which then revealed a Christian/non-Christian ration of 6 to 5, a figure then used to allocate political positions among the different religious communities.

against the different demands of the Axis and the local nationalists. The high point of possible Axis gains in the Fertile Crescent came with the anti-Hashimite Iraqi bid for power, reversed by a quick British military strike against Rashid Ali's government in May 1941.

The British were then in a position to oust the Vichy regime from Syria and Lebanon. Aided by a token Free French force (all the Free French had available—the limited numbers in no way indicated a lack of Gaullist interest in the Levant), British troops overran the Vichy government in June and July 1941. Thereafter, a tenuous wartime arrangement gave the Free French administrative control over the mandates, with the British exercising over-all military responsibility.

Later that year the Free French representative, Georges Catroux, issued proclamations of independence (in September for Syria, November for Lebanon). This was in accord with Free French promises (and Allied pressure), but what de Gaulle's government hoped for was substantive French predominance in Syria and Lebanon similar to what Britain had worked out in Iraq or Jordan.

Instead, the French position simply could not hold—even in Lebanon—against the combined onslaught of:

1. Determined nationalists who remembered the 1936 treaties that France had never ratified and earlier promises during the First World War
2. Britain intent on keeping the area under easy military control by, if necessary, sacrificing French interests
3. The United States, with its open door and anti-imperialist policies, also supporting independence

This particular multiparty diplomatic game was not ended until after the Second World War, in 1946, when France withdrew her last troops from the area. A year later the entire Fertile Crescent area was plunged into the struggle for Palestine. The year following the first Arab-Israeli war in 1948 brought three military coups to Syria. Thereafter, the country has been engaged in an agonizing search for governmental

stability and acceptable territorial definition of political legitimacy (i.e., greater Syria, union with Iraq, absorption of Lebanon, a larger Arab union as with Egypt from 1958 to 1961,
or even possibly the notion of loyalty to Syria in its present
borders).

Nor could Syria's political elites move at their own pace.
Iraq, Egypt, Saudi Arabia, Jordan, the Palestinians, Lebanon,
Turkey, the three major Western powers—Britain, France, and
the United States—and after the mid-fifties the Soviet Union
have all been intimately involved in Syria's politics. *The Struggle for Syria* was the title Patrick Seale chose for his book[8]
mapping the labyrinthine inter-Arab and Middle Eastern great
power politics especially of the 1950s. The title could not have
been more apt.

The torments of Lebanon during this period have been no
less hectic but much more bloody. The civil war of 1958,
which provoked U.S. military intervention, was followed less
than a generation later by the cataclysmic strife that began in
1975 and continues to this day. Moreover, since 1975 Lebanon has become the principal battleground of the continuing
Arab-Israeli confrontation. As a result Lebanon has been af-
flicted with such massive interventions on the part of the PLO,
Syria, and—most of all—Israel that by 1982 the poor country
no longer existed as a viable state and hardly even as a society.

Not a single year of Lebanon's recent stormy history can be
adequately interpreted without simultaneous attention to the
local, regional, and international dimensions. At the local level
the constant push and pull of communal separatism opposed
to cross-confessional political integration has remained the
fundamental issue. Regionally, it has been a battle over the
degree of Lebanon's commitment to the Arab world as well
as Lebanon's position in the lineup of pro-West and anti-West
forces (these terms—pro— and anti-West—are quite inadequate and even misleading, but other dichotomous terms such
as left-right or moderate-radical or progressive-reactionary are

[8] London, Oxford University Press, 1965.

no less so). Internationally, Lebanon has played the unhappy role of shuttlecock in the ongoing great power struggle for influence in the Middle East.

Examples of all three levels and of the confused intertwining of local, regional, and international are numerous, including:

1. The landing of the U.S. Marines in 1958 in response to the appeal of Lebanon's president, Camille Chamoun, was ostensibly a great power move directed against "international communism" consistent with the Eisenhower Doctrine. It is more appropriately seen as a last-ditch American stand against Nasserist advances in the Middle East.

2. Chamoun was vulnerable locally because of his ill-advised attempt to consolidate his power at the expense of traditional leaders from the several different religious communities. The restoration later achieved under the presidency of General Shihab worked because the familiar pattern of communal power-sharing was accepted.

3. The 1975 Lebanese civil war is closely linked to King Husayn's crushing defeat of PLO forces in Jordan in 1970 ("Black September"). Thereafter, the PLO could not operate against Israel from Jordan. It had never been permitted a free hand from Syria or Egypt. This left Lebanon, whose precariously balanced and fragile political alignment make it impossible to line up wholeheartedly either with or against the PLO. Lebanon was too weak to treat the PLO as the other Arab confrontation states have done—lip service to the Palestinian cause plus strict control of the PLO. Sensing the steady political erosion, Lebanese nationalists (both the incipient "separatists" and those who would have been satisfied with a return to the terms of the 1943 "National Pact") took steps that set off the war.

4. The later intervention of Syrian troops, followed by a largely unsuccessful effort to stymie Syrian unilateralism

through Arab League action, the Israeli invasion of Lebanon in the spring of 1978, and Israel's continued support of avowed Christian separatists, all demonstrated the lack of a dividing line between local and regional concerns. The U.S. government's persistent but largely unsuccessful efforts to mediate a settlement that would maintain Lebanese political integrity reveals, equally, the international nature of the dispute.

5. The major Israeli invasion of Lebanon in the summer of 1982 seems at this writing to have crippled the PLO as a military force (but then the PLO strength never lay in its military threat). Whether, as some hopeful analysts suggest, the way is now clear for the eventual removal of all foreign troops from Lebanon and the reconstruction of a viable Lebanese state is unclear. That Lebanon seems destined to remain the twentieth-century Eastern Question shuttlecock appears more likely.

In short, the Fertile Crescent since the First World War has been moved to center-stage in Eastern Question politics and taken over the uneasy role played a century ago by the Balkans.

* * *

There were, of course, several examples of sustained, intensive colonizer/colonized bilateralism in the period of Western imperial rule, especially in French North Africa. Viewed in region-wide terms, however, the disjunctive and variegated nature of the Western imperial period is most striking.

Moreover, this disjointed Western imperial rule facilitated the development of separate Middle Eastern states whose bureaucracies and armies have henceforth become vested interests favoring kaleidoscopic international politics. This is markedly true in the Fertile Crescent, but the many small political units of the Persian Gulf—as well as South Yemen—were also nurtured by Western imperialism.

The more conventional territorial divisions used in studying the modern Middle East do have their utility. In many contexts it does make sense to concentrate on states as they now exist and to trace the roots of these states back into the past. Even so, viewing the region as a whole and as an ongoing international relations system has decided advantages. In many important respects no part of the area—certainly not a Syria or Israel, but not even an Egypt or Tunisia—can be studied in isolation. Western imperial rule adapted to the existing constraints of the Eastern Question system more than it changed them. Such a perspective does not belittle the impact of Western imperialism. It simply places that phase in a larger context.

Elizabeth Monroe's inspired title for her study of the period of British imperial predominance in the area—*Britain's Moment In The Middle East*—is more than British understatement. British, and for that matter Western, imperial domination in the Middle East was only a moment in an era that began earlier and exists still.

CONTINUING GREAT POWER RIVALRIES

The same can be said for the seeming move among the great powers from Eastern Question style multilateralism to a stable division of the spoils between only two powers—Britain and France. The apparent shift proved to be short-lived and not sufficient to change the basic kaleidoscopic rules of the game.

Russia did not play its customary great power role in the Middle East for roughly a quarter-century after the October Revolution, but thereafter the Soviet Union regained its place at the table. Even in the period from 1917 to roughly 1941 Soviet diplomacy in the Middle East, although muted because the new regime concerned itself largely with consolidation at home, was not voiceless.

Italy, with a minor Middle Eastern imperial position after

1911, remained bent on challenging the status quo and enlarging its stake from that time until its defeat in the Second World War. In the 1930s Mussolini increased the pressure on both the Middle East and the powers with Middle East interests, producing among all parties a flurry of responses reminiscent of earlier nineteenth-century Eastern Question crises.

Nazi Germany entered Middle Eastern diplomacy in a major way during the years of the Second World War, after at most a few tentative propaganda probes earlier. Somewhat like Napoleon almost a century and a half earlier, Nazi Germany attempted to use the Middle East to outflank its European opponents, was frustrated (with the October 1942 battle of El Alamein as the turning point), and ended up facilitating developments it had no interest in—the acceleration of decolonization.

The United States in these years also entered Middle East politics. There was a rapid and intensive political involvement during the short period from Woodrow Wilson's enunciation of his Fourteen Points until the U.S. lapsed into political isolation.

These few years spawned efforts by several different Middle East nationalist leaders seeking U.S. support for national independence, talk by different parties of possible U.S.-administered mandated territories (as Armenia or Syria) and the dispatching of an official American investigating team, the King-Crane Commission (1919), to canvas the wishes of the Syrian inhabitants concerning their political destiny. The King-Crane Commission was a very American gesture and doomed to futility. At the same time, it was in the tradition of those national liberation tendencies such as the West had been exporting willynilly to the area for over a century.

After Wilson and isolationist America pulled back politically, the commerical interests of private American oil companies in the inter-war years maintained a minimal U.S. presence. Then during the Second World War the United States became involved in the area as a great power and has continued so until this day. It might be recalled that the first commitment of American troops to combat during World War II was in North Africa.

From the European side the multilateral, musical chairs nature of the diplomatic game continued after the First World War and continues still. It is true that usually only two major outside powers or blocs determined the pace of the game—Britain and France from roughly 1917 until the fall of France in 1940, and following the Second World War the United States and the Soviet Union.

These powers or blocs, however, never totally pre-empted the action of outsiders. Other players had their impact on events (such as the United States in 1917-1920, Italy in the 1930s, France under deGaulle's Fifth Republic). This continues a pattern that had existed throughout the nineteenth century (e.g., Napoleonic France *v.* a coalition, Britain *v.* Russia, Britain *v.* France until 1904, while sundry other powers intervened from time to time, as Austria at different times, or the period when Bismarck held the ring).

Such are the broad lines of the argument that the Eastern Question as a system did not die with the dismemberment of the Ottoman Empire but exists to this day. That twentieth-century Eastern Question players have continued to play the same game, even though often to accompaniment of quite different political rhetoric, is well illustrated by the two most ambitious efforts to establish a position of predominance in the Middle East. In each case those seeking hegemony showed by their actions an appreciation of Eastern Question rules. Yet, they later were lured into assuming that it might be possible to edge out rivals and to organize a major part of the Middle East under their leadership. In each case these ambitions were shattered by the stubborn reality of persistent kaleidoscopic Middle Eastern politics.

One effort was that of a great power, Britain, beginning in the heyday of its imperial strength. This was Britain's Arab policy. The other effort came from within the region. This was the rise of Arabism, beginning in the last decades of the

Ottoman period and reaching its diplomatic heights in the age of Nasser.

Much of modern Middle Eastern political history has been organized around these two themes but not usually examined in relation to the distinctive Middle Eastern diplomatic culture. This is done in Sections II and III respectively.

II. BRITAIN'S ARAB POLICY

As Britain's longstanding policy of supporting the Ottoman Empire began to come apart in the last decades of the nineteenth century a search for possible alternatives became imperative. This started developments that led to Britain's Arab policy, but the new policy was long in emerging, and can best be explained by beginning the story in the heyday of Britain's support for the Ottomans.

THE OTTOMAN BACKGROUND

From the time of the first Syrian crisis of 1832-1833, pitting Muhammad Ali against Sultan Mahmud, Britain had backed the Ottoman Empire as the best means of denying outside powers (mainly Russia) a position in the Middle East that might threaten communications with India. This policy initiated by Palmerston and staunchly maintained by him during the many years he dominated British political life (he died in 1865, two days before his eighty-first birthday) began to be questioned by the time of the Eastern Crisis (1875-1878).

Disraeli, with his imperialist flamboyance and distrust of Russia, did manage to keep the pro-Ottoman and anti-Russian policy inherited from Palmerston more or less intact throughout this crisis, but even he had to hedge at times. More important for the future, two powerful statesmen—one destined to be the Conservative leader and the other the Liberal leader, Salisbury and Gladstone—were each inclined to move away from reliance on the Ottoman Empire. This was

107

perhaps the only thing the two men did agree on, and they arrived at similar conclusions about the Ottomans from quite different premises.

Salisbury, a perceptive and supercilious aristocrat, who believed that the world should be ruled by the great powers,[9] had become convinced that the Ottoman Empire would soon fall. What he saw as the Ottoman government's stubborn resistance to British pressures to "reform" further inclined him to see the old Palmerstonian policy as a bad bet. It was much better to cut losses then rather than later when all was in shambles.

Gladstone, the Christian moralist, saw the Ottoman Empire as an abomination. The 1876 massacres in Bulgaria provided him the occasion to call into question British support for the Ottomans. The Bulgarians, who revolted in the spring of 1876, almost overran the limited Ottoman security forces on the spot and massacred a number of Muslims. The Ottoman suppression that followed, largely by the notorious irregulars, the Bashi-Bazuks, was fierce. Mr. Gladstone now had his cause, so well attuned to the late Victorian mood of genuine moral concern mixed with a healthy dose of self-righteous nationalism. His pamphlet *The Bulgarian Horrors and the East*, published in September 1876, quickly sold 200,000 copies. From this campaign came the celebrated Gladstonian dictum that the Ottomans should clear out of Europe "bag and baggage." Later historical scholarship has shown that Gladstone was actually cautious in demanding Ottoman withdrawal.[10] Moreover, the public uproar in Britain died down by the following

---

[9] During the 1878 Congress of Berlin, Salisbury summed up his personal discomfort: "At Potsdam [where he was residing during the Congress] there are mosquitoes—here (Berlin) there are minor powers. I don't know which is worse." Cited in B. H. Sumner *Russia and The Balkans, 1870-1880* (Oxford University Press, 1937), p. 506.

[10] See R. T. Shannon, *Gladstone and the Bulgarian Agitation, 1876* (London, 1963, revised edition 1975), who also argues the case of Gladstone as reluctant leader of a popular protest movement.

year. Gladstone's second pamphlet on the subject, which appeared in January 1877, sold only 7,000 copies.

Indeed, by 1878, after a victorious Russia had imposed the harsh Treaty of San Stefano on the Ottomans, British public opinion reverted to its more customary Russophobia. The man in the street was for the nonce willing to forget about Turkish baggage in order to follow Disraeli's brinkmanship against Russian baggage trains a day's march from Istanbul. This was the age that gave to the English-speaking world the word "jingo."[11] Disraeli's success in restoring Palmerstonian policy on the Eastern Question was, however, temporary. Britain's support of the Ottoman Empire could never be the same. The well-springs of visceral antipathy to everything "Turk" that Gladstone had tapped remained just under the surface.

Even more important, at the height of the 1878 Anglo-Russian war scare Britain had obliged Sultan Abdul Hamid to permit British occupation of Cyprus. This was in return for a British guarantee of remaining Ottoman territory in Asia. Cyprus was to serve as a British military depot close enough to resist a possible Russian military thrust. The hard-pressed Ottoman government gave in, but without enthusiasm. It was galling to cede territory to one's ally after having suffered such massive losses at the hands of one's enemy. Ottoman dismay at the turn of events was increased when it became clear that Britain had agreed to France's taking Tunisia, legally an Ottoman pashalik. This France proceeded to do in 1881.

A year later, in 1882, the point of no return for both Britain and the Ottoman Empire was reached with the British occupation of Egypt. That Gladstone's government had not really meant to do this and did make seriously intended ges-

---

[11] From the London music hall song that drummed up the British martial spirit:

> We don't want to fight,
> But, by jingo, if we do,
> We've got the ships,
> We've got the men,
> We've got the money, too.

tures about evacuation was not likely to mollify the Ottomans. They had been hearing just such talk ever since Navarino. From the Ottoman side increasingly came new ventures in diplomacy including pan-Islam plus a reliance on Germany as the least harmful of the European powers.[12]

Thereafter, British statesmen continued to express the old maxims about the Ottoman Empire as a necessary buffer and the need to insure that Constantinople not fall into the hands of a great power such as Russia, but with less enthusiasm. Certain British statesmen became open to other possibilities, not excluding the final partition of the Ottoman Empire. This is the import of Salisbury's initiatives with Germany and with Russia in the 1890s. Naval and military leaders were advising Salisbury that forcing the straits to forestall a possible Russian seizure of Istanbul was no longer militarily feasible. Among other reasons, the Franco-Russian alliance of 1891 meant the French fleet could endanger British naval operations against Russia in the Eastern Mediterranean and the Black Sea.

Although Salisbury believed his military were being excessively cautious,[13] this warning signal plus the continued British occupation of Egypt, with after 1890 no further talk about evacuation, turned his mind to not unattractive alternatives: The true lifeline to India for a seapower such as Britain lay south of Istanbul. The key was Egypt and the Suez Canal. This route and Britain's position in Egypt were best protected by a strong British stand in the Persian Gulf, Arabia, and the Fertile Crescent.

The areas of Ottoman Asia claimed by Britain during the First World War secret negotiations neatly fitted this emerging British strategy of relying on Egypt, Arabia, and a contig-

[12] Abdul Hamid is reported to have said, "The Germans do me as much good as they are permitted to do, whereas the rest of Europe do me as much harm as they can." A. Vambery, "Personal Recollections of Abdul Hamid and his Court," *Nineteenth Century, LXVI*, July 1909, p. 81.

[13] Salisbury had a healthy skepticism about all specialists. "Never trust experts," he insisted. "If you believe the doctors nothing is wholesome; if you believe the theologians nothing is innocent; if you believe the soldiers nothing is safe."

8. Disraeli had just bought the indebted Egyptian khedive's Suez Canal share. To imperial Britain Egypt was not so much a country as a route to India (*Punch*, 1876).

uous belt of territory in the Fertile Crescent. All of this territory was occupied by Arabic speakers, a point which British policymakers fully realized but only later shaped into an ambitious policy.

Until the First World War the occasion for a decisive break with the Ottoman Empire never developed. Indeed, the Young Turk Revolt of 1908 brought a brief period of pro-British sentiment among the new Ottoman rulers, who identified with the exemplar of parliamentary democracy. Nor did the Young Turks in their subsequent disappointment with Europe (e.g., the Austro-Hungarian annexation of Bosnia and Herzegovina in 1908, the Italian invasion of Libya in 1911, Great Power indifference to a Balkan coalition against the Ottomans during the First Balkan War) have reason to single out Britain for blame.

Even after the outbreak of the First World War Britain hoped for Ottoman neutrality. Things did not work out that way, and by 5 November 1914 Britain and the Ottoman Empire were at war. If Britain needed any additional stimulus to take action, the Ottoman sultan/caliph provided it nine days later, on 14 November, when he declared a *jihad* against the Allies.

Britain, possessing India and soon to convert its occupation of Egypt into a protectorate (December 1914), was the greatest Muslim power in the world. Most of the Indian army and virtually all of the Egyptian army were Muslims. There was no sure way to calculate what impact the sultan/caliph's declaration would have on Muslims (almost none as it turned out), but British officials most conversant with the Muslim world did sense that if the Allies could assure their Muslim subjects uninterrupted pilgrimage to Mecca the worst would be forstalled. If they could deny the Ottomans control of the Holy Cities, that would be even better. And if they could find someone with a legitimate title to religio-political authority in the Holy Cities to rise up against the Ottomans and denounce their religious claims, that would be best of all. Suddenly, Sharif Husayn, Ottoman-appointed Sharif and Amir of Mecca, seemed a very important figure.

Moving Toward the Arabs

As early as April 1914 Abdullah, the son of Sharif Husayn, had called on Lord Kitchener in Cairo and asked if Britain would support his father with arms if he were attacked by the Ottomans. The answer was negative, but the door had been left ajar. The British had long known of the Sharif's difficulties with the authorities in Istanbul. They also saw Sharif Husayn as a very ambitious man.

Even earlier in 1912 and 1913 Kitchener had noted the possible utility of an eastern hinterland to the Suez Canal embracing Palestine from Acre to the Gulf of Aqaba. Kitchener's recommendations to the British government offer another sign of the emerging imperial strategy that would position Britain's defense perimeter well south of Istanbul. Kitchener had persuaded his government to prepare contingency plans some six weeks before Britain and the Ottomans plunged into war. On 24 September 1914 Lord Kitchener, by then Secretary of State for War, cabled Cairo: ". . . send secret and carefully chosen messenger from me to Sharif Abdallah to ascertain whether 'should present armed German influence in Constantinople coerce Sultan against his will, and Sublime Porte, to acts of aggression and war against Great Britain, he and his father and Arabs of the Hejaz would be with us or against us.' "[14]

From this date Britain's Arab policy arose, phoenix-like, from the ashes of Britain's Ottoman policy. Many of the geographical pieces needed for this new strategy were already in place.

— Britain had held Aden since 1839.
— She had enjoyed a predominant position in the Persian Gulf since the 1820s.
— Kuwait, long in the British orbit, was declared an independent state under British protection on 3 November 1914.
— Egypt became a British protectorate the following month.
— Britain ruled the vast Sudan to the south (in spite of the name, Anglo-Egyptian Sudan, Egypt was in no position to exercise influence), and this meant control of the Western littoral of the Red Sea.
— British contact with the Sanusis of Libya beginning in armed dispute over border demarcation had, by the end of the First World War, developed into a close relationship destined to be reactivated a generation later during the Second World War.

Moreover, only Britain was in a position to pursue contacts with tribal or provincial leaders in the Arabian peninsula. British officials managed to do just that during the years of the

[14] Sir Ronald Storrs, *The Memoirs of Sir Ronald Storrs* (New York, 1937), p. 163.

113

First World War, not without awkward overlapping, by entering into treaty relations with Sharif Husayn of Mecca, Ibn Saud of the Najd, and the Idrisi Sayyid of Sabya (north of Yemen).

Then, the complicated negotiations among Britain, her European allies, and her Middle Eastern allies (or, more realistically, clients) throughout the war years left Britain in control of what became Iraq, Transjordan, and Palestine. This was an impressive swatch of Arab territory under British paramountcy. From the perspective of later times a British Arab policy seems so plausible that one can easily assume it looked obvious to the policymakers of the day. In fact, the British moved toward a fully elaborated Arab policy in fits and starts.

There were always strong countervailing tendencies within the British diplomatic establishment. The most tenaciously long-lived was the tension between foreign policy orientations of British India and of the British Foreign Office. In the years during and immediately after the First World War the Arab Middle East provided the arena for the sharpest clashes between these two separate wings of the British foreign policy establishment.

To the rulers of British India the idea of creating ostensibly independent Arab states was dangerous nonsense. They preferred the time-tested British Indian tactics of dealing with tribal leaders beyond their borders. These tactics ranged from subsidies to punitive expeditions. The last thing that the British in India sought was to help these disparate tribesmen and petty principalities come together to form a larger political entity.

The Foreign Office thinking, on the other hand, as crystallized in the Arab Bureau (formed in 1916) with its headquarters in Cairo, was more attuned to the recent history of Europe and the Mediterranean world, where Italian and German unification, Hungarian, Polish, and Armenian nationalism, and the rise of Greece and Balkan states seemed to argue that nation-state building was the wave of the future. Better to reap the benefits of playing a role in what would come in any case than waste precious diplomatic assets trying to hold it back.

The Arab Bureau thinking, reflecting its Foreign Office roots, was not that of an Asian empire always ready to send its army to quell the turbulent frontier. They thought, instead, of maintaining the balance of power without tying down military resources, of keeping the area open to trade, and of letting regional political clients have the headaches of daily government. In a sense, the Arab Bureau thinking was the child of Britain's Eastern Question experience, a more subtle diplomatic game than countenanced by British India. The game was played, unlike in India, with the awareness that not just one other Great Power (Russia) but several Great Powers were involved. An overly aggressive forward policy by any one of those powers would almost certainly create a coalition of great power opponents to dismantle and distribute among all parties the gains achieved by one. It was, accordingly, better to keep buffer states in existence and work through ostensibly independent regional clients.

The contending diplomatic philosophies of the Arab Bureau and British India clashed in the Middle East. British India signed a treaty with Ibn Saud and granted him a subsidy (December 1915). The Arab Bureau put their money on Sharif Husayn. Of course, the different British diplomatic actors were aware of the enmity between the two leaders in Arabia, but at the top there was the hope—so common among Great Powers—that their clients would confine themselves to opposing enemies they both shared.

The two different views also clashed in the immediate postwar years, with Arab Bureau personnel and thinking predominating in Palestine and Transjordan, while the men and ideas of British India (especially Sir Percy Cox and Sir Arnold Wilson) prevailed in Iraq.

By 1923, with the signing of the Lausanne Treaty, neither diplomatic tendency could point to a clear superiority over the other in terms of results. The Arab revolt organized around Sharif Husayn had provided military support to General Allenby's successful campaign against the Ottomans in Palestine and Syria, but it was not nearly so important as the later myth-making associated with the name of T. E. Lawrence implied. Such use of a regional client also embroiled Britain in a bitter dispute with France over the post-war settlement in the Middle East while leaving the very Arabs they had backed with a bitter feeling of having been let down. The infinitely more modest subsidy to Ibn Saud and the eventual British conquest of Mesopotamia, without pretending to put forward local Arab leadership, the work of British Indian officialdom, appeared in hindsight more realistic.[15]

Then, after the French had driven Faisal out of Syria (July 1920) and Ibn Saud had driven Husayn out of Arabia (1924)[16] the British backing of the Hashimites looked shaky indeed. In the meantime, however, things had happened to discredit the British Indian philosophy as applied to the Middle East and to make the emerging British Arab policy look promising in spite of these earlier difficulties. An insurrection in Iraq (June-September 1920) was the response to Sir Arnold Wilson's effort to apply the no-nonsense methods brought from British India. Quelling the revolt was not easy, and it was costly. Furthermore, the disturbances that had broken out in India itself as well as in Egypt, coming at a time when the war-weary British public was in no mood for imperial expenditures, combined to impose severe restraints on what London would permit its agents in the field to consider.

[15] "Indeed, the officials of the India Office, had they been driven into a corner by infuriated British tax-payers, might have represented with some plausibility that in purchasing Ibn Sa'ud's benevolent neutrality at £5,000 sterling a month they had made a better bargain than their colleagues at the Foreign Office who had contracted to pay £200,000 a month of the tax-payers' money for Husayn's military cooperation." Arnold J. Toynbee, *The Islamic World Since the Peace Settlement, Survey of International Affairs, 1925*, Volume I (Oxford University Press/Royal Institute of International Affairs, 1927).

[16] In October 1924 King Husayn abdicated in favor of his son Ali, and soon left the Hijaz. Ali was able to hold out against Ibn Saud's forces only until December 1925, when he, too, departed.

Other matters also intruded. Wilson's intervention into world affairs may have been brief, but the ideas he personified survived. The revolutionary challenge from Lenin and Bolshevism served to undergird the same tendencies. All this obliged old-fashioned imperialists of post-war Britain to accept a much more indirect form of rule which received legal expression in the League of Nations mandate system.

Franco-British Rivalry and the Emerging Arab Policy

Playing within these restricted rules, the British government also found itself on collision course with its war-time ally, France, over division of the Ottoman spoils. France had good reason to believe that the British sought to undermine the French position in the Middle East. The French sense of grievance centered on Syria.

The British argument was that Britain had promised Sharif Husayn and his followers what amounted to an independent state in an area including most of Syria in return for military support against the Ottomans. The Arabs under Sharif Husayn had fulfilled their part of the bargain. In addition, the Arabs of Syria were making it quite clear that they wanted no tie to France. They sought, instead, independence in a constitutional monarchy led by Sharif Husayn's son, Faisal.

The French held that the Allies had agreed to an equitable division of Ottoman holdings in Asia, and Britain should stick to its commitments. France had already made considerable concessions in this area (e.g., Mosul and Palestine), but intended to make no more. Neither Sharif Husayn and his following nor political spokesmen in Syria demanding independence represented real political forces, in the French view. They were simply being encouraged by British actions.

The several different groups who sought to speak for the Arabs of this area agreed without exception on at least one principle: They sought independence if possible, but in any case they wanted to keep Great Power domination to the min-

117

9. Faisal and party at Versailles, 1919; note T. E. Lawrence in Arab headdress.
To the French the Arab revolt was largely Britain in Arab headdress
(By permission of Imperial War Museum, London).

imum. This meant that they might accept a loose American
mandate or even, as a second choice, British; but they feared
that French ambitions amounted to imperialism of the old
school.[17] The three-cornered dispute finally came to a bitter
end in July 1920 when French General Gouraud marched on
Damascus, defeating en route a small body of hastily mustered
Syrian volunteers. The French then forced Faisal into exile.

Relations between France and Syria under the mandate were
destined to remain to the end based on brute force and mutual

[17] Except for most of the Maronite community in Lebanon who saw a close
tie to France as the best insurance against being dominated by the overwhelmingly Muslim majority of greater Syria.

suspicion. France and Syria thereafter lurched and stumbled from one crisis and confrontation to another:

— Creation of "greater Lebanon" at Syria's expense in 1920
— The Druze rebellion of 1925-1926
— French bombardment of Damascus in October 1925 and May 1926
— The frustration of an acceptable Franco-Syrian treaty signed in 1936 but never ratified by the French parliament
— France's cession of Alexandretta to Turkey in 1939
— The last-ditch French effort in 1945-1946 to maintain a position of strength by keeping control of locally recruited *troupes speciales* (the deadlock being broken by British armed intervention)

From the Syrian and Arab perspective, indeed from the perspective of any impartial observer, France's conduct in Mandated Syria was inexcusably heavy-handed. Inexcusable, yes, but the French actions were understandable. France's Syrian policy provides a useful case study demonstrating the continuity of Eastern Question thinking even after the demise of the Ottoman Empire. To French statesmen the British arrangement with Sharif Husayn was a ruse to create and then push forward a local puppet who could be manipulated to erode French interests in the Levant. The more the British stressed these commitments to the Arabs, the more suspicious the French became.

Further, when Lloyd George indelicately advanced the argument that most of the Allied fighting in the Near Eastern theatre had been done by British troops, the French response was one of scarcely controlled rage. France had made by far the major contribution in soldiers, and in casualties, on the Western front.[18]

[18] Lloyd George at a meeting of the Council of Four (of which only three were present—Wilson, Clemenceau, and Lloyd George) in May 1919 observed that France's help in the "Turkish campaign" was negligible, "perhaps 2,000 men out of 200,000, 1 percent." Yet, at the time Allenby's forces were

Faisal, for his part, had a difficult role to play. Perceptive and realistic, he just might have been able to accommodate the French, but he was limited in his maneuverability by the nationalist forces of Syria, organized into the Syrian Congress, which in March 1920 had declared Syria an independent constitutional monarchy. The Hashimite dynasty had the essential contacts with the outside world, but they were suspect for that very reason. Many of the earliest Arab nationalists in the Fertile Crescent, whose political societies pre-dated any such activity by Sharif Husayn's family, had all along feared that the Hashimites, with a great power sponsor, might dominate a movement they saw as their own.

Believed by the French to be only a catspaw of the British and suspected by the Syrian nationalists of being prepared to make a deal with the great powers, Faisal was trapped from the start. Any concession to the French would have been repudiated by the Syrian nationalists as a betrayal. Yet, complete acceptance of the Syrian nationalists aspirations for full independence, with no tie whatsoever to France, would only confirm the French in their suspicions that Britain was behind the entire affair, working, as the outspokenly anti-French T. E. Lawrence once put it, to "biff the French out of Syria." Faisal, and Syrian nationalists too, were thus left with only the weak card of previous commitments (but, then, the French staked their claim on that, too—proper treaties drawn up by sovereign states which also happened to be great power allies) plus the even weaker card of appealing to Wilsonian principles.

If the French policy was under the circumstances understandable (although not wise in the long run, for France in Syria never really recovered from its unfortunate beginning), what then can be said about the British? Interestingly, most of the controversy has been over whether or not the British had deceived, or at least had let down, the Arabs. That ques-

---

winding up the campaign in Syria, France had 103 divisions on the Western Front. The British had 61. See Zeine N. Zeine, *The Struggle for Arab Independence* (New York Edition 1967), pp. 90 and 210.

tion is perhaps best blended into an even larger one: Did the British play a double game in dealing both with allies and clients?

The British did work to create on-the-spot situations that could modify in their favor earlier agreements, while disingenuously pleading the force of new circumstances. If the British had shown any inclination to forego advantages gained from the war-time Allied agreements commensurate with what they were asking France to give up, their case would have been both consistent and honorable. They did no such thing. Moreover, they defended the weaker parties only until it became inconvenient. It seems fair to conclude that the British policy was both self-serving and devious.

This debacle for Britain and for Faisal[19] served to accelerate the development of Britain's Arab policy, contradictory as that might seem. This was for two quite different reasons. First, Abdullah shrewdly seized upon the unhappy event, raised a small party of men, and announced that he was marching against the French in Syria to avenge the insult to his brother. Realizing that the French would interpret this as a plot hatched by Perfidious Albion, the British officials induced Abdullah to remain in Transjordan, where he was duly recognized as amir in 1921. The following year Transjordan, part of the Palestine Mandate, was excluded from the Jewish National Home provisions of the Mandate.

Second, while these developments were taking place, British officials decided that Faisal should be king of British-mandated Iraq, and so arranged things, not without some arm

[19] Upon being expelled from Syria, Faisal took the train to Haifa. Lord Samuel, Britain's first civilian high commissioner in Palestine, has written: "I decided that he (Faisal) should be received on Palestine territory, not as a defeated fugitive, but as a respected friend; ordered a guard of honor to parade when his train arrived; went, with Storrs, to meet him at a stopping place on his way through. . . . I was told afterwards that when the Emir saw the soldiers drawn up on the platform on his arrival he did not know whether they were not there to arrest him; and, after the emotional strain of the previous days, almost broke down when he found that they were a guard of honor." Herbert L. Samuel, *Memoirs* (London, 1945), pp. 138-319.

twisting, that he was accepted in 1921. British motives would seem to have been mixed. There was the sense of noblesse oblige and of compensating an ally whom Britain had let down.

There was also the genuine recognition of Faisal's leadership qualities. After the developments in Syria and the insurrection in Iraq, the British realized that their task in Iraq would not be easy. The available Iraqi leaders were either anti-British or possessed an overly narrow power base. The choice of any Iraqi to become ruler of Iraq was likely to displease all save the community from which the successful candidate came. Nor did it escape the attention of the British that an outsider with no power base of his own would be more beholden to Britain.

Accordingly, Faisal was chosen king of Iraq. Since the Syrian National Congress had earlier, before the French march on Damascus, passed a resolution declaring Faisal king of Syria and Abdullah king of Iraq, the British were obliged to get involved in Hashimite intra-family negotations. Abdullah did give way, picking up in the process one more claim to British gratitude.

THE INTERWAR ILLUSION OF HEGEMONY

Thus, in less than seven years from the time Abdullah had been politely rebuffed by Ronald Storrs in his request for arms against the Ottomans, the British found themselves supporting a band of contiguous Hashimite principalities in the Hijaz, Transjordan, and Iraq. Ibn Saud later ousted the Hashimites from the Hijaz, but all was not lost. Britain had ties with Ibn Saud and could aspire to adjudicating disputes between these two families.

By the mid 1920s British officials could survey the Middle Eastern scene and feel that they had a workable policy. The earlier sharp differences in orientation between British India and the Foreign Office had been rendered irrelevant by new circumstances. A Britain engaged in retrenchment required a Middle Eastern policy that tied down a bare minimum of money and manpower.

Sir Percy Cox personified the resolution of this old issue. As British High Commissioner in Iraq, this former official in British India skillfully handled the establishment of the British mandate and the selection of Faisal as Iraq's first king, playing the game according to the new, restrictive rules.

The one potential rival to British predominance in the Middle East was France. Russia, the major rival of the nineteenth century, would not again pose a threat until the Soviet government was organized and felt secure enough to look beyond its own borders.

The United States, with the capacity to challenge and the advantage of being regarded with favor by most political forces within the Middle East, chose isolation. Private U.S. oil interests increased significantly from the twenties onward and private U.S. philanthropic and educational concerns continued to play a role, but official American interest was to be activated only much later.

The British dispute with France over the fate of Syria left its legacy of bitterness betweeen the two powers, but by a strictly Machiavellian reckoning Britain had come out best. The nature of France's entry as mandatory power in the Middle East insured that she would not be able to exert any diplomatic influence beyond Syria and Lebanon.

Nor did it seem likely that France could patch things up with Syria. This left France with only the Maronites providing a firm political base in the area. Support for the essentially separatist aims of the Maronites thus took France out of contention in the game Britain was seeking to play—that of organizing the area, of creating and supporting one or a limited number of larger political units that would take the place of the Ottoman Empire.

Admittedly in Palestine the British, by championing the idea of a Jewish national home, went against the logic of their evolving Arab policy. A number of British officials and observers, realizing this from the beginning, opposed Zionism. Such pressures did not deter Britain from the policy enunciated in the November 1917 Balfour Declaration, but they helped nudge Britain toward the concept of "equal obligation" (i.e., to Zionists and Palestinians) in administering the Palestine Mandate.

In the early years of the Mandate the conflicting commitments to Palestinian Arabs and Zionists appeared manageable. Later in the thirties (with Hitler's rise to power, the upsurge of Zionist immigration, and the 1936-1939 Arab revolt) it was to be a different story. Nor did the British face any temptation in the immediate post-war years to support Ataturk's Turkey as the keystone of their post-Ottoman Middle Eastern policy. They had gambled and lost by backing Greece against what was to become the Republic of Turkey, and, even assuming a diplomatic revolution might thereafter have been feasible, Ataturk did not look like the kind of leader a great power would be able to control. A policy building on existing British strengths from Cairo to Kuwait looked more promising.

This line of thinking makes more comprehensible Britain's early termination of the Mandate in Iraq. The 1930 Anglo-Iraqi treaty provided the essentials from imperial Britain's point of view—military bases, transit rights, mutual aid in wartime, and consultations on foreign policy. Two years later Iraq was accepted into the League of Nations, and the Mandate officially came to an end. Britain had secured her strategic requirements while managing to escape the economically and politically costly obligations of daily colonial administration.

The 1930s brought what seemed at the time to be a promising upturn in the always stormy Anglo-Egyptian relations. In 1936, after so many previous efforts had failed, Britain and Egypt negotiated a treaty and in the following year Egypt, too, was admitted in the League of Nations. Again, as in the case of Iraq, Britain obtained the necessary base and transit rights while granting Egypt in return the appearance of independence, including formal termination of the British military occupation, with British troops to be quartered only in the Suez Base.

The British realized that Egypt was not satisfied with Britain's continued military presence in the country nor with Britain's continued control of Sudan. There was no Egyptian change of heart concerning Britain. The threat posed by Mussolini in Ethiopia and Libya motivated the Egyptian leaders to come to terms. Even though the impetus was thus more fear of something worse than a positive response to British imperial needs, this 1936 Anglo-Egyptian treaty was, for Britain, a silver lining to the otherwise darkening clouds coming out of Europe.

Throughout the interwar period the British government, consistent with its role of king-maker and general arbiter for the Arab East, was often to be found overseeing regional agreements. As mandatory, for example, Britain had arranged satisfactory treaties settling border and related issues between Iraq and Turkey as well as between Iraq and Saudi Arabia. Britain was intimately involved in all Arabian peninsula negotiations. British ambassadors, whether in Cairo or Baghdad or Jidda, could feel that they were heirs to the tradition of Stratford de Redcliffe.

The extent to which British policymakers by the thirties were thinking in terms of an Arab policy transcending any single political unit may be seen in the British reaction to their thorniest problem in the Middle East—Palestine. The Palestinian Arab general strike of 1936 protesting British mandatory policy was brought to an end following an appeal by the Arab rulers of Iraq, Saudi Arabia, and Transjordan. That the démarche was a carefully arranged face-saving device for all concerned in no way detracts from its importance. Britain had accepted, indeed encouraged, Arab good offices.

Then, after the Peel Commission (1937) had recommended the partition of Palestine, only to have this plan challenged as impracticable by the follow-up Woodhead Commission, the British government made another effort to bring the concerned parties together. This was the 1939 London round-table discussions. To the great consternation of the Zionists, the British definition of the concerned parties included Arab delegations from Egypt, Iraq, Saudi Arabia, and Transjordan as well as from Palestine. Nothing came of the London talks, and Britain was left to impose a policy unilaterally. The result was the well-known, or in Zionist eyes notorious, 1939 White Papers, which, if implemented, would have resulted in a permanent Jewish minority in an independent Palestine.

Commentators on this controversial 1939 policy statement agree that Britain, rightly or wrongly, felt the need to make a significant gesture to the Arabs by way of preparing for the world war that was imminent. This confirms the extent to which British Middle Eastern thinking, roughly one generation after the Husayn-McMahon correspondence, tended to be based on assumptions of an over-all Arab strategy.

WORLD WAR II

Britain's darkest days in World War II from the fall of France (June 1940) until the battle of El-Alamein (October 1942) put these assumptions to a severe test. In Palestine the Arab nationalist forces were still in disarray following the 1936-1939 Arab revolt, but Britain was unable to turn this to positive account.

Hajj Amin al-Husayni and most of the leadership of the Palestinian Arab Higher Committee were in exile when war began. Their influence had prevailed in the Palestinian Arab rejection of the 1939 White Paper, by far the most pro-Arab policy statement in the entire Mandate period. The extreme bargaining position imposed by Hajj Amin and his followers hardly augured well for Britain's rallying Palestinian Arab support during the war. Britain, however, seemed prepared to settle for quiescent neutrality.

The less influential, traditionally pro-British, Palestinian politicans led by the Nashashibi family did support Britain when war was declared. Britain offered only polite noises by way of response. Presumably, they sought to keep open the door for the much more influential Hajj Amin to come to terms or at least stay on the sidelines. They were soon to be disabused.

126

In Egypt the overwhelming majority of the political elite favored Egyptian neutrality, and several openly deplored the 1936 Anglo-Egyptian Treaty, which obliged Egypt in case of war to be at least a passive ally. The Egyptian government did, however, avoid challenging Britain, and the spirit of the 1936 treaty. Egypt broke diplomatic relations with Nazi Germany and interned German citizens living in Egypt.

Even so, at the beginning of the war Britain had cause for concern. In August 1939, shortly before the outbreak of war young King Faruq appointed a government headed by Ali Mahir, a shrewd, autocratic politician and palace favorite of decidedly anti-British orientation. Moreover, the chief of staff of the Egyptian army was Aziz Ali al-Misri. His uncompromising nationalism, Anglophobia, and unconcealed admiration for the German military frustrated British-Egyptian military cooperation. Early in 1940 the British were able to pressure the Egyptian government to have al-Misri removed,[20] and additional pressure brought Ali Mahir's resignation in June of that year. The worst had been avoided.

In Iraq the situation was even more delicate. The staunchly pro-British Nuri al-Said, then in office as prime minister, was prepared to declare war on Germany, but was stopped by strong opposition from within the cabinet. Then, in October 1939, Hajj Amin al-Husayni and several of his colleagues arrived in Baghdad. The Palestinian leader had no difficulty finding Iraqi political figures willing to consider the possibility of ties with Britain's enemies.

Most important, the Iraqi army was by 1939 much more politicized than the armies of other Arab countries. General

[20] Aziz Ali al-Misri later conspired with the then very young Free Officers (destined to overthrow Faruq's corrupt regime in July 1952) in an effort secretly to leave Egypt in 1941 and establish contact with the Axis powers; but the plane on which he was to make his escape crash landed. Al-Misri was later arrested and interned. See Anwar al-Sadat, *Revolt on the Nile* (New York, 1957), pp. 32-42 and Majid Khadduri, "Aziz Ali al-Misri and the Arab Nationalist Movement," *St. Anthony's Papers* (London, 1965) No. 17 (*Middle Eastern Affairs*, No. 4), pp. 158-159.

Bakr Sidqi's 1936 coup had given Iraqi officers a taste for political involvement, and most of the young officers were adamant nationalists chafing under British tutelage.

Grudging Iraqi and Egyptian cooperation consistent with a narrow construction of treaty obligations that marked the period from the outbreak of the war until the fall of France gave way thereafter to a much more dangerous trend for the British. With the fall of France the idea that Britain would soon suffer the same fate became increasingly thinkable in the Arab world. The limited Arab political support for Britain immediately became clear. Only strong counter-pressure kept the situation from becoming, from the British point of view, much worse.

First, most Arabs, leaders as well as rank-and-file, preferred a prudent non-commitment. This attitude, the heritage of those many Ottoman centuries when politics passed them by, had been reinforced by the disappointing experiences growing out of World War I diplomacy. A wait-and-see mentality prevailed over what otherwise would have been the more normal reaction—that of seize-the-moment.

Second, with Italy's entry into the war on Germany's side, the question of which path led to genuine decolonization became confused. Germany looked to many like a safe bet. She had no colonies in the Middle East. She had no apparent imperial aims in the Middle East. Her strongly revisionist diplomacy was largely directed against the two European powers that dominated the Arab world, Britain and France. Germany's outspoken opposition to Zionism was another important weight on the Arab side of the balance.

Mussolini's Italy, on the other hand, was notorious for its brutal conquest of Libya. This was then followed, beginning in 1935 by Il Duce's settler colonization designed to make Libya Italian forever. Hitler's demands for *lebensraum* seemed to Arabs to be safely directed against Europe. Mussolini and his overpopulated Italy, by contrast, looked toward Arab lands.

Third, during that critical period from June 1940 until October 1942 Nazi Germany never made a strong bid for dominance in the Middle East. The few tentative bids tried proved to be too little too late. Hitler's strategy focused on Europe. The important question was whether Britain or the Soviet Union was to be the next primary target after France. All else, including the Middle East, was incidental. Other constraints gave pause to the Nazi regime. Germany had virtually conceded the Levant and the Arab lands of Northern Africa as the Italian sphere of influence.

As if this were not deterrence enough, Nazi Germany harbored the hope of turning Vichy France from defeated enemy into ally, or at least keeping Petain's government popular enough to withstand the Gaullist challenge for support of the French people. Germany thus had to avoid giving Vichy reason to suspect that plans were afoot to dismantle France's Arab empire. This latter constraint prevailed until the launching of Operation Torch, the American landing in North Africa, in November 1942. By then the time for bold Axis bids to win over the Arabs was past. Even the earlier sending of German troops to North Africa (beginning in February 1941), was done more to shore up a sagging Italy than to begin a venturesome Nazi push into the Arab world.

These limitations on the Axis side were, however, obscured from the Arabs. If ever the more desperate or more daring spirits were to collaborate with Britain's enemies (just as Sharif Husayn had done against his Ottoman overlord in the First World War) then the time was from June 1940 until the turning of the tide at El Alamein in October 1942. Britain during that time did face two challenges. One was in Iraq, the other in Egypt.

Iraqi nationalist and anti-British politicians had considered seeking help from the Axis even before the fall of France. That dramatic event accelerated such moves. So pervasive was the belief in Iraqi circles that Britain would go down in defeat that even the staunchly pro-British Nuri al-Said sought to hedge his bets by soliciting contacts with the Axis.[21]

---

[21] See Majid Khadduri, "General Nuri's Flirtation with the Axis Powers," *Middle East Journal*, 16, no. 3, Summer 1962.

Rallying the anti-British forces were the politician Rashid Ali al-Gaylani and a few other leading Iraqi politicians plus military officers. Their political strategy was typical of those unsure of their own power base who are attempting to change their client status from one great power to that power's wartime enemy. They simultaneously tried to negotiate with Britain to gain concessions while maintaining clandestine contacts with the Axis (especially Germany, for, as explained, the Iraqis suspected Italian ambitions in the Arab world). They were especially concerned to get firm commitments from the Axis and worried over the timing of any possible outright break with Britain. The break must not be too late to reap the full advantage of concessions offered by the other side; but, even more important, it must not be too soon. That would risk being defeated by a British attack before sufficient Axis support was forthcoming.

The showdown came in spring 1941, begun by a military coup that brought Rashid Ali al-Gaylani back into power. Not having yet received any arms aid from the Axis, al-Gaylani played a waiting game, but the British, deciding that he was only playing for time, struck first in early May. By the end of May British forces had prevailed over the Iraqi military, forcing Rashid Ali and his followers to flee the country. The British-Hashimite connection in Iraq was restored. The regent, Abd al-Ilah, and other prominent pro-British politicians such as Nuri al-Said who had gone into exile after the Rashid Ali coup returned to take over the reins of government. Britain had no further trouble with Iraq for the remainder of the war.

The Egyptian challenge took a less dramatic form, but the stakes involved were perhaps more crucial. In January 1942 General Rommel started an offensive that achieved immediate gains. That the Axis might overrun Egypt, and thus destroy Britain's Middle Eastern military position before U.S. troops could be engaged (the Soviet Union was still reeling from the German invasion that began in June 1941), suddenly seemed likely.

King Faruq and his entourage, who had been in secret contact with the Italians and the Germans for over a year, stepped up these activities. At the same time, Faruq's animosity to Britain came to be expressed more publicly. There were also sporadic contacts with the Axis by representatives of the major Egyptian parties. The plans of Faruq and others in Egypt remained, however, much more circumspect than that of Rashid Ali and his colleagues. Rather than exploring details of possible Egyptian military action against the British they were more inclined to offer a benevolently neutral and receptive Egypt once Rommel's armies defeated the British.

Even this was more than the embattled British were willing to countenance. King Faruq continued his subtle games by engineering the resignation of a weak Egyptian government which had British backing. Faruq hoped both to signal to the Axis the changing political climate in Egypt and to form a government more under his direct control. Britain recaptured the initiative with a surprising step. Ambassador Sir Miles Lampson (later Lord Killearn) demanded that the king appoint a Wafdist government.

This reversed a long-standing British antipathy to Egypt's only genuinely popular party. Shortly before, the British and the Wafd had come to terms—a free hand for the Wafd to govern Egypt in return for a Wafdist commitment to maintain the domestic public order necessary for the Allied war effort.

King Faruq tried to temporize, but Lampson arrived at the royal palace the night of February 4, 1942 accompanied by British troops. Within an hour the ultimatum was accepted. Egypt's majority party, the Wafd, that had so often been denied office by British or royal machinations (or both) was now brought to power on British bayonets. The Wafd fulfilled its part of the bargain, maintaining public order during those months leading up to the decisive battle of El Alamein (just 65 miles west of Alexandria).[22] Britain had survived this crisis, too.

---

[22] The sequel to the surprising wartime alliance between Britain and the Wafd is instructive. Britain permitted King Faruq to dismiss the Wafd in 1944. By this time the party had, admittedly, become mired in corruption. Even so, the timing and manner in which Britain let the Wafd be dropped displayed a will to return to control of politics from the British Embassy. Nor

Pinnacle of Success?

By the end of 1942 Britain could breathe easier in the Arab world. A hard-eyed examination of how Britain got through the period up to El Alamein might well conclude that it was more a matter of daring British initiatives and good luck than a depth of Arab loyalty or even acquiescence. Perhaps, but however they arrived at the conclusion British policymakers faced the last three years of World War II strengthened in the conviction that their Arab policy was a winning strategy.

Britain *seemed* on the threshold of attaining a new monopoly political position in the Arab world from Libya to the Persian Gulf—something no great power had ever come close to achieving since the beginning of the Eastern Question. In Libya the Sanusi brotherhood under Idris (later independent Libya's first and only king) had willingly enlisted in a British-sponsored Libyan Arab force to fight alongside the British during the entire North African campaign. Thus began a British-Sanusi working alliance and comradeship in arms.

As early as January 1942 Foreign Minister Eden gave a pledge in the House of Commons that Cyrenaica (the Sanusi stronghold, the brotherhood being much less important in Tripolitania) would not return to Italian rule. The statement was one of the important milestones on the road to Libyan independence achieved in 1951. Thus, after the successful conclusion of the North African campaign Britain's position in Libya rested on a solid foundation.

In the Fertile Crescent the British strike against Rashid Ali's government in Iraq was quickly followed by an equally successful British and Free French campaign to oust the Vichy government from Syria and Lebanon (June-July 1941).

---

did Britain make any effort to work with sounder political elements either within the Wafd or elsewhere. They would later pay for their cynicism. In the stormy post-war period of Anglo-Egyptian negotiations, the British faced only a corrupt court, an embittered Wafd, a handful of politicians without any power base, and a xenophobic mass movement of Muslim fundamentalism—the Muslim Brethren. This made satisfactory negotiations impossible, until after the 1952 Free Officers coup.

Later that year the Free French issued proclamations of Lebanese and Syrian independence, but it soon became clear that the Free French notion of independence included French base rights and a privileged position. The political leadership of Syria plus (an unpleasant surprise for France) even an important segment of the Maronite community in Lebanon wanted total independence.

A replay of the three-cornered British-French-Syrian struggle that had taken place after the First World War occurred, but this time France was outmanned. After 1918 France was weak on-the-spot in Syria but sufficiently strong in Europe to prevail. This time France was again weak in the Middle East, but also weak in Europe. Free France did not have the resources to stand up against British (at times British and American) pressures. Britain's representative, General Edward Spears, must have seemed to the hard-pressed French as the reincarnation of the Francophobe T. E. Lawrence, only now with the rank and power to work his will.

To size up the power situation: the Syrian and Lebanese nationalists kept up the pressure, and General Spears could apply the screws under the plea of military necessity. The Free French fought tenaciously but in a losing cause. De Gaulle never got his preferential treaties, and after several crises Syria and Lebanon were admitted into the new United Nations and the French *troupes speciales* obliged to withdraw (1945-1946). The Anglo-French rivalry in the Middle East that could be traced back to Napoleon's landing in Egypt almost a century and a half earlier now appeared to be coming to a conclusion with a single winner—Britain.

In this heady context Britain was also developing ambitious plans for regional organization under British guidance. One such plan grew out of immediate war-time needs of supply and distribution. This was the Middle East Supply Center (MESC), created in 1941. There seemed no reason why the region-wide approach to economics, and to economic development, could not continue after the war, with Britain providing the expertise and the over-all direction. Such patterns

133

of indirect rule, long favored by British imperialism in political and administrative matters, could thus be extended to economics.

The only possible Great Power rival for such a role appeared then to be the United States, which Britain had needed to bring in as an equal partner in sharing the economic burden as early as 1942. There was, however, reason to hope that the American recognition of the Middle East as a British responsibility in wartime would extend to the post-war period. Britain also took a leading role in encouraging Arab unity. As early as May 1941 Eden had announced British support for any Arab unity plan "that commands general approval." This announcement, taken alone, could be discounted as a bidding for regional support in wartime when the outcome was far from assured, but it was followed by an equally positive statement from the British foreign secretary in February 1943 (thus four months after El Alamein).

Eden at that time emphasized that the initiative for such unity should come from the Arabs. This was seen by the Arabs and by other observers as one more example of Britain's preferred way to operate in the Arab East—behind the scenes. After all, the pro-British Nuri al-Said had been first off the mark with a proposal for Fertile Crescent unity in December 1942.

Thereafter, the several different Arab leaders began negotiations in the knowledge that a form of Arab unity could be openly worked for with British support. The Alexandria meeting of 1944 with delegates from Egypt, Iraq, Lebanon, Saudi Arabia, Syria, Transjordan, and Yemen (and observers from Palestine and the Maghrib) produced a protocol which, when signed by those states the following year, brought into existence the Arab League. No better sign of Britain's bullish attitude toward its future in the Arab world can be found than Britain's role as recruiting sergeant for what became the Arab League.

With the end of the war Britain's position, instead of becoming consolidated at this apparent peak of influence never before reached by a great power in modern times, quickly began to come apart. It would be tempting to attribute the setback to the Palestine problem, which had already bedeviled British officialdom for over a quarter-century and was in the years 1945-1948 heading for a decisive show-down. Palestine was in fact only the most dramatic of Britain's problems with the Arab world in the post World War II era. Events in Egypt and Iraq were no less discouraging for Britain's Arab plans. In Iraq a treaty signed in January 1948 to replace the 1930 Anglo-Iraqi treaty had to be abandoned following severe nationalist riots in Baghdad and tension throughout the country. Immediately after the war, Egypt and Britain became embroiled in abortive treaty negotiations and bitter mutual recrimination over the two issues of British troops in Egypt and the Sudan question. Neither was to be resolved until 1954, two years after Nasser and his Free Officers had seized power.

PALESTINE

Events in Palestine did, however, provide a general pan-Arab animosity toward Britain which kept Arab opposition virulently alive. How this happened is common knowledge, but the extraordinary nature of this development is not always sufficiently noted.

The first Arab-Israeli war in 1948 assured the sovereign existence of Israel and left Abdullah controlling the major part of what the United Nations had allocated for a separate Palestinian Arab state (the remainder having been conquered by Israel during the war, except for Gaza, which fell under Egyptian tutelage). Abdullah soon absorbed this portion of Palestine into his state, the name of which was changed from Transjordan to Jordan (1949).

Measured by the crude, and often cruel, divisions of peoples and territories that had characterized Eastern Question politics for over a century, this carving up of Palestine was not unusual. The Arab-Israeli confrontation thereafter might well have continued to fester as one more struggle of national groups

135

over the same small territory, or it might even have been resolved. The British phasing out of Palestine, while hardly a
creditable performance, might also by that same Eastern
Question standard have seemed a realistic cutting of losses.
Instead, the Arab-Israeli confrontation became the central regional issue around with other issues, conflicts, and alliances
tended to be organized. Moreover, the Arab world saddled
Britain with the blame.

Why did developments take this turn? The most satisfactory
answer would seem to lie—as so often in Eastern Question
issue—in the kaleidoscopic arrangement of many factors including the following:

1. The Great Powers and the United Nations assumed that
   a peace treaty would soon be signed after the 1948 war.
   The agencies they set up to assure temporary order and
   relief of suffering (e.g., mixed armistice commissions,
   Palestinian refugee relief) actually made it possible for all
   parties to avoid a settlement. The situation soon jelled
   into a no war-no peace confrontation, with the immediate antagonists dealing through third parties and the Palestinian refugees as a hostage community.
2. The miserable performance of the Arab armies (except
   the Arab Legion of Transjordan) induced the political
   leaders of these shaky regimes to seek a scapegoat. Britain and Abdullah satisfied this need.
3. The long-standing division within the Arab area, pitting
   those who favored accommodation with the imperial
   presence against the rejectionists was exacerbated to such
   an extent that pragmatic politics became virtually impossible.
4. Ostracized, Israel was under no pressure to seek a settlement with her neighbors. When the resulting policy of
   wait-and-see while building up at home was joined to
   the tactic of retaliation in force, all the elements necessary
   for keeping the confrontation in stalemate broken by short-
   term lapses into violence were in place.

5. None of the power wielders either in the region or beyond had a sufficiently strong motivation to work for a
settlement. Only Palestinians, especially the refugees, had
this motivation, but they were powerless.

Britain had always been vulnerable to Arab attacks on the
Palestine question. The Balfour Declaration had been the first
official state recognition of Zionism. Britain had, in fact, shown
signs early and late in the mandate period of wanting to hedge
on its commitment to Zionism, but Great Powers in dealing
with regional clients usually require some help in finding a
face-saving formula before watering down commitments.

The accommodationists, such as Abdullah, Nuri al-Said of
Iraq, the Nashashibis in Palestine, were willing to play this
game, but the rejectionists, who dominated politics in mandate Palestine, and ultimately elsewhere in the Arab East, would
have none of it. Further, the rejectionists' major weapon in
attacking their Arab opponents was the accusation of toadying
to, or even being paid hirelings of, the imperialists and Zionists.[23]

Then—such is the perversity of human nature—once the
rejectionists saw that their tactics, especially when unmatched
by any effective military or diplomatic action, had lost Palestine, they turned in paroxysms of rage against the British and
the Hashimites, whose tactics (however impure their motives
might have been) could have gained a more favorable outcome.

[23] Not without some basis in fact. Certainly, the Hashimites and those
politicians who worked faithfully with them received invaluable support from
Britain. The Nashahibi clan in Palestine was receptive even to the idea of
Zionist subsidies in the 1920s. See Y. Porath, *The Emergence of the Palestinian-Arab Nationalist Movement, 1918-1929* (London, 1974), p. 224 and in
general Chapter V. Hajj Amin al-Husayni, on the other hand, received large
subsidies from the Axis during the Second World War. Diplomatic historians
and international relations specialists are inclined to take the extreme positions of ignoring or exaggerating the influence of under-the-table subsidies.
The phenomenon needs to be studied more rigorously. "An honest politician
is one who when bought stays bought." That is the viewpoint of the patron.
The client morality would have it that an honest politician is one who can
use bribes effectively to advance his group's goals.

That the old enemy of the Palestinian rejectionists, King Abdullah, was the only Arab leader to come out of the first Arab-Israeli war with some gains only increased the pain, and the anger, of the frustrated Arab nationalists.

DECLINE AND FALL

Yet, for all its importance in the sudden plummeting of British-Arab relations in those immediate post-war years, the Palestine problem was only a major catalyst, setting in motion what was bound to happen. Britain would have faced essentially the same challenge in roughly the same manner even if the Palestine problem could have been somehow magically conjured away. The workings of the system itself produced such a reaction. By reaching a pinnacle of power in the eastern Arab world, Britain automatically became the focus of all discontent in the area.

No one any longer needed Britain to help get France out of Syria and Lebanon. The Soviet Union, while baring its teeth in Iran and Turkey, posed no threat to the Arabs. Only Britain stood in the way of an appreciable transfer of power to the region. If Britain had demonstrated a strong will to consolidate its position in the area and had allocated the considerable means required to back up that policy, then something might have been achieved before other great powers posed a challenge.

To present the matter in this way is to underline how unavoidable the decline really was. Britain had been bled white by its efforts in World War II. She was well along in the last phase of decolonization in India. In 1947, Britain was obliged to pass the front-line defense of Greece, Turkey, and Iran against the Soviet Union to the United States, a changing of the guard that led to the Truman Doctrine. Under such circumstances British statesmen simply could not be expected to succeed in the only game plan their country's dire economic straits permitted them to try—that of light-touch British hegemony in the Arab world.

Even if native Arab political power had ever been as solidly in the hands of the Arab accommodationists as the British strategy assumed, a rearrangement of power with more ending up in the hands of regional political forces was indicated. Under such circumstances, and without the trauma of Palestine, the change could have taken place more smoothly, but the change itself was not to be stopped.

Britain had no such luck. The Palestine problem took the worst possible turn for a would-be great power organizer of the area—an explosion of war followed by no settlement at all. Palestine, instead, remained to exacerbate the many other problems. Radical nationalism was on the rise throughout the Arab world. The existing Arab regimes in almost all cases had only a shaky claim to political legitimacy and even less to popular support. The complex post-war transition thus took place in an atmosphere of extreme tension and no little violence until Suez made a mockery of British dreams to organize the Arab world.

Playing a dominant role since the beginning of the Eastern Question, Britain had twice tried to organize the Middle East, the first based on support for the Ottoman Empire and the second building on a slowly evolving Arab policy. The historical context of each was necessarily very different, just as the world of Lord Palmerston and Lord John Russell was not that of Anthony Eden and Harold MacMillan. Even so, the structural similarity of the two developments that span the last two centuries is striking. Moreover, in neither case could Britain attain a hegemony sufficient to change the rules of the Eastern Question game.

Another twentieth-century effort to organize the Middle East came from within the region. This was Arab nationalism.

III. ARABISM IN THE EASTERN QUESTION CONTEXT

Arabism is appropriately classified with the several old-new nationalisms that came to maturity while the Ottoman Empire was slowly dying. Like these others, Arabism was new insofar as the notion of the nation-state composed of participating citizens was new to the Middle East. It was new, moreover, in advancing as the criterion of political loyalty a common identity based on language and culture.

Arabism was, equally, a reordering of very old bonds of social solidarity. There was the common language—Arabic. Moreover, even the most superficial examination of the Arab world reveals a common culture to be seen in such basic matters as architecture, cuisine, relations of the sexes, idea of the family, and aesthetic expression.

Just as with the other old-new nationalisms of the nineteenth and early twentieth centuries (indeed, more than for most other nationalisms) Arabism drew inspiration from an earlier golden age. If the Greek could look back to the Byzantine Empire and to Hellenic civilization, the Arab could lay claim to the Abbasids, to Islam itself, and also to that idealized Eastern equivalent of Europe's noble savage—the bedouin Arab.

Arabism, just as these other nationalisms, arose because the old political system—that represented by the Ottoman Empire—was breaking down, and the dynamic nation-state ideology of dominant Europe was at hand to be borrowed. Unlike the nationalism of the Ottoman Balkans, however, Arabism was not separatist nor was it necessarily anti-Ottoman. To the Arabs, roughly 90 percent of whom were Muslims, the Ottoman Empire represented them. The enemies of the Ottomans were their enemies. Their normal impulse was to help shore up the Ottoman Empire if they were politically active, to sympathize in silence if they were not.

Until the years following the Young Turk Revolt of 1908, the main current of Arabism may properly be described as an effort to assure a larger share of power for the Arabs in a reformed empire. The role of the Arabs in the Ottoman Empire may be compared, *grosso modo*, to that of the Hungarians in the Austrian Empire, except that the Hungarians got their dual monarchy, whereas the Ottoman Empire after the Young Turk Revolt went down the road of Turkism.

Even the anti-Ottoman Arabism of the early days entailed more nearly an ideology of replacement rather than of separation. The ideological struggle was over the leadership of the Muslim Middle East, with the range of options bounded, on the one side, by the view that the Arabs should have an equal role in the empire and, on the other, the idea that the Arabs should, rightly, have a predominant role.

In another sense, early Arabism was an ideologically uneasy juxtaposition of the classic "pan" movement (as Pan-Slavism, Pan-Turanism) alongside a more circumscribed nationalism. Certainly, the "pan" nature of the movement is revealed in the eventual expansion of Arabism from the Fertile Crescent to embrace all of Arab Asia, then Egypt, then the Maghrib.

The disapproval with which most Arabs greeted Sharif Husayn's revolt against the Ottomans during the First World War attests to this underlying current of unity that has always informed Arabism. Sharif Husayn and his allies in the Fertile Crescent were able to ride out this adverse reaction from many of those they claimed to be liberating because of a combination of favorable circumstances:

1. They had chosen the winning side. Otherwise, the "revolt in the desert" would have been only one more footnote in the long history of provincial uprisings against imperial unity.
2. The harsh regime in Syria of the Ottoman Young Turk leader, Jamal Pasha, during the First World War, coupled with an increasingly inflexible policy of Turkification emanating from Istanbul, moved many Arab leaders of greater Syria to sense that an Arab-Turkish separation had already been decided—by the Young Turks.
3. Sharif Husayn himself chose the ambiguous framework of both a "pan" movement and a more narrowly limited nationalism by keeping open the idea of an Arab caliphate.

Among the intriguing historical might-have-beens is the course of developments if Sharif Husayn and the Arab nationalists of the Fertile Crescent had been able to strike a bargain with the Young Turk leadership of the Ottoman Empire. There were contracts. Each side knew rather well not only the options available to the other but what the other side was up to. Such a bargain between the Ottoman government and the Arab nationalists, reviving in different form Abdul Hamid's thinking concerning an Arabo-Turkish Ottoman Empire, could well have substituted for Jamal Pasha's divisive policies in Syria during the war years a common Arabo-Turkish loyalty.

Then, after defeat, what if Ataturk had pitched his resistance movement in terms of an Arabo-Turkish Muslim nationalism? (Not a religious nationalism per se. That would have been out of character for Ataturk. A Muslim cultural nationalism, akin to the Zionism of David Ben Gurion, would, however, have been conceivable.) There *were* contacts after the war between Ataturk's forces and the disparate Arab political leadership in the Fertile Crescent. The forces of inertia—four centuries of common history are not easily shucked off—just might have kept them together.

Or the might-have-been speculation concerning a common Arabo-Turkish political future becomes even more compelling if the Ottoman Empire had managed to remain neutral in the First World War. Then Arabism would even more clearly have been pushed into the role of a separatist, divisive movement,[24] and for that very reason it might have withered on the vine.

Arab nationalism eventually became a powerful—although elusive and imprecise—ideological force for a variety of reasons:

1. The steadily increasing evidence that the old political order represented by the Ottoman Empire was doomed made imperative the search for alternatives.

[24] This line of speculation is influenced by the Arab nationalist ideologue Sati' al-Husri's important *Al-Bilad al-'Arabiyya wa al-Dawla al-Uthmaniyya* (Beirut, 1957, and later editions) and by Zeine N. Zeine's *The Emergence of Arab Nationalism with a Background Study of Arab-Turkish Relations in the Near East* (Beirut, revised edition 1966). Both emphasize the Young Turk revolt of 1908 as a decisive turning point. Both provide a healthy corrective to earlier accounts that trace Arabism as a movement of an oppressed nationality against imperial (Ottoman) oppression. Both show that the eventual break between Arab and Turk was caused at least as much by the latter as the former.

2. Nationalism appeared especially attractive since it was associated with the West that represented power and efficacy.

3. Remaining scruples among Arab Muslims and certain Arab Christians about undermining the beleaguered Ottoman Empire began slowly to fade as the Young Turk ideology captured the Ottoman government.

4. For a political culture in which the jealous loyalty to a small-group particularism (religious, ethnic, linguistic, tribal) was countered by the bleak wisdom that these many political particularisms if unrestrained led to anarchy, Arabism could appeal as a plausible universalist alternative to Ottomanism. Arabism could be presented as the ideological matrix for a great state that would assure order and justice.

5. Rather than challenge the Arab Muslims' fundamental loyalty to Islam, Arab nationalism may be said to have nationalized Islam. The religion of Islam was depicted as a major component of the Arab heritage, and from this position it was but a short step to the implicit argument that loyalty to the Arab nation was virtually a religious duty.

6. Arab nationalism could be presented to non-Muslims as an organizing principle, transcending religious difference, that all Arabs shared equally.

7. To the modernist and the secularists Arab nationalism was seen as a move away from older patterns of social and political organization and toward modernity.

8. At the same time, Arab nationalism, by emphasizing the Arab heritage, could appeal to those who deplored the massive introduction of new, foreign ideas and artifacts.

THE POLITICS OF ARAB NATIONALISM

Such are Arab nationalism's diverse ideological roots. When emphasis is shifted from the ideological background to political history a more precise chronology is possible. The fifteen-year-period from the Young Turk Revolt in 1908 to Ataturk's

143

creation of the Republic of Turkey constitutes the turning of the tide. Before that time, Arabist ideologies were the work of insignificant numbers of persons who entered politics from diverse backgrounds and sought diverse goals. Before 1908, their political challenges to the status quo could be made to appear as a foolish (if not malicious) siding with Europe, the outside oppressor, against one's own beleagured leadership. Even as late as 1915-1916, after the Young Turk leadership in Istanbul had moved far in the direction of Turkism, Sharif Husayn's revolt against the sultan was not viewed with favor by most politically concerned Arabs of the Fertile Crescent.

After 1923 there was no longer an established political order standing in the way of Arabism. The Ottoman Empire was no more, and Kemal Ataturk was urging the inhabitants of Anatolia to choose Turkish nationalism.

Moreover, Arab nationalism henceforth had an unambiguous enemy to oppose—European colonialism, which after the First World War held sway everywhere in the Arab world except for the heart of Arabia itself.

To the Arabs of the Fertile Crescent, the disappointment of emerging from one imperial yoke which was harsh and remote but not culturally or religiously alien (the Ottoman Empire) only to fall prey to clearly alien imperial systems was exacerbated by having had wartime hopes for independence so rudely dashed. That European colonialism not only denied the Arabs of the Fertile Crescent their freedom but also divided them into separate political entities subject to two different imperial overlords—Britain and France—gave even greater symbolic appeal to the goal of Arab unity.

In the years immediately following the First World War, Arab nationalism continued to be, as it had been from the beginning, a program advanced by—and appealing most of all to—Arabs of the Fertile Crescent. Egyptian nationalism was already a good two generations old and had brought into existence two mass-based political parties: first, the Watani Party founded by Mustafa Kamil (1874-1908), and then the Wafd organized in 1919 under the leadership of Saad Zaghlul. But while Egypt was thus effectively politicized, its commitment to Arabism was yet to come. A similar development in the Maghrib would take place even later.

FERTILE CRESCENT ARABISM

Fertile Crescent Arabism during the interwar years developed in the context of two political confrontations. There was, first, the struggle between traditional political elites which generally took the form of Hashimites against anti-Hashimites. The former attempted to make the most of their close ties to Britain. The latter often obtained the support of Ibn Saud, who, as the nemesis of Sharif Husayn's ambitions in Arabia, sought to keep the family of his defeated rival from growing in strength.

Second was the challenge posed by newly emerging political elites against both the traditional leadership of whatever stripe and the Western imperial order. Almost all these Fertile Crescent political figures found themselves espousing Arabism either from conviction or convenience. Even the principal imperial power, Britain, was moving in that direction, as has been seen.

The basic similarity in Arabist ideology of the traditional leadership is revealed in the careers of Hashimite Nuri al-Said and anti-Hashimite Hajj Amin al-Husayni who each presumed to lead the Arabs to unity. That hardy perennial of Iraqi politics, Nuri al-Said (1888-1958) belonged to the generation of Arab political leaders who made the transition "from the Ottomanism to Arabism." (The phrase is C. Ernest Dawn's, whose book by that title is one of the best treatments of early Arab nationalism.) The son of a minor Iraqi religious functionary, the young Nuri received a military education, the last three years of which were spent at the military academy in Istanbul. He was graduated at the age of 17, commissioned in the Ottoman army, and first saw service in his native Iraq. Returning to Istanbul in 1910 for training at the military staff

college he soon became active in politics, joining in 1912 the
'Ahd society.

Nuri became increasingly disaffected by Young Turk politics. In 1914, after the British had occupied Basra Nuri, al-
Said crossed his Rubicon. He contacted the British, was interned as an Ottoman officer but soon released to begin his
work with the British and the Hashimites in what was destined to become the Arab revolt. Several other Arabs serving
as Ottoman officers abandoned the Ottoman cause early in
the Great War. Others, such as the leading Arab nationalist
thinker, Satiʿ al-Husri, or Nuri's compatriot and fellow Ottoman officer, Yasin al-Hashimi (1884-1937), remained loyal
Ottomans until the end of the war, but thereafter switched
"from Ottomanism to Arabism."

The arch-rival of the Hashimites in Palestine, Hajj Amin al-
Husayni (1897-1974), had an early career paralleling that of
Nuri al-Said. Al-Husayni also studied at the military academy
in Istanbul and served as an Ottoman officer during the First
World War. In 1917, he defected to the Arab revolt. A major
difference between the two is that Nuri came from a very
modest family, while Hajj Amin belonged to one of the most
eminent families of Jerusalem. The former needed a patron to
advance his political career; the latter because of family connections could aspire to leadership in his own right. Hajj Amin
emerged as the natural leader of the Palestinians opposing the
British Mandate. In the twenties and even in the thirties certain British officials believed that Hajj Amin might be won
over to at least a grudging cooperation with British imperial
aims, but he and his following only hardened in their opposition.

In this rivalry of traditional political elites, personified by
Nuri al-Said and Hajj Amin al-Husayni, neither side took a
position against Arabism as a political ideology. Both sides
favored Arab unity and differed only over means to attain that
end. The pro-British Hashimites could argue that their standing with Britain made it possible for them to influence decisions favoring the Arabs. Their opponents could counter that

the Hashimites were toadying to the imperial overlord. Those opposed to the Hashimites, lacking a powerful imperial sponsor, relied on anti-Hashimite or anti-British elements such as Ibn Saud and Egypt, whose politicians—whatever their domestic rivalries—all wished to limit British power in the area. Egyptian politicians also perferred—again, regardless of their opposition on other points of Egyptian politics—to see Egypt remain the dominant power in the Arab world.

It is significant commentary on France's political weakness in the Fertile Crescent that no important Arab political leader, aside from those in the Maronite community, openly advocated the type of working alliance Britain enjoyed with the Hashimites.[25]

Most Western observers in those years regarded those collaborating with Britain as moderates and their opponents as extremists. In fact, neither the Hashimites nor anti-Hashimites were politically or, even less, socially revolutionary. The political alliances available to them did, however, push the one toward accepting the existing imperial order (working within that order to effect evolutionary change), while the other was moved to an uneasy cooperation with increasingly revolutionary forces.

What, then, of the newly emerging Arab political elites in the Fertile Crescent? They have been the most consistently misunderstood. Outsiders tend to project their own political preferences upon them and either praise or condemn them uncritically.

It is rather like European appraisals of the Greek independence movement a century or more earlier. Those who embraced the Romanticist and French Revolutionary traditions saw the Greeks through rose-colored glasses. Those favoring the established order had a jaundiced view of the Greek rebels. In each case the outside West was not simply "watching the

[25] France's poor political position in the area probably helped lull the British into an overly sanguine appraisal of their own standing among the Arabs. Later the same sort of false optimism characterized American policymakers while observing Britian's decline in the area following the Second World War.

147

show" but actually encouraging or supporting certain political figures. The same involvement of Western public opinion has held for the twentieth-century Middle East.

The rising Arab elites shared an exposure to the intrusive Western culture. They had access to Western education (often abroad) and were integrated into the colonial apparatus of bureaucracy or army. Others, while outside formal government, pursued Western-style professions as lawyers, doctors, schoolteachers. They were caught between the old and the new, the indigenous and the alien, and their educational experience left them dissatisfied with the old but not really integrated into the new. Lacking a solid power base in either the old or the new worlds, they pressed on vigorously lest they lose their precarious gains.

By no means were all revolutionaries. In the interwar years most were from well established middle-class families with a small, but growing, segment of lower-middle-class representation. Several worked with the traditional political elite, and not a few collaborated with the colonial apparatus. Nevertheless, the basic orientation of their politics was revolutionary, for they sought, sooner or later, to replace both the traditional political elite and the colonial apparatus. Moreover, their numbers slowly increased with growing educational opportunities, the expanding scope of modern government, and the continued absorption of their societies into the Western, capitalist economy. Eventually, there would be beleaguered small farmers and even a number of industrial workers ready to serve as political constituencies, for those would challenge the notables. For the most part, however, during the interwar period the traditional political elites were still firmly in the saddle. The men destined to create what might be called the new politics were still testing their wings. Only two partial exceptions to dominance by old guard politicians deserve comment.

First, General Bakr Sidqi's military coup of October 1936 toppling the existing Iraqi government and bringing Hikmat Sulayman to power began what was destined to become a dominant theme in modern Arab politics—military intervention in politics. This would, at first sight, appear as a clear example of the "new politics," for the interlocking themes of the military as an avenue of upward mobility for those of modest social origins and the militarization of politics loom large in any review of the modern Arab world.

On the other hand, this coup of 1936 seems rather closer to the reactionary, establishment politics of Latin American juntas than to the revolutionary coups associated with Nasser's Free Officers or the later Ba'thist military interventions in Syria and Iraq. Bakr Sidqi was a popular general at the very top of the military hierarchy. He was not an obscure colonel or major (as with the Egyptian Free Officers Movement, for example), concerned that the establishment politicians and generals at the top were blocking his advancement and the country's interests. Moreover, although the coup had the last-minute support of a small body of Iraqi politicians who were attempting to move their country along the modern liberal or socialist path (the Ahali group), these Iraqi examples of the rising political elite were soon cast aside.

The second partial exception to old guard political dominance occurred in Palestine. There the Arab revolt that broke out in 1936 and continued until 1939 is most plausibly interpreted as a popular uprising against Zionist expansion and British rule while also repudiating the socio-economic domination of the Arab urban notables. The countryside failed in its bid for nationalist leadership, which was, instead, recaptured by the traditional urban notables aligned with Hajj Amin al-Husayni.

BASIC CHARACTERISTICS OF INTERWAR ARABISM

Two general themes relevant to the study of Arabism within the larger context of the special Middle Eastern diplomatic culture emerge from the above pages. First, the multiparty and kaleidoscopic nature of Middle Eastern politics is confirmed for this period immediately following the demise of the Ottoman Empire. In the Fertile Crescent—the sole important arena of Arabism during the interwar years—the traditional elites were struggling among themselves; the British and French imperial powers maintained constant, even if at times muted, rivalry; and newly emerging political forces were beginning to be heard from.

All these different groups made constant efforts to co-opt or to crush political rivals. The imperial powers usually worked with the more cooperative of the traditional political elite, but they occasionally succumbed to the temptation to treat with the hard-line opposition, either to reach agreement with those seemingly representing a broader spectrum of native opinion or to prevent their customary supporters from becoming too complacent.

The traditional elite usually perceived the challenge to their standing represented by the emerging new political groups, but this did not stop them fron often seeking short-term tactical advantages against traditional opponents by working with those native political parvenus whose ideology and operating style they deplored. And the rising new political forces, whether meliorist or revolutionary, liberal or socialist, had good reason to consider both the established traditional leadership and the colonial apparatus as obstacles to the goals they sought. Nevertheless, they, too, occasionally compromised with one or the other.

This thorough diffusion of political power with its continually shifting alliances maintained the environment that fostered the second general characteristic. In the absence of a single, predominant indigenous power center sustained by a political doctrine of wide-ranging appeal, the different political groups in the Fertile Crescent fell into the habit of outbidding each other in support of Arab nationalism.

A plethora of positive inducements and almost no negative drawbacks drew all in this direction:

1. The lack of attractive alternatives. An appeal to an Iraqi, Palestinian, Transjordanian or Syrian patriotism fell on barren ground. There was no historical, cultural, reli-

gious, or linguistic justification for choosing such small political units as the ultimate goal. The clearly separatist ambition of many Lebanese Maronites—the one exception to the above—only served to make the idea of small-state nationalism suspect. And the greater Syria ideology of Sa'adeh's SSNP, although stopping far short of unifying all Arabic speakers, was in the context of the times a force for unity and against separatism.

2. Arab nationalism provided a convenient justification for those of pragmatic expansionist intentions such as Transjordan's Abdullah.

3. The best tactic for frustrating the expansionist designs of one's opponents was to label the scheme as an imperialist plot that actually would defeat genuine Arab unity efforts.

4. Those in politically weak positions in any specific Fertile Crescent country could openly seek support from neighboring Arab countries in the name of Arab unity and thus avoid the stigma of bringing outsiders into domestic quarrels.

5. The modernizing elites, lacking a traditional political base, could use the appeal of Arab unity to discredit the local power of the traditional notables.

These practical reasons, pushing virtually all political actors in the Fertile Crescent to take a public stand for Arabism during these years, should be set alongside Arabism's emotionally powerful attractions. Doctrine and deed became mutually reinforcing. Thus unchallenged, Arabism earned political legitimacy throughout the Fertile Crescent.

PALESTINE AND ARABISM

The spread of Arabism from the Fertile Crescent to the rest of the Arab world is most readily traced in terms of Palestine, for the confrontation between Arab and Jew in that tiny territory under British mandate (the size of New Jersey) eventually came to concern Arabs from Morocco to the Gulf. In the process the touchstone of Arabism, itself, became support for Arab Palestine. Palestinian Arab leaders during the first two decades of this century all viewed Palestine as part of a larger entity, either the Ottoman Empire or an Arab state embracing at least the Fertile Crescent.

In the years following the First World War the Palestinian leadership held to the argument that Britain had broken its promise, set out in the Husayn-McMahon correspondence. Not only, they insisted, was the promised independent Arab state pushed aside; but Britain compounded its perfidy by imposing the idea of a Jewish national home upon Palestine, which was to be part of that larger Arab political entity.

There is no need here to rehearse the many subtle lucubrations that have since been developed to support or refute this argument. It is, however, important to emphasize how this approach kept the Palestinian leadership wedded to a greater Arab orientation. This the Palestinian leadership never abandoned. Of course, the day-to-day problems of dealing with the mandatory administration and of resisting Zionist activities on the spot restricted much of their activity to Palestine itself. That the Arab leaders of the neighboring states had their own immediate concern with colonial rule also diverted them from Palestine. Even so, the recurrent political crises in Palestine that the Zionist-Palestine confrontation triggered always managed to spill over into the neighboring Arab countries.

Outside Arab concern for Palestine steadily increased. Among the milestones along the way to total Arab involvement in the Palestine issue were the following:

1. In 1925 the very personification of Britain's commitment to Zionism, Lord Balfour, made his only visit to Palestine. Returning by way of Damascus, he was faced with such hostile mobs that the French authorities, fearing for his life, hurried him out of the country.
2. Following the Wailing Wall incident of 1929[26] the Mus-

[26] Muslim-Jewish disorders growing out of a dispute over access to reli-

152

lim leadership of Palestine organized an Islamic congress held in Jerusalem in 1931. The principal agenda item of the congress over which Hajj Amin al-Husayni presided was the protection of Muslim holy places in Palestine. One result of this campaign was increased concern for the fate of Palestine throughout the Arab world, and indeed throughout the Muslim world.[27]

3. In 1936 the Palestinian general strike called in April and the subsequent acts of guerrilla violence in the countryside had by that autumn caused considerable economic hardship in the Palestinian community without any apparent compensating damage done to the Zionists or effective pressure on the British to change their policy. The traditional political elite sought a way to abandon the general strike without losing their political standing. The needed face-saving formula was found in a joint note from King Ghazi of Iraq, Ibn Saud, and Abdullah, urging "our sons the Arabs of Palestine" to rely "on the good will of our friend the British government." This was one more significant step in the direction of Arabizing the Palestine problem.

4. In the following year, 1937, soon after the British Royal Commission (the Peel Commission) had reported in fa-

gious shrines—for the Jews the Wailing Wall, a portion of the Second Temple destroyed in 70 of the Christian era, but this Jewish shrine for prayers and lamentations is at the southwest corner of the Haram al-Sharif, the third holiest site in Islam.

[27] "The Wall affair marked the beginning of the development of the Palestine question from a local question into a Muslim, pan-Arab one. Thanks to the propaganda carried out by the SMC (Supreme Muslim Council established by the Mandate Government in 1922 as a concession to the Muslim population) during the twenties, Muslim public opinion in general began directing its attention to Palestine and its Holy Places. . . . Of no less significance is the fact that when in 1930 the League of Nations' Commission of Inquiry into the rights of Jews and Muslims at the Wailing Wall was set up, the Palestinian spokesmen skillfully represented this issue as affecting the Muslims of the entire world." Porath, *Palestinian-Arab Nationalist Movement, 1918-1929*, p. 272. The Palestinians had taken a leaf from the Zionist book and managed to internationalize their case.

vor of partitioning Palestine into separate Jewish and Arab states, a large pan-Arab congress was held in Bludan, Syria, to reject the Peel Commission proposal. Some 400 delegates from the Arab world attended. An eminent Iraqi politician and former prime minister (1929-1930), Naji al-Suwaydi, was elected chairman of the congress. Other notables included an Egyptian politician, a Christian bishop from Syria,[28] and the well-known advocate of Arabism, Shakib Arslan, a Druze from Lebanon.

5. In October 1938, an interparliamentary congress in defense of Palestine met in Cairo in response to an appeal from the Palestinian leadership. Both the strength and weaknesses of the Palestinian cause in inter-Arab politics were reflected in this Cairo congress. A decision was taken to send a delegation to London protesting the partition plan, but by the time it arrived Britain had already abandoned the Peel Commission proposal. Aside from this action and other quite general resolutions of protest, the congress accomplished little, but it did reveal the sharp inter-Arab rivalries that were destined to plague the Palestinians. No delegates were permitted, for example, from Transjordan or Saudi Arabia. Moreover, the large delegation of Egyptian parliamentarians (60) appears less impressive when it is noted that the major Egyptian party, the Wafd, boycotted the congress.[29]

6. In early 1939, the British government, in one last effort to reach a negotiated settlement before the outbreak of

[28] Muhammad Ali ʿAlluba and Bishop Huraykan, See Y. Porath, *The Palestinian-Arab National Movement, 1929-1939* (London, 1977), p. 231. ʿAlluba was a founding member of the Wafd Party. He later abandoned Zaghlul and the Wafd to participate in the creation of the Liberal Constitutionalist Party. He was one of the small number of prominent Egyptian politicians (Abd al-Rahman Azzam was another) who supported the Society for Arab unity organized by students at Cairo University in 1936. See Sylvia Haim (ed.), *Arab Nationalism*, p. 49.

[29] See Porath, *Palestinian Arab Nationalist Movement, 1929-1939*, pp. 376-377, and E. Rossi, "Il Congresso Interparlamentare Arabo E Musulmano Pro Palestina Al Cairo (7-11 Ottobre), "*Oriente Moderno*, November 1938.

the Second World War, invited Arab and Jewish representatives to round-table talks in London. The substantive "internationalization" of the Palestinian issue was
manifest on both sides. The Jewish Agency (representing
both Zionist and non-Zionist Jews) was invited to select
its delegation to the talks, and the delegation from the
Arab side was not confined to Palestinian Arabs but included such notables as Amir Abdullah; Nuri al-Said, then
serving as Iraq's foreign minister; and Ibn Saud's son
Faisal.

7. The Alexandria Protocol of October 1944 and the Arab
League Pact, signed on 22 March 1945, both contained
statements fully supporting the Palestinian Arab case.

The Alexandria Protocol spoke of creating an "Arab
national fund" to "safeguard the lands of the Arabs of
Palestine." (The term, itself, is significant—an Arab national fund to prevent the loss of Arab-owned land in
Palestine as a counter to the Jewish national fund, which
worked to purchase land for Zionist settlement.) The pact
itself asserted that Palestine was, legally speaking, independent ("Her international existence and independence
in the legal sense cannot, therefore, be questioned . . .")
but as yet unable to exercise that independence. The
Council of the Arab League was itself to choose an Arab
representative from Palestine.[30]

8. Thereafter, the Arab states, strongly divided on many
political issues, were always able to reach at least formal
unity on Palestinian independence and resistance to
Zionism. That mutual rivalries among the several different Arab states (not to mention among politicians within
the same state) led often to competitive overbidding on

[30] Texts of the Alexandria protocol and the Arab League Pact are in J. C.
Hurewitz (ed.), *The Middle East and North Africa in World Politics: a Documentary Record)*, Vol. II, *British-French Supremacy, 1914-1915* (Yale University Press, 1979), pp. 732-738. A good short account of the events leading
to the creation of the Arab League is found in Robert W. MacDonald, *The
League of Arab States* (Princeton, 1965), pp. 33-42.

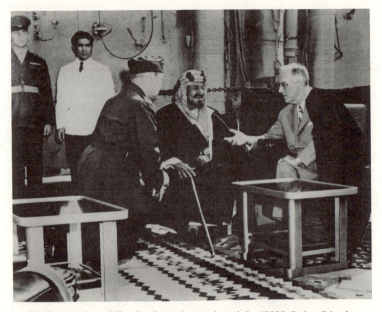

10. Roosevelt and Ibn Saud meeting on board the "USS Quincy" in the Suez Canal, February 1945 (By permission of AMIDEAST, Washington, D.C.).

the Palestine issue is beyond doubt. At the same time, the genuine concern about Palestine among all Arabs, and not just the leaders or the politically articulate, also determined actions taken. For those last years before the creation of Israel in 1948 and the ensuing first Arab-Israeli war, only a few of the more representative examples of the pan-Arabization of the Palestine need be given:

a. Ibn Saud, when meeting with Roosevelt in February 1945 and in a follow-up exchange of notes, obtained Roosevelt's commitment that he would take no action on the matter of Palestine "which might prove hostile to the Arab people."[31]

[31] Roosevelt and Ibn Saud met aboard the *U.S.S. Quincy*. The following month, Ibn Saud sent Roosevelt a long statement devoted exclusively to defending the Palestinian Arab case. The President responded in a letter dated

b. A boycott against Zionist goods was proclaimed by the Arab League in December 1945.

c. Bludan, Syria, again served as the site of a special meeting on Palestine, this time in June 1946 under the auspices of the Arab League. Here the first decisions were taken (secret at the time) concerning possible Arab military intervention to protect Palestine.

d. In a last effort to break out of its quandary, the British government called in July 1946 another London congress. This was boycotted by both the Jewish Agency and the Palestinian Arab Higher Committee, but accepted by the Arab states. For later sessions (in early 1947) the Arab states convinced the Arab Higher Committee to send delegates.

e. Arab League meetings in Sofar, Lebanon, in September 1947, in neighboring Aley the following month, and then in Cairo in December (after the UN General Assembly had voted to accept partition) laid the plans for raising a volunteer army to support the Palestinians in their efforts to prevent partition and the creation of a separate Jewish state.

f. In April 1948, the Arab League drew up plans for military intervention.

g. In May 1948, with the termination of the mandate and the establishment of the State of Israel, armies from the Arab states of Egypt, Iraq, Lebanon, Syria, and Transjordan intervened in Palestine.

The first Arab-Israeli war was disastrous for the Arab cause. Inter-Arab political rivalries, the woeful state of Arab military preparedness (except for Transjordan's tiny Arab Legion), and the total lack of military coordination were mercilessly ex-

---

5 April 1945, just one week before his death. See the little book by William A. Eddy (who served as interpreter), *F.D.R. Meets Ibn Saud* (New York, 1954). Texts of the official U.S. memorandum on that meeting and of the letters later exchanged are in Hurewitz, *Middle East and North Africa*, II, pp. 752-760.

posed in this ill-chosen confrontation with a unified and determined Israel. After a few weeks of warfare, broken by two UN sponsored truces, hostilities came to an ambivalent end, with a series of bilateral military armistices between Israel and the outside Arab states signed between February and July 1949.

No peace treaty followed, and indeed it was only after three more Arab-Israeli wars and three more decades that the first peace treaty was signed between Egypt and Israel in 1979, an action strongly opposed by the other Arab states. Moreover, the original issue pitting Zionists against Palestinian Arabs remains unresolved.

After 1948, the Palestinian impact on Arab politics and Arab nationalism took a more virulent form. The debacle of that year, more than any other event in recent Arab history, accelerated the decline of the established political elites.

The collapse of the political old guard came first in Syria, always the heartland of Arabism, where three military coups in 1949 inaugurated a new era of military rule broken only by brief periods of turbulent civil government that always dissolved into still more military rule. In this process, started in 1949, the old Syrian politics of notables has given way to new personalities, new political classes, and new ideologies.

The coup that brushed aside Egypt's ancient regime was somewhat longer in coming—July 1952—and can be attributed to other factors as well, but Egyptian politics-as-usual never quite recovered from the regime's miserable performance in the 1948 Arab-Israeli war.[32] Nasser's coming to power in Egypt is thus, in certain respects, to be set alongside the history of Syria since 1949. In both cases military intervention in politics growing out of the sense of frustration and betrayal that set in after the 1948 war undermined the old political elite.

The extent to which the Palestinian problem gave shape to

[32] Nasser, who served in that war, related the last words a fellow officer said to his friend before dying: "Listen, Kamal, the biggest battlefield is in Egypt." Gamal Abdul Nasser, *Egypt's Liberation: The Philosophy of the Revolution* (Washington, 1955), p. 22.

the politics of Arabism is revealed in the way the four Arab-Israeli wars—1948, 1956, 1967, and 1973[33]—were the most important crises and the most important turning points in recent Arab history.

An equally dramatic way to demonstrate the Palestinian dimension of Arabist political activity is to note the thirteen different Arab summit conferences that were held during the years 1964-1982. The idea of Arab summitry, itself, illustrates how the more informal diplomatic initiatives of a few Arab politicians in the period before the Second World War had become both institutionalized and generalized to embrace the entire Arab world. Yet, if the various interests subsumed under the banner of Arabism had expanded well beyond the confines of the Fertile Crescent, the Palestine issue continued to serve as the major occasion causing Arab heads of state to convene and take decisions:

TABLE III. ARAB SUMMIT CONFERENCES, 1964-1982

Date	Place	Major Issues or Decisions Taken
1st January 1964	Cairo	Proposed Arab joint action to counter Israeli plans for use of Jordan River
2nd September 1964	Alexandria	Establishment of Palestinian Liberation Organization
3rd September 1965	Casablanca	End inter-Arab rivalries (But Tunisian boycott against Egyptian "hegemony")

[33] Many speak of five Arab-Israeli wars, including the 1969-1970 Egyptian-Israeli war of attrition. In terms of commitment of resources (and casualties), the war of attrition belongs in the series. In seriousness of casualties and political impact one must now add the Israeli invasion of Lebanon, beginning in June 1982 as the fifth (or sixth) Arab-Israeli war.

TABLE III (*cont.*)

Date	Place	Major Issues or Decisions Taken
4th August 1967	Khartoum	Following disastrous June War. The "three nos"— no negotiation, no recognition, no peace with Israel; settlement Egyptian-Saudi dispute over Yemen; oil-state economic support to Arab confrontation states
5th December 1969	Rabat	Inconclusive and heated discussion on combined Arab economic-military strategy against Israel
6th November 1973	Algiers	General economic and diplomatic issues following October 1973 war
7th October 1974	Rabat	PLO recognized as representing the Palestinians
8th October 1976	Riyadh	Lebanese civil war
9th November 1978	Baghdad	Rejection of Sadat's agreement to establish peace with Israel. Decision to move Arab League headquarters from Cairo to Tunis
10th November 1979	Tunis	Second Arab summit without Egypt. Continued efforts coordinating strategy concerning Palestine question and Israel
11th November 1980	Amman	Ostensibly to establish new

Date	Place	Major Issues or Decisions Taken
		common policy toward Israel, but actually unsucessful effort to close Arab ranks after outbreak Iraq-Iran war. Boycotted by PLO, Algeria, Lebanon, Libya, South Yemen, and Syria
12th November 1981	Fez	Failure to act on proposed Saudi (Fahd) Plan for Arab-Israel settlement
13th September 1982	Fez	Effort to establish common Arab policy following Israeli invasion of Lebanon

* * *

In short, the principal agenda item for at least 10 of the 13 Arab summit meetings was the issue of Palestine and the concomitant drive for an Arabist front against Israel. Whether the different Arab leaders gathered for these different summit meetings were prepared to make tangible sacrifices for the Palestinian cause can be disputed. Whether Arab summitry fostered or frustrated the Palestinian movement can be debated. That Palestine has become the hallmark of Arabism is beyond question. Even when the issue to be considered has been something quite different, as with the 1980 Arab summit meeting, there has been a marked inclination to use the Palestinian cause as a rallying call for unity.

In the Arab world since 1948 only one other subject can approach Palestine as a focal point of Arabist interests and a stimulus to Arabism. This was Nasser and Nasserism. From

161

soon after his arrival to power in 1952 until his death in 1970 Nasser dominated Arab politics. By embracing pan-Arabism Nasser changed the political orientation of the largest Arab state and set a generation of Arabs on a new political course. The major question to be posed here concerning the man and his age are: Why did Nasser and his colleagues opt for Arabism? And why did the choice have such an electrifying effect on the Arab world?

THE NASSER ERA

Earlier interpretations of the political era begun by Nasser and his Free Officers, penned in the heat of ongoing political battles, often tended toward extremes. Either Nasserism was seen as a long overdue progressive development which native forces of reaction in league with foreign imperialism had hitherto held in check. Or, Nasserism was deplored as the work of unscrupulously ambitious but unrepresentative small groups, relying on support from the Communist bloc, and upsetting the political balances that sustained Middle Eastern society.

Now, in the post-Nasser period during which his successor, Anwar al-Sadat, championed Egyptianism over Arabism, not without success, a more dispassionate view is possible. Nasser's Arabism was by no means the only realistic choice open to him. Egypt's long history demonstrates that a policy of strong Egyptian self-identity (either isolationist or expansionist) is often well-received. Moreover, in geopolitical terms a more natural route of Egyptian expansionism would be up the Nile southward into Sudan and East Africa. Indeed, the years preceding the 1952 revolution in Egypt had been filled more with efforts to achieve "unity of the Nile valley" than with the Arabist ambitions.

Nor was post-revolutionary Egypt necessarily saddled with the "dishonor" of 1948. This responsibility could be laid at the feet of the discredited old regime. Nasser and his group had the opportunity to start afresh.

Arabism—like other nationalist or "pan" movements—is in-

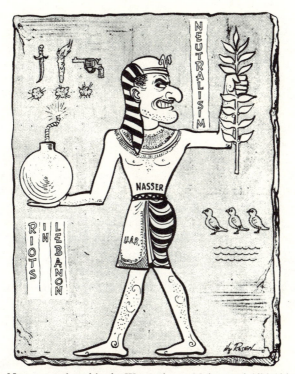

11. Nasser was viewed in the West rather as Muhammad Ali had been over a century earlier. Both were deemed behind most of the trouble roiling the Middle East (By permission of Hy Rosen, *Albany Times-Union*).

trinsically neither progressive nor reactionary. Nasser's revolution could have been directed toward Egyptian domestic issues ("listen, Kamal, the biggest battlefield is in Egypt") or to unity of the Nile valley.

Yet, the Arabist option chosen—while by no means the only one available—had its attractions. Throughout history a common bond linking all revolutionary regimes, especially in those heady first months after seizing power, is the belief that theirs is a universal mission, not confined to a single country. This sense of mission tempted Nasserists to champion Arabism, for

163

as Nasser put it: ". . . it seems to me that within the Arab circle there is a role, wandering aimlessly in search of a hero."[34]

The Nasser regime was not, however, immediately embraced with open arms by the Arabs of the Fertile Crescent. They had long been trying to involve Egypt more directly in Arab affairs, using Palestine to break down the walls of Egyptian isolationism. The Egyptian response up to 1952 had been reasonably promising in terms of commitment to Arabism but woefully discouraging in performance, as 1948 had demonstrated. After the Egyptian revolution there was reason to fear that the Free Officers might well soft-pedal Egypt's commitment to Arabism.

The Palestinians and other Arabs of the Fertile Crescent regarded the new Egyptian regime first with cautious hesitation and then with downright antipathy after Nasser ousted the better-known General Naguib and mounted a campaign against the Muslim Brethren (who, whatever their faults, were in the eyes of other Arabs fervent supporters of the Palestinian cause).

Nasser was right that in those years after 1948 there was among the Arabs a role wandering in search of a hero. Traumatized by their poor performance and the loss of Palestine in 1948, the Fertile Crescent Arabs were politically divided. They were antagonistic, or at the very least ambivalent, toward existing Fertile Crescent regimes because of their continuing ties to Western imperialism.

Arabs passionately sought a strong leader who would reject the past with its bitter disappointments, who would lash out against the old enemies—Zionism and Western imperialism—and who would provide strength through unity. When Nasser seized that role wandering in search of a hero by adopting an unambiguous position of Arab leadership against Israel,

---

[34] *Philosophy of the Revolution*, p. 87. That this political treatise in the form of an introspective memoir is generally thought to have been written for Nasser by his friend, the journalist Mohamed Heikal, does not detract from its importance in this context. It is an authentic statement of the way in which the regime sought to be perceived on its early days.

bringing the Soviet Union into the arena to counter previous Western hegemony (with the so-called Czech-Egyptian arms deal of 1955), and nationalizing the Suez Canal (July 1956), the earlier Arab antipathy gave way to adulation. The Nasser regime had won the Arabs of the Fertile Crescent to Egypt's cause, and the Arabs had won Nasser's Egypt to the cause of Palestine and Arabism.

If Nasser had known what paroxysms of praise from other Arabs awaited his acts in 1955 and 1956, there would have been little hesitation in adopting the course chosen, but this is to reason from hindsight. What needs to be answered—with due regard for the context of the times—is why Nasser chose the path of daring but dangerous innovation instead of remaining within the bounds of prudent half-measures? Many inducements made the gamble appear worth taking:

1. The Egyptian leadership could sense that other powers were successfully challenging Britain's position in the Arab East—the United States from within the Western alliance and the Soviet Union from the outside.
2. The favorable standing vis-à-vis the West enjoyed by the Hashimite kingdoms, Israel, and Saudi Arabia (however much they differed among themselves) indicated that these three rival poles of political power within the Middle East would be favored over Egypt in any regional political strategy that accepted the continued hegemony of the West.
3. Cooperation—even at arms length—with the West at that time was the natural strategy only of those satisfied with the status quo. Egypt, challenging the British military presence in Suez, looking to achieve unity with Sudan, and seeking a predominant position in the Arab East, was a revisionist regional power. Nasser's only reliable political allies were those favoring revisionist politics.
4. A cautious policy of collaboration with the West and of settling for limited concessions would have undermined the Nasserist revolutionary elan. It would have been ask-

ing a Garibaldi to act like a Metternich. Active defiance against those forces that had for so long kept regional political actors on a very short leash offered the immediate bonus of enthusiastic support at home. It also cut the ground from under those who might seek to mount an opposition movement under the banner of "the revolution betrayed."

5. Many observers pin-point February 1955 as the time when Nasser decided to challenge Israel, embrace pan-Arabism, and cooperate with the Soviet Union. In four days, Nasser confronted two major challenges. On 24 February Iraq broke ranks with the Arabs and signed a defense treaty with Turkey. This was the beginning of the Baghdad Pact. Then on 28 February Israel launched a major raid against Egyptian-controlled Gaza. In Nasser's eyes Egypt was being shown its limited power and put in its place. He chose to fight back.

6. The subtle diplomacy of the post-Stalinist Soviet Union made it easier for Nasser to spring his daring démarche. The arms deal with the Soviet Union (arranged in May 1955 and made known to the world in September) was modestly disguised as a Czech-Egyptian transaction, and the Soviet Union was careful in other ways to underplay its own ambitions.

7. The new Nasser strategy conveniently coincided with the heyday of the non-aligned movement symbolized by the Bandung Congress of April 1955, where Nasser found himself accepted as an equal partner with Chou en-Lai, Nehru, and Sukarno. In those early months during which the new Arabist, anti-Western policy was launched, the Egyptian leaders probably sensed that they could mitigate the danger of a violent Western reaction by linking their policies to the larger Bandung spirit. Even those Western leaders inclined to old-school gunboat diplomacy[35] might hesitate to challenge an Egyptian leader who

---

[35] That is, the view of international politics as rightly a Western game (including Russia) epitomized by the alleged jibe of an American official who characterized the Bandung Congress as "the darktown strutters' ball."

had obtained the support of India, China, Indonesia, and Yugoslavia, not to mention a number of lesser non-Western powers. Nasser seemed to be in a position to play the small power game of balancing off great power blocs at minimal risk, because a great power attempt to get rid of this small power "nuisance" carried with it not inconsiderable penalties elsewhere. (The Suez crisis exhibited the limits of Nasser's immunity, but the division within the Western ranks illustrated the soundness of his gamble.)

8. Finally, there was that elusive quality of momentum, so important in all situations of confrontation from games to diplomacy and war. The first fruits of Nasser's new Arabist policy backed by a pro-Soviet/anti-Western stance were so bountiful (or, at least, appeared so at the time) that it would have seemed perverse to have turned back. Nasser became a prisoner of his own early successes. After his several anti-Western ripostes in 1955 any genuine accommodation with the West would have been politically dangerous and psychologically devastating.

Nasser gave his name to a period of Middle Eastern history. From the mid-fifties until the death of Nasser (or, to take a more conservative estimate, at least until after the June 1967 Arab-Israeli war) Egypt maintained the initiative in regional politics.

Even the most abbreviated listing of events conveys both the perfervid quality of those years and the way in which these activities all seemed linked to Egyptian initiatives or responses (especially the latter for Nasser was a born counter-puncher):

TABLE IV. PRINCIPAL DIPLOMATIC EVENTS OF THE NASSER ERA

July 1956	Nasser's nationalization of the Suez Canal
29 October to 7 November 1956	Anglo-French-Israeli invasion of Egypt
February 1958	Egyptian-Syrian unity to form United Arab Republic
Summer 1958	Lebanese civil war, Lebanese government charging Egyptian interference
July 1958	Iraqi coup overthrowing pro-Western, anti-Nasserist Hashimite kingdom
	U.S. troops to Lebanon at request of Lebanese President Chamoun
December 1958	Announcement of Soviet aid for building Aswan High Dam
September 1961	Syrian withdrawal from United Arab Republic
September 1962	Coup in Yemen. Beginning of Yemeni civil war, with Republican forces supported by Egypt, royalists by Saudi Arabia
January 1964	First Arab summit conference to counter Israeli plans concerning Jordan River development
May 1964	Khrushchev visit to Egypt on occasion completion of Aswan High Dam
June 1967	Six-day War. Third Arab-Israeli war
Spring 1969	Beginning "war of attrition" between Egypt and Israel
January-March 1970	Israeli deep-penetration air raids against Egypt/arrival Soviet missiles and military advisors.
7 August 1970	Egypt and Israel accept U.S.-sponsored cease fire
6 September 1970	Popular Front for the Liberation of Palestine (PFLP); guerrillas hijack western commercial aircraft, landing them in Jordanian desert, as response to cease-fire.
17-27 September 1970	War between Jordan and Palestinian guerrillas ("Black September"), stopped by Arab League mediation.
28 September 1970	Death of Nasser

✳   ✳   ✳

Why Did Nasserist Arabism Fail?

From the mid-fifties until his death in September 1970 Nasser dominated politics and diplomacy in the Middle East, but he did not succeed in unifying the Arabs. Why did Nasserist Arabism fail? Some would argue that Nasser's approach was too heavy-handed and too obviously centered on Egyptian hegemony. Certainly, the Egyptian record during those years is not lacking in examples of intimidation, coercion, and subversion directed against other Arab leaders.

The ups and downs in the relationship between Nasser and another dynamic Arab leader, Tunisia's Habib Bourguiba, are illustrative in this regard. Indeed, if Bourguiba had ruled a more populous and more powerful state (Tunisia lacks the "oil weapon" or other significant economic muscle and has a population about one-seventh that of Egypt), the pattern of Arab politics might have been different.

Egyptian bullying of Jordan's King Husayn was even more obvious. Husayn was the heir in both blood and spirit of his grandfather, Abdullah. Probably the most realistic of Fertile Crescent Arab leaders in his times—and certainly the most self-serving—Abdullah was the only Arab winner in the 1948 war with Israel, absorbing into his kingdom the Arab portion of partitioned Palestine (less what a victorious Israel had taken in battle from the Arab share set out in the 1947 UN Partition Plan and excepting the Gaza Strip, which lay beyond his reach and fell under Egyptian administration).

In retrospect, Abdullah's power grab can be seen as the least unfavorable outcome available to the divided and defeated Palestinians. Had the fait accompli been accepted Palestinians would have lived under Arab rule with a good chance to increase Palestinian participation in that political community, the refugees could have been settled, and the even more crushing defeat and territorial losses of 1967 would have been avoided.

This was not the way matters worked out. Most Palestinians felt betrayed, and many saw Abdullah as the very personification of treachery. Other Arab leaders saw themselves as

having been tricked by Abdullah and had little trouble viewing the entire outcome as part of a devilish Anglo-Hashimite
plot. Abdullah was, accordingly, branded as at worst virtually
a traitor and at best a man who had willfully broken Arab
unity ranks. He paid with his life. Abdullah was assassinated
by a young Palestinian just as he was entering al-Aqsa mosque
in Jerusalem on 20 July 1951.

Husayn, who succeeded his father Talal[36] in August 1952,
was saddled with this bitter legacy. To the Arabs he represented a dynasty that cooperated with Britain and the West;
had a record of secret, bilateral negotiations with Israel; and
had—worst of all—violated Arab unity. Nasser had only to
play on these animosities that predated his rise to power in
order to keep Husayn in line.

Hashimite Iraq, led in those years by that seasoned veteran
of inter-Arab and international politics, Nuri al-Said, was not
so easily manhandled. Yet, the regime was eventually destroyed in a bloody coup that, while not engineered by Nasser, was certainly inspired by the Nasserist political ideology.

Other examples of Nasserist policies of no holds barred in
dealing with the Arab world may be found in the Sudan. An
earlier generation of old Arab hands remembers "the dancing
major." He was Major Salah Salim, member of the original
Revolutionary Command Council whose photograph in leop-
ard skin dancing with pagan tribesmen of the Southern Sudan
titillated readers of news magazines in 1954. Behind the farci-
cal photo was a policy not so pleasing to many British or
Sudanese of the day—bribes of Sudanese politicians, newspa-
permen, religious figures, and any others who might help Nasser
push the Sudan toward union with Egypt.

Equally illuminating were Nasser's fluctuating relations with
Saudi Arabia, at times embraced in Arab brotherhood and at
other times savagely attacked as the bastion of regional reaction and the catspaw of American imperialism.

Yet, the many examples that can be amassed to demonstrate

---

[36] After a short reign of just over a year, Talal who was mentally ill was
declared unfit to rule.

Nasser's use of intimidation, coercion, and subversion against other Arabs in the drive for Egyptian-controlled Arab unity do not add up to a convincing explanation for why his policy failed. The use of strong-arm, as well as subversive, tactics was hardly the monopoly of any party, Arab or great power, during the Nasser years. Moreover, major changes in territorial boundaries and in the very basis of political legitimacy are seldom achieved without force. Italian and German unity in the previous century were finally realized not by unarmed ideologues but by the likes of Cavour, Garibaldi, and Bismarck.

Nasser's most severe critics would be hard put to argue that Nasserist "blood and iron" tactics exceeded those of Bismarck. Nasser's tactics were more in the public eye than those of his opponents, if only because one usually pays more attention to the winners, and Nasser was winning because his cause did have Arab support.

Nasser made mistakes, as do all political leaders, but to many contemporaries—friend or foe—there seemed to be a touch of genius in the man. Those who remember his speeches on Egypt's Voice of the Arabs, beamed to the entire Arab world, can attest that the Egyptian drive for Arab leadership did not falter through neglect of media coverage. He was flamboyant to a fault, and his dangerous ploy of raising the ante in confrontation with stronger opponents brought a shattering defeat in the Six Day War of June 1967, but that same flamboyance made his name during the period from the Bandung Congress through the Suez crisis.

Nasser was on other occasions both prudent and patient. His acquiescence to Syria's 1961 defection from the United Arab Republic, his realistic line concerning military confrontation with Israel in the early sixties in opposition to the impatient leadership of Syria and Iraq, and his cautious maneuvers leading to Egyptian acceptance of the Rogers initiative for an Egyptian-Israeli cease-fire a few weeks before his death (with the concomitant careful balancing of the two superpowers) reveal another, more careful, side of Nasser.

171

If Arab unity was to be achieved, Nasser was the man to do it and the Nasser years the time for it to be done. Yet, Arab unity as a political reality is today no more advanced than it was before that handful of middle-rank Egyptian army officers seized power in July 1952. Arab unity even as an ideal has hardly advanced either. The most satisfactory explanation for the failure of Nasser's bid for Arab unity is to be found in the very nature of Middle Eastern politics.

This brings the matter squarely back to the Eastern Question pattern. Nasser's Arab unity bid, backed by Egyptian power, put him in a position to be stronger than any single Arab adversary and indeed than any combination of Arab opponents. Since his Arab opponents could rely on Western support, Nasser's move toward the Soviet Union may be seen as an effort to neutralize the outside forces in order assure Egypt's preponderance in the Arab world. In these efforts he achieved considerable success, but one that fell far short of being decisive. The homeostatic quality of the over-all system was never overcome. His regional forces were not sufficient to defeat Israel militarily, but his confrontation strategy foreclosed the possibility of winning over or neutralizing Israel. The best Nasser could achieve by bringing in the great power opponent of Israel's great power supporter was a great power balance of forces reflecting in global dimensions that which pertained in the Middle East.

He could penalize the West by keeping in existence an anti-Western Arab coalition while using Western support of Israel to cow those Arabs who opposed him. This was sufficient to make Western statesmen, from time to time, seek an accommodation, but Nasser could not reach a satisfactory working relationship with the West without putting in jeopardy his ability to keep Arab radicals in line.

NASSER AND THE SOVIET UNION

The limits on Nasser's maneuverability were revealed in relations with his newly found great power patron, the Soviet

Union. The Soviets could enthusiastically support a regional leader who was contributing to the dismantling of established Western positions, but once this was accomplished they had no interest in strengthening someone bent on creating a regional political force capable of resisting all outside powers, including the Soviet Union.

Nasser always kept Arab Communists under tight control, if not behind bars. Nor should it be overlooked that a major catalyst for the 1958 union with Syria was Nasser's response to Syrian Ba'thist fears of being outflanked by Syrian Communists.

The Soviet problem in dealing with Nasser was a mirror image of that often facing the Western democracies. The latter have often agonized over whether to support a local despot who shared their immediate global interests but who oppressed democratic forces at home. Substitute local Communists for local democrats, and the dilemma that the Soviets faced in dealing with Nasser is neatly drawn.

The Soviet Union faced another problem that was as old as the Eastern Question itself—that of balancing changing policies and strategies in the great power arena with regional goals. When the Cold War began to give way to detente, the Soviet Union found itself obliged to decrease support of Middle Eastern clients in order to achieve the more important goal of a working relationship with the United States. Somewhat like the British after the First World War, who finally had to accept that good relations with France took priority over their "Arab policy," the Soviet Union in the age of detente chose to emphasize its great power relationships over regional considerations.

Soviet-Egyptian relations in the Nasser era may be seen as a short honeymoon in the mid-fifties, when both parties felt that they were making progress toward their different goals, followed by a much stormier relationship. Later Soviet efforts to hedge their Egyptian bet by establishing better ties—at different times—with Syria or Iraq or Algeria within the circle of Arab states revealed the limits of the relationship.

These Soviet initiatives were answered (or, at other times,

provoked) by Nasser's diplomatic probes outside the Soviet
bloc, such as the periodic openings to the West, the relationship with Yugoslavia, or the friendly ties to China maintained
even after Soviet-Chinese relations worsened. Most of all, Nasser
resisted Soviet efforts either to dominate or to divide the Arab
world.

The Soviet role in events leading up to the June 1967 Arab-
Israeli War illustrates the tangled web the Soviets and Egyptians had managed to weave within twelve years after their
close relationship had begun. The most plausible interpretation of the crisis would seem to be that the Soviets certainly
contributed to the crisis but could not control it. Nor could
Nasser.[37]

Following Nasser's crushing defeat, the Soviets did replen-
ish Egypt's shattered military forces. This, too, seems consistent with the Eastern Question pattern: a great power will
not readily permit the total defeat of its regional client but
will not mind keeping that client indefinitely in a state of dependence.

Nasser's Failure: The Eastern Question Answer

Nasser's drive for Arab unity under Egyptian leadership, in
sum, was not derailed by an antagonistic West, nor by Israel,
nor by "reactionary" Arab politicians, nor by impatient Arab
radicals determined to force the pace, nor by Soviet reluctance
to continue supporting the Nasserist strategy that it had been
so instrumental in inaugurating, nor by clumsy Egyptian diplomacy in dealing with other Arab states. Arab unity faltered
as a direct result of all these causes acting simultaneously. From
this perspective one can link together in frustrated ambition
the two most dynamic leaders of nineteenth- and twentieth-
century Egypt, Muhammad Ali and Gamal Abdel Nasser.

Moreover, the British and Egyptian efforts to organize the
Middle East in this century establish a tragic bond between

---

[37] The causes of the June 1967 war are considered on pp. 201-212 (Part
III).

12. Eden's self-inflicted knockout at Suez prefigured Nasser's in the June 1967 war. Neither of these old enemies succeeded in controlling Middle Eastern diplomacy (Fischetti, reprinted by permission of Newspaper Enterprise Association).

two individuals who have nothing else whatsoever in common, Nasser and Anthony Eden.

*   *   *

IV. AFTER BRITAIN'S "MOMENT"—THE GREAT POWER PATTERN IN THE MIDDLE EAST

In recent times no regional effort to organize the Middle East has rivalled that of Nasser. Nor does another such ven-

175

ture seem likely in the foreseeable future. The most plausible candidate, in geopolitical terms, would be Turkey, but Ataturkism seems to have immunized Turkey against Eastern Question activism.

Iran, just beyond the borders of the Middle East as defined in this book, briefly showed hegemonic pretensions in the last years of the Pahlavi dynasty, but beginning in 1979 the Iranian Revolution shattered the Shah's dreams. Ayatollah Khomeini's Islamic Revolution has shown expansionist tendencies, and a strong Iran is always to be reckoned a regional force. Iran's surprising resistance to Iraq has already had important repercussions, sending tremors throughout the conservative, oil-rich Arabian peninsula while reducing to shambles Saddam Husayn's bid for Iraqi preeminence in the Gulf. At this writing, however, it remains questionable whether the present Iranian regime has the cohesion or even the intention to play a dominant role in the region.

In spite of its small population, Israel today is a regional military power, but its pariah status (only partially overcome by the Egyptian-Israeli treaty) rules out any possible claim to lead region-wide political programs.

In the post-Nasser period certain states of the Middle East, such as Saudi Arabia, are playing larger roles. From time to time since its independence in 1962, Algeria has made claims to regional leadership. None of these, however, can match the potential for regional hegemony to be found in strong leadership ruling Egypt or Turkey. None now shows signs of harboring such pretentions.

What, then, of great power ambitions in the Middle East following the collapse of Britain's Arab policy? The two obvious contenders are the United States and the Soviet Union. The starting positions of the two were totally different. The United States had to work out its Middle Eastern policy within the framework of alliance politics. As the leader of the Western coalition against the Soviet bloc in the Cold War, the United States sought regional adjustments within the framework of Western solidarity. This had many advantages. The

176

United States could use its overwhelming economic, military, and political power to ease the British out of their dominant role in the Middle East while avoiding outright confrontation. It seemed a low-risk, high-gain policy.

Often, circumstances were such that Britain, exhausted from its efforts during the Second World War, took the initiative in inviting the United States to do just that. For example, Britain's warning that the Western position in Greece and Turkey was threatened by the Soviets led to the Truman Doctrine. Earlier, Britain's Labour government had shrewdly attempted to involve the United States in a settlement of the Palestine issue, but with limited success.

The U.S. advantage of working with an alliance partner more or less reconciled to conceding power in the area was offset by the disadvantages of inheriting all the anti-imperialist fervor that the peoples of the Middle East had developed as a result of the long Western domination. The Soviet Union, on the other hand, had the advantages and disadvantages of an outsider.

Such were the starting positions. What does the historical record indicate concerning their different aims and achievements? A case can be made that the U.S. drifted into a policy of seeking predominance. Certain parallels with the way Britain's Arab policy emerged come to mind. The overall American strategy would seem to have been composed of two major considerations which, it was believed, could be fitted together:

1. Defense of Western interests in the area, especially oil, global communications and an important link in the "containment" chain around the Soviet bloc, and
2. an orderly decolonization that would induce independent Middle Eastern states to remain within the Western camp.

The most explicit American enunciation of this strategy came with the ill-fated Eisenhower Doctrine of early 1957, following the Suez crisis. Claiming that a power vacuum existed in

the Middle East which was likely to be filled by Soviet infil-
tration unless effective counter-action were taken, the Eisenhower Doctrine offered economic and military support to those
states of the Middle East threatened by international Communism. The Doctrine made sense only if the premise were
accepted that the protective parasol of Western (or, after Suez,
American) tutelage was required to maintain the political freedom of Middle Eastern states. This premise, however, was
totally at odds with the conclusions drawn by most Arabs.

With the recent Suez experience in mind, the Arabs believed that the West remained more in a position to call the
political shots in the Middle East than the Soviet bloc. Radical
Arab opinion welcomed the seemingly more revolutionary
message that the Soviet Union preached, but even dyed-in-
the-wool conservatives recognized the utility of balancing off
the great powers. As a result, only political leadership relying
on what might be dubbed a separatist power base could afford
to embrace the Eisenhower Doctrine openly. This explains the
response of Lebanon's President Chamoun. The dizzying pace
of change begun with Nasser's simultaneous turn toward the
Soviet Union and championing of Arabism led many Lebanese Christians, and especially the Maronite community, to
doubt whether Lebanese independence could survive unless
explicitly linked to a Western patron.

Many other Arab governments, or at least certain of their
leaders, did indeed, signal their support of a strengthened
American position in the Middle East (e.g. Sudan, Saudi Arabia, Jordan, and Iraq), but they were not keen to be formally
lined up in treaties or even in "doctrines."

Those Arab leaders who offered some measure of positive
response to the Eisenhower Doctrine, either on or off the
record, feared, not Communist, but Nasserist domination. Even
so, they were all—except for Lebanon, whose communal situation was unique—concerned not to leave themselves open
to the charge of breaking Arab ranks.

The American strategy was thus based on these two inter-locking illusions:

1. The Middle Eastern states would be satisfied with a pattern of informal Western (increasingly American) control, provided the more direct and formal ties of Western domination were removed. The implicit quid pro quo for American support of decolonization plus American economic and military aid was Arab acceptance of a junior partnership in the Western alliance to contain the Soviet Bloc.

2. The Arab states agreed that the Soviet Union and Soviet-supported Communism posed a threat at least equal to those provided by many inter-Arab power struggles and the Arab-Israeli confrontation. The United States *assumed* that its interpretation of Middle Eastern politics in terms of great power rivalry was shared by Middle Easterners themselves.

A policy so totally at odds with the perceptions of those it was designed to influence was bound to fail. The Arabs, after years of Western control, saw the reassertion of Western tutelage as the principal outside danger. They, or at least the more daring, were inclined to bring in Soviet influence to loosen the still heavy Western hand. Beyond this, their major immediate diplomatic concerns were regional (summed up in two words—Nasserism and Israel). All this the Eisenhower Doctrine blithely ignored.

The contrast between the Eisenhower Doctrine and the Truman Doctrine illuminates the limits of great power effectiveness in the Middle East. The Truman Doctrine was well received by the Turkish government (Greece and Iran as well), because the American commitment offered the support immediately needed to counter pressure from another great power source—the Soviet Union. The situation at the time of the Eisenhower Doctrine did not permit such regional receptivity.

The fate of Camille Chamoun's government in Lebanon attests to the wisdom of those Arab leaders who steered clear of the Eisenhower Doctrine. In simplest terms, the 1958 Lebanese Civil War grew out of two conflicting tendencies:

1. Maronite fears that Nasserist pan-Arabism was undermining Lebanese independence
2. Chamoun's upsetting the balances on which Lebanon was based. Chamoun sought a second term as president, but this required a constitutional amendment for which he needed a two-thirds majority in Parliament. Chamoun and his followers set out to get this—with U.S. help—in the 1957 parliamentary elections. Their overwhelming victory boomeranged. The many defeated political leaders, deprived of their parliamentary seats, sought other means to continue the struggle.

Lebanon faced a domestic and regional crisis, not a threat from international communism. The crisis was resolved by domestic and regional compromises which involved the removal of one "extremist," President Chamoun, and the implicit acceptance by the other radical challenger to the status quo, President Nasser, of Lebanon's political independence.

Before this settlement, which saw General Fuad Shihab (descendant of Amir Bashir Shihab, who ruled Mount Lebanon between 1788 and 1840) installed as president of Lebanon, the beleaguered President Chamoun had invoked the Eisenhower Doctrine, and the U.S. had sent troops to Lebanon. This action followed the most dramatic regional event in the immediate post-Suez years—the overthrow of the Hashimite Kingdom of Iraq by a military coup.

Did the brief American military intervention in Lebanon signal "thus far but no farther" to the Soviet Union? Such an interpretation is still popular, especially among those who concentrate on great power diplomacy. An eminent American diplomatic historian writes, for example: "Dulles met this danger promptly and effectively, responding to President Chamoun's request for assistance by sending U.S. Marines to the imperilled country. This action dispelled the prospect of Communist domination of the Near East and made idle Khrushchev's hope that he might be able to exploit the Near Eastern troubles so as to force a summit conference on his own terms."[38]

A more plausible interpretation, however, is that the signal sent by the landing of U.S. troops in Lebanon was directed at Nasser, not Khrushchev. Moreover, the effectiveness of the American military intervention was assured by an American political willingness to back away from its effort to line up an anti-Nasser coalition in the name of anti-Communism.

The 1958 American landings in Lebanon thus exemplify great power misperception arising from a tendency to see regional conflict too much in terms of great power rivalry. U.S. policy immediately thereafter was, by contrast, a brilliant example of realistic "damage control." The U.S. supported the compromise presidential candidate, General Shihab, and quickly withdrew American troops. This was a clear signal that the U.S. had abandoned its dream of organizing the Arab portions of the Middle East. Pragmatic limited commitment replaced illusory overcommitment.

Arabs fearing the hegemonic drive of Nasserists—Saudi Arabia, Kuwait (soon to call on British military intervention to stop an Iraqi effort to take over the country), the smaller states of the Perisan Gulf, and the Maghrib countries of Libya, Tunisia, and Morocco—were pleased to see a continued American presence, provided they were not pressed into overt alliance with the West. The United States after 1958 had learned to cease insisting that its friends in the Arab world must stand up and be counted. The plight of President Chamoun, even more of the Hashimites in Iraq, revealed that those who did so were quite likely to be counted out.

In the meantime, the Soviet Union appeared to be going from strength to strength in the Middle East throughout the fifties. Earlier Soviet thrusts against Greece, Turkey, and Iran

---

[38] Gordon Craig, "Dulles and American Statecraft," in his *War, Politics, and Diplomacy* (New York, 1966), p. 277.

had been effectively countered, but with the Soviet-Egyptian arms deal of 1955 the Soviet Union had managed to leapfrog over the "northern tier" into the Arab heartland.

Did the Soviets then hear the same siren song that had earlier lured the British and then the Americans to think of organizing the Arab world? Many observers believe this to be the ultimate Soviet goal, but a more modest interpretation of Soviet intentions also fits the facts. The Soviet Union, it would appear, saw a golden opportunity effectively to neutralize the Middle East, undercutting vestigial Western positions of strength. Beyond this, the Soviet government would seem to have looked toward Western acceptance that Middle Eastern affairs could not be settled without Soviet participation.

Whatever their maximum goal might have been, the Soviets, too, soon learned the limitations of great power influence in the Middle East. As early as February 1958, only slightly more than a year after the Suez war, Egypt and Syria united to form the United Arab Republic. The stimulus for this union came from Ba'th party leaders in Syria who feared increasing Communist control in their country. Nasser's response to Syrian pleas was merely the most dramatic of his actions against regional Communist parties, in Egypt or elsewhere.

Thereafter, from time to time Premier Khrushchev would scold Nasser and other "progressive Arab leaders" for their attacks on Arab communists. For example, Khrushchev took both Nasser and Iraq's Qasim to task in his January 1959 report to the 21st Congress of Soviet Communist Party; but Nasser, speaking in Damascus on the first anniversary of the creation of the United Arab Republic, countered with a defiant assertion of Arab independence from all great powers.[39]

Throughout the sixties, while continuing to regard Egypt as the linchpin of their Middle Eastern policy, the Soviet leadership sought alternatives. Much of this expanded interest in the Arab world came to center on Syria. Soviet steps to help

[39] See Mohamed Heikal, *The Sphinx and the Commissar: The Rise and Fall of Soviet Influence in the Middle East* (New York, 1978), pp. 103-104.

its Syrian client at a time of domestic difficulties contributed to the June 1967 Arab-Israeli war. That war demonstrated the limits of great power maneuverability. Neither the United States nor the Soviet Union was especially decisive in the days leading up to the outbreak of hostilities. The most that can be said is that "hot line" diplomacy worked, and the great powers did avoid stumbling into confrontation or being led down that path by their respective clients.

With the United States and the Soviet Union thus neutralizing each other, the overwhelming Israeli victory ran its rapid course undeterred by outside forces. Among the results was a loss of Soviet prestige in the area. Indeed, the Arab defeat in the Six Day War set in motion Egypt's strategic rethinking that resulted in President Sadat's later de facto alliance with the United States.

After the June 1967 war the Soviet Union faced unattractive choices. They could cut their losses and abandon their "Arab policy" begun with such promise some twelve years earlier. Or they could pay the price of replenishing the shattered armies of Egypt and Syria, continue their activist policies in the Middle East, and work for the day when Soviet Middle Eastern clients might prove to be a stronger strategic asset.

The latter option was chosen. Massive Soviet military aid helped Egypt and Syria to rebuild their military, and Soviet diplomatic support enabled Nasser to resist any temptation to come to terms with Israel or, more likely, to call on the United States to play the role of honest broker. Nor did the Soviet support stop there. When Nasser's war of attrition against Israel (begun in spring 1969) provoked an Israeli response of deep-penetration air raids into the heart of Egypt, Nasser obtained a protective Soviet air and missile presence in Egypt itself. Close Soviet/Egyptian strategic cooperation was again demonstrated at the time of the U.S. initiated cease-fire between Egypt and Israel (August 1970), when Soviet and Egyptian technicians continued—in violation of the agreement—to place missiles along the west bank of the Suez Canal.

This violation, the strong reaction of the Israelis, and the ambiguous American response to the Israeli protests wrecked the slight chance that the August cease-fire would start a series of steps toward Arab-Israeli peace.

Yet, if the Soviet government continued to support radical Arab forces and even took some risks in so doing, the men ruling from the Kremlin did appear intent on keeping Middle Eastern crises under control. Certainly, Nasser's successor, Anwar al-Sadat, so interpreted Soviet policy.

President Sadat sensed that the Soviet Union valued detente with the United States over restoring Arab losses in the June 1967 war. From this reading of the great power and regional situation, President Sadat was moved to break out of an intolerable "no war-no peace" status quo by taking the risk of war in October 1973 to demonstrate that the post-June 1967 status quo was unstable.

Earlier, in July 1972, Sadat had suddenly asked that Soviet military advisers leave Egypt. This dramatic démarche had both domestic and international aims. Domestically, Sadat realized that Egyptians who for generations had suffered the plague of foreign advisers would respond with enthusiasm.

Internationally, Sadat was frantically signaling his desire for rapprochment with the United States, but the message was ignored until the seriousness of Sadat's intentions was underscored by his launching the October 1973 war.

Egyptian and Syrian military action in the October war had demonstrated that Israel could not impose the results of the June 1967 war upon the Arabs without heavy cost. The Israeli military response made it clear that the Arabs could not impose conditions upon Israel. Each side had the ability to frustrate indefinitely the maximum goals of the other. Each side, accordingly, was more disposed to reduce its expectations. This enhanced the possibilities of a negotiated settlement.

The two superpowers had also been sobered by the war. As in the previous Arab Israeli war, the United States and the Soviet Union avoided direct involvement, but brinksmanship was in evidence. A Soviet announcement of its intention to send troops, unilaterally if necessary, to prevent Israel's destruction of Egypt's Third Army had provoked a U.S. global alert of its military forces. Having thus for a few days lived with the awesome prospect of confrontation, the United States and the Soviet Union had strong incentives for sponsoring a negotiated settlement.

The Middle Eastern crisis of October 1973 began just one month after Henry Kissinger had become U.S. Secretary of State. He immediately brought an atmosphere of theatrical drama to diplomacy. This became so much a part of his modus operandi that it is easy to lose sight of where his actions were leading. While the world watched with fascination his "shuttle diplomacy," something else was unfolding. The United States leadership scoured the Middle Eastern political horizon and seemingly saw that old mirage of a single great power organizing the Middle East.

As with most drives for great power predominance in the Middle East this enticing temptation was viewed in defensive terms. U.S. policymakers saw only an opportunity to dismantle the Soviet gains achieved in the Arab world since the mid fifties. That others might view U.S. actions as provocative was, it seems, not considered.

This second American effort to organize the Middle East, coming a mere fifteen years after the collapse of the Eisenhower Doctrine in the setbacks of 1958, bore another resemblance to earlier great power ambitions in this part of the world. The new American policy developed in fits and starts. Just as the British moved slowly into a policy of supporting the Ottoman Empire, thereafter to take an equally tortuous road away from the Ottomans and toward an Arab policy, so the United States leadership let themselves slide into a strategy that would ease the Soviet Union out of the Middle East. The critical difference is that while the full flowering of the earlier British policies was in each case a matter of years that of the United States after October 1973 evolved in weeks, at times even in days.

To understand the new American policy orientation follow-

185

ing the October war, it is important to consider Soviet options. In simplest terms the Soviet Union saw itself as the patron of Egypt and Syria while the United States was Israel's patron.

The Soviet Union had a weak hand to play. Their clients had done much better militarily than previously, but Sadat's Egypt was seeking independence from the Soviet connection so painstakingly put together since the days of Premier Khrushchev. Moreover, other regional powers took initiatives that the Soviet Union might be able to exploit but could hardly pretend to control (such as the Arab oil embargo). Because of its relative weakness the Soviet Union appeared in a mood to accommodate, if only to avoid exposing the slipping Soviet control. Nor would it seem that the men in the Kremlin relished the economic cost that a more assertive Soviet diplomacy would bring.

Those in Moscow who had always questioned the cost effectiveness of support for the Arabs since 1955 could build a strong case against major new commitments of arms and aid to the Arabs at a time when Egypt, the leading Arab state, showed signs of changing sides. If, however, the Soviet position had weakened it was by no means desperate. Soviet options were clearly better than those faced immediately after the June 1967 war, and in the meantime the world energy crisis had increased enormously the perceived strategic importance of the Middle East. There is no reason to believe that the Soviet leadership felt obliged to accept a major loss in the Middle East, but they were, seemingly, in a mood to negotiate an easing of regional and great power tensions.

From the American side, Secretary Kissinger quickly grasped President Sadat's desperate but sophisticated plan to:

1. Secure the return of Egyptian territory held by Israel
2. Obtain an Arab-Israeli settlement in order to reverse policies that had cost Egypt so dearly in men and resources during the Nasser years
3. Lessen Soviet influence in Egypt and the region.

Kissinger maneuvered so as to present the United States as the sole great power able to achieve all these aims. The Kissinger strategy was, first, to provide massive military aid to Israel in order to signal both to the Soviet Union and to the Arabs that the U.S. would not permit its client to lose. That part of the strategy, alone, would have been of little long-term value to the United States. Indeed, it would have provided one more step toward the Middle Eastern alignment that the Soviets have long sought—the United States and less than 4 million Israelis versus the Soviet Union and 150 million Arabs.

The other arm of the Kissinger strategy was to present the United States as the indispensable great power mediator, shrewdly keeping before the regional parties the awareness that:

1. The United States would frustrate any Arab effort, even if fully supported by the Soviet Union, to defeat Israel, but
2. Only the United States could put effective pressure on both sides—the Arabs and Israel.

The subtle diplomacy of showing both Arabs and Israelis the right mix of pressure and support had to be matched, if the Kissinger plan was to succeed, by yet another level of subtlety. The Soviet leadership had to be given the semblance of full partnership, for although lacking the diplomatic maneuverability to achieve what Kissinger was after (an Arab-Israeli settlement), the Soviet leadership did have the power to frustrate any over-all settlement that excluded them.

The challenge for American policy, therefore, was to give the Soviets the impression that the proposed regional readjustments involved minimal losses to them and were, on balance, preferable to the available alternatives. If, on the other hand, the Soviet leadership became convinced that the United States was intent on driving them out of the Middle East then they would adopt a policy of unremitting obstructionism. The regional component of Mr. Kissinger's strategy was amazingly effective. He had more success in moving matters toward an Arab-Israeli peace than any of his predecessors among world statesman during the twenty-five years between 1948 and 1973.

The great power component was less successful. Whatever his original mindset Mr. Kissinger began to act, soon after the October war had been brought to a shaky cease-fire, as if he believed the U.S. could aim for a double diplomatic coup—a negotiated settlement of the Arab-Israeli conflict *and* a significant reduction of Soviet influence in the area.

That the author of *A World Restored: Metternich, Castlereigh, and the Problems of Peace, 1812-1822*, a book demonstrating a finely honed appreciation of the balance of power reality governing great power diplomacy, could have convinced himself that the two aims—regional peace and a major American diplomatic victory over the Soviet Union in the Middle East—were compatible seems hard to believe. Whatever his own inner thoughts, the growing unilateralism of Kissinger's shuttle diplomacy was duly noted by the Soviet government.

As the Kissinger diplomacy achieved significant piece-meal gains (restoration of U.S. diplomatic relations with Egypt and Syria, two different Egyptian-Israeli disengagement agreements, a Syrian-Israeli disengagement agreement, re-opening of the Suez Canal, and an especially close relationship with Saudi Arabia), American thinking, both official and private, leaned toward ambitious Middle East projections that blithely ignored the previous century and a half of Eastern Question history. There was even talk of an American-sponsored Egyptian-Israeli-Saudi Arabia axis.

With Greece and Turkey members of NATO (overlooking the many problems dividing the two and the recent dismal relations of each with the U.S.), with the Shah's Iran firmly attached to the West, the new alignments in the "southern tier" of the Middle East augured a Middle East Pax Americana. The reality was much different. Syria, the PLO, even Husayn's Jordan (too easily taken for granted as a Western client) each in different ways took their distance from what was seen as overly assertive American policy. This, plus the

13. Kissinger's shuttle diplomacy (1973-1975) made him world-famous, but did he try to do too much? (By permission of Hugh Haynie, *The Louisville Courier-Journal*, 1975).

influence of the consistently "rejectionist" states such as Iraq, Libya, South Yemen, and Algeria, gave the Soviet Union adequate manueverability to frustrate American plans.

By the time the Carter administration came into office in 1977, it was generally conceded that the Kissinger approach had run out of steam, although the American discussion of alternatives remained bogged down in tactics. The more useful task of looking for possible flaws in the over-all American strategy concerning the Middle East was less in evidence.

Yet, change and reconsiderations were taking place within the new administration. On 1 October 1977 a joint U.S.-Soviet statement on the Arab-Israeli confrontation appeared to usher in a major American démarche, accepting that one could not realistically expect a negotiated settlement between Israel and the Arabs in the teeth of Soviet opposition. The joint statement, which included the phrase "legitimate rights of the Palestinian people," raised a storm of criticism in the United States. Whether the Carter administration would have held its course against the combined pressure of pro-Israeli and anti-Soviet groups plus those supportive of strong, unilateral American diplomacy was never tested. Later that month President Sadat surprised the world by agreeing to go to Jerusalem and address the Israeli Knesset.

Only the great power dimension of the fascinating Sadat initiative leading ultimately to the Egyptian-Israeli peace treaty signed on the White House lawn on 26 March 1979 is relevant here. The U.S. government, faced with a choice imposed not from the rival superpower but from within the area, quickly supported President Sadat's surprising venture. Thereafter, the United States adopted an adamantly unilateral role, getting completely involved in the tortuous process leading to Egyptian-Israeli peace, while largely disregarding the Soviet Union, Western Allies, and other Middle Eastern powers.

The result has been an impressive break-through to peace between Israel and Egypt, the largest and most important Arab state.

Another result has been a new alignment of outside powers and Middle Eastern powers. Neither the American nor the Soviet attempts to achieve predominance in the Middle East have proved capable of changing that region's stubborn penchant for kaleidoscopic equilibrium.

V. CONCLUSION: STABILITY AND FLUX

The concluding section of Part One began with the observation that the Middle East in 1923 was a radically different place from the Middle East of 1774. An equally strong statement contrasting the Middle East of the early 1980s with that of 1923 is surely in order. By 1923 most of the Middle East

"TELL THE TRUTH, ANWAR,—I WANT TO KNOW...... THERE'S SOMEONE ELSE, ISN'T THERE?"

14. Middle Eastern leaders have greater motivation and greater opportunity, to change sides in great power politics, than is usually realized (Doug Marlette, *The Charlotte Observer*, 1976).

had fallen under colonial rule. Today, from Morocco to the Persian Gulf and from the Black Sea to the Arabian Sea, the Afro-Asian lands of the Ottoman Empire are divided up into sovereign states. The peoples from the largely bedouin areas of the Arabian peninsula and much of Libya have moved from penury to per capita incomes that rank among the world's highest, thanks to oil. In the process they have ceased to be isolated folk whose distinct way of life was known only to the rare Western traveller or anthropologist and have become, themselves, a new breed of international travellers, with flats in London, Bombay, and New York, while the world's largest banks and business firms rush to open offices in their countries. Throughout the area the percentage of literate, educated, and urban have increased many times over. So, too, have expenditures on arms and armies.

Yet, for all the change from 1923 to the present—just as the great change from 1774 to 1923—that tenacious international relations system, which is the two-centuries old Eastern Question, survives intact.

191

The conclusion of Part One emphasized that systemic stability was consistent with massive, even revolutionary, change within the system. Part Two has demonstrated that the same holds for the period since 1923.

To illuminate this pattern of systemic stability largely impervious to change induced either from within the region or from outside, Part One concluded with a Table on "Eastern Question Team Standings and Strategies, 1774-1923." The equivalent table for the period covered in this chapter appears below:

TABLE V. EASTERN QUESTION TEAM STANDINGS AND STRATEGIES, 1923-1980s

1917-1923	Russia faded as Middle East Power following Bolshevík Revolution. Largely bipolar great power struggle in Middle East between Britain and France won by former, but France maintained unrivalled hegemony in Maghrib. Regional power bids with fissiparous results, e.g., Ataturkism, Arabism, Zionism
1920s	The Western Imperial system consolidated. The three outside powers (Britain, France, Italy) accepted the imperial division of the area. Imperial efforts to keep the "colonized" on a short leash created problems (Italian Libya, French in Syria), but looser British system seemed to be working (nominal independence for Iraq; easy, indirect control in Jordan; light touch dominance in the Persian Gulf)
1930s	Assertive Italian challenge to the imperial division of Middle Eastern spoils (strongest impact on Libya's neighbors, French-controlled Tunisia, and British-controlled Egypt). Palestine as catalyst for anti-imperialism and pan-Arabism. Turkish absorption of Alexandretta widened gulf between Turkey and Arabs. Decline in standing of collaborate-with-imperial power political groups (as Hashimites of Iraq and Jordan)
1940-1942	Nazi defeat of France and Italian entry into war seemingly augured complete reversal great power standings in the

192

TABLE V (*cont.*)

	Middle East. British stopping Rommel's forces at El Alamein (as Soviets turned back Nazis at Stalingrad) consolidated Western position in region. Muted, circumspect response to wartime crises from regional political forces (e.g., Palestinian groups largely in disarray, short-lived challenges to British control from Iraq readily suppressed, and anti-British/pro-Axis elements in Egypt easily outbalanced by surprising British/Wafd wartime alliance)
1943-early 1950s	Apparent British dominance in region, but war-weakened Britain proved unable to bear "burden of empire." Eclipse of French influence in Levant. Major Russian efforts to reestablish standing as Middle Eastern power (immediate post-war crises in Greece, Turkey, Iran) stymied by Western ripostes. Entry of United States as Middle Eastern great power—in gestation throughout wartime as result of U.S. economic and military muscle—formalized with 1947 Truman Doctrine. First Arab-Israeli War and creation of Israel deepened Arab political malaise and shook legitimacy existing regimes.
1952-1956	Early Nasser period. Consolidation Western standing in "northern tier" (Greece and Turkey into NATO, restoration of Shah, and overthrow of Mossadegh) offset by failure Western efforts organize "southern tier." Accelerated decolonization (e.g., Sudan, Tunisia, Morocco in single year, 1956) increased potential for bolder regional initiatives. Dramatic re-entry of Soviet Union into area with Soviet-Egyptian arms deal. Rapid increase in prestige of Nasserist Arabism. Disastrous Western response in Suez crisis
1957-early 1960s	Apogee of Nasserism (1958) followed by slow decline (breakup of UAR, Yemen war). Similar sharp rise and then levelling off of Soviet influence. Bottoming out of United States standing (ill-fated Eisenhower Doctrine, overthrow of Iraqi Hashimites, U.S. intervention in Leb-

193

TABLE V (*cont.*)

	anon). Final dismantling of French imperial rule in Maghrib, with Algerian independence (1962). Beginning era vastly increased revenues in oil producing states with its impact on regional and world geopolitical balances
Mid 1960s–1973	Relative balance-in-flux of great power standing in region, tested and proved in the 1967 Arab-Israeli war. Regional forces came forward to disturb that balance—death of Nasser and end of Nasserism, emergence of PLO as independent factor, Sadat's moves away from Soviet ties, increased strength of oil producing states
1973-present	October war bringing new U.S. attempt achieve predominance stalled with Arab rejection of Camp David initiative. Double "diplomatic revolution" of Sadat's Egypt in substituting U.S. for Soviet Union as "patron" and in gambling on negotiated peace with Israel. Bottoming out of Soviet losses after 1973. Sharply enhanced diplomatic standing of Saudi Arabia in particular and oil-producing states in general. Sustained period of domestic troubles in Turkey, plus estrangement from U.S. over Cyprus. Subtle but sustained re-entry of other outside powers into regional politics, plus relative isolation U.S. (Camp David initiative, difficulties with Turkey, overthrow of Shah), augured return to fully elaborated kaleidoscopic pattern.

✳ ✳ ✳

Parts One and Two have presented the argument that the Middle East has been characterized for roughly two centuries by a distinctive international relations system. Implicit throughout Part Two, and explicitly affirmed in the last two sections, is the related argument that the Eastern Question system is by no means a thing of the past. The Eastern Question system still shapes Middle Eastern diplomacy. Part Three offers observations on the Eastern Question as a system at work.

194

PART THREE

PART THREE

--- ✳ ---

The Eastern Question System
at Work

PARTS One and Two have set out the major theses of this book:

1. The Middle East possesses a distinctive diplomatic culture.
2. That diplomatic culture came into existence during the period c. 1774-1820s (when the Middle East fell prey to a stronger Europe) and was consolidated throughout the period historians call the age of the Eastern Question.
3. Seen as a system, however, the Eastern Question did not go out of existence with the end of the Ottoman Empire following the First World War. The Eastern Question *system* characterizes international relations in the Middle East to this day.

It follows that similar perceptions and policies should characterize politics in the nineteenth and twentieth centuries. Muhammad Ali and Nasser, Palmerston and Dulles, Tsar Nicholas I and Brezhnev have been playing the same game. Points of systemic comparability linking the two centuries of Eastern Question history have been noted in the preceding pages. Part Three now addresses the issue of systemic durability more directly. This is done in two different ways. First, one enduring mindset that great power statesmen have brought to their Middle Eastern diplomacy is examined. This is the notion that the rival great power *really* determines developments and the regional political actors are more-or-less puppets on strings. Thereafter a few other examples of systemic

197

durability are briefly presented, not in detail but as agenda times for future research.

I. THE MYTH OF THE GREAT POWER PUPPETEER AND REGIONAL PUPPETS

(A) TWENTIETH-CENTURY EXAMPLES

Writing of the situation in Egypt and Iran throughout 1953, Dwight D. Eisenhower observed, with his famous idiosyncratic approach to English syntax, "The evidence of Communist meddling was evident. . . . Because of European dependence on the Suez Canal, the interests of the entire Free World were at stake in Egypt. . . ."[1]

A later American president, Lyndon B. Johnson, offered the following retrospective view in discussing events leading to the June 1967 Arab-Israeli war: "In an effort to gain influence in the radical Arab states, the Soviet Union shifted in the mid-1950s from its original support of Israel to an attempt to push moderate Arab states toward a more radical course and to provide a Middle East base for expanding its role in the Mediterranean, in Africa, and in the areas bordering on the Indian Ocean. The Soviets used Arab hostility toward Israel to inflame Arab politics to the boiling point. Country after country had shifted to the Russian view. The expanding Soviet presence in this strategic region threatened our position in Europe. Soviet leaders called publicly for the withdrawal of our Sixth Fleet from the Mediterranean, as well as for the liquidation of NATO. If they gained control of the seas, the oil, and the air space of the vast arc between Morocco and Iran, all that had been done since President Truman's time to achieve stability and balance in the world politics would be endangered."[2]

---

[1] Dwight D. Eisenhower, *Mandate for Change* (New York, 1963), p. 150.
[2] Lyndon B. Johnson, *Vantage Point* (New York, 1971), p. 288.

Richard M. Nixon's *Memoirs* sums up the 1970 crisis in Jordan: ". . . one thing was clear. We could not allow Hussein to be overthrown by a Soviet-inspired insurrection. . . ."[3]

Such statements by recent American presidents can be matched by those of other public figures. Let one example suffice. Admiral Elmo R. Zumwalt, Jr., who had recently left a distinguished career in the U.S. Navy and was seeking a niche in national politics, insisted in 1976: "After all, the principal fomenters of trouble in the Middle East are the Soviets, who have the long-range objective of gaining control of the oil there. They not only keep Arab hatred of Israel burning high, but provide the Arab states with the wherewithal to turn their hatred into action."[4]

The similar American perception of Middle Eastern international politics is clear: "evidence of Communist meddling," "Soviets . . . inflame Arab politics to the boiling point," "Soviet-inspired insurrection," "principal fomenters of trouble in the Middle East are the Soviets."

But for the outside Soviet meddling, these statements imply, Middle Eastern problems would be easily resolved. Instead of seeing these different Middle Eastern disputes as a complex interweaving of local, regional, and international interests, with many players in the game, such analyses reduce the problem to one cause—the outside meddler. It may be useful to review the Middle Eastern diplomatic context of the four American statements cited above.

EISENHOWER, 1953

Soviet interest in the Arab world blossomed following the death of Stalin (March 1953) and developed into a significant new policy after Khrushchev's arrival to power (February 1955). The Stalinist image of the Arab nationalists had been decidedly negative. These Arab nationalists might keep Western powers off balance with their insistent demands for decolon-

---

[3] Richard M. Nixon, *Memoirs* (New York, 1978), p. 483.
[4] Elmo R. Zumwalt, *On Watch* (New York, 1976), p. 442.

ization and their concern over Palestine, but to Stalin they remained unreliable bourgeois nationalists. Stalin regarded the early post-coup Egyptian government of Naguib and Nasser as virtually an American client. It took the cunning of Khrushchev to see the advantage in playing the non-alignment card.[5]

President Eisenhower's detecting of Communist meddling in Iran in the early fifties was on target, but he is anachronistically reading back later Soviet policy in the Arab world when he assumes important Soviet activities in Egypt before 1955. The specific Egyptian context in which President Eisenhower's charge of Communist meddling was raised was the continuing dispute between Britain and Egypt over the British military base at Suez. The British wanted to keep the base. The revolutionary Egyptian government wanted British troops out of Suez and British influence out of Egypt. Nasser's Free Officers government could scarcely afford to be less firm than the regime they had toppled from power. Whatever can be said against pre-1952 Egyptian politicians they had a consistent record of opposing British presence in Egypt. At least, they all had a consistent rhetorical record.

Moreover, the immediate catalyst for the July 1952 coup had been the notorious breakdown of public order in Cairo dubbed "Black Saturday," 26 January 1952. This unfortunate incident had been set off by a harsh British move against Egyptian government forces in the Suez Canal city of Ismailiyya, which left over 50 Egyptian police and gendarmes dead and many more wounded. This British military strike came in response to the long-standing Egyptian guerrilla actions against British personnel and property in the Suez base.

[5] That is, for countries in or claimed by the Western camp. Non-alignment remained an unmitigated evil for those countries in or claimed by the Soviets. "After Bandung, much was heard of the virtues of non-alignment. The Soviets liked this coming from Nasser, but disliked it from Tito. . . . The Americans, of course, saw things exactly the other way round, and sometimes when I have been in Moscow and heard Gromyko talking about non-alignment I have felt that if I closed by eyes I could be listening to Dulles." Mohamed Heikal, *The Sphinx and the Commissar*, p. 57.

The guerrilla activity was largely the work of the well-organized Muslim Brethren, which Egyptian governments of those days treated with caution. Fearing the power of the Muslim Brethren Egyptian governments did not dare openly oppose them, especially on such a popular issue as resistance to the British. The Free Officers who overthrew Faruq had ties with, but were already taking their distance from, the Muslim Brethren.

The principal actors on the Egyptian stage in this period to which President Eisenhower refers were, therefore:

1. A shaky new government in Egypt (Nasser's great popularity came much later, after he confronted Israel and the West)
2. An Egyptian populace glad to be free of Faruq but disposed to accept the new government wholeheartedly only when it demonstrated its nationalist fervor
3. A Britain that had dismantled the British Raj in India but was perversely digging in its heels over Egypt and the Suez Canal
4. A United States attempting to work out a negotiated settlement between Britain and Egypt.

The Soviets chose to remain in the wings.

The many obstacles to good Western relations with the Arab world in the years before 1955 do explain the success Khrushchev's policies achieved, but if Western policymakers before the mid-fifties had concentrated more on Western vulnerabilities in the region and less on presumed Soviet actions they might not have offered Premier Khrushchev such an easy target.

JOHNSON, 1967

President Johnson had the timing right concerning the Soviet move toward the Arab world, but in claiming to see a long-range Soviet strategy to "gain control of the seas, the oil, and the air space of the vast arc between Morocco and Iran" he offers a Manichean interpretation of Soviet strategy which ducks the difficult questions. Any student of bureaucratic politics—whether of totalitarian or democratic states—would question the compounded assumptions that:

1. Members of a large bureaucratic apparatus could be in unanimous agreement over policy.
2. They could rise above daily decisionmaking to develop and agree upon a long-term strategy.
3. Then, finally, they could consistently adhere to that long-term strategy, not being influenced by the challenge of unanticipated events breaking on the international scene.

Nor would students of diplomacy be satisfied with an argument that moves imperceptibly from the worst-case scenario of an adversary's possible actions to the untested assertion that the adversary has consistently embraced that policy and thence to the equally untested assertion that the adversary is well on the way to realizing his policy goal.

President Johnson wrote these lines in treating the diplomatic crisis ending in the June 1967 war. A useful test of this sweeping interpretation is to ask if the Soviets, acting consistently with their presumed long-range Middle Eastern strategy, did play a decisive role in the events leading to the Six Day War. This is a more complex question than that of alleged Soviet influence on Egyptian actions in 1953. By the mid-sixties the Soviet Union had become a major factor in Middle Eastern politics. Having won over Nasser's Egypt with the 1955 arms deal, support during the Suez Crisis, and massive economic aid symbolized by the building of the Aswan High Dam, the Soviet Union was no longer simply a welcomed counterweight to an oppressive Western presence. By its very successes and by Western failures the Soviet Union had become Egypt's sole great power patron.

This changed the nature of Egyptian-Soviet relations. There were no more dramatic—and largely risk free—actions to be found in the Soviet bag of diplomatic tricks. As with so many patron-client relationships, the great power found itself recalling past favors while the regional client complained: "But what have you done for me lately?" In such circumstances both sides sought more freedom of maneuver. This helps to account for President Nasser's opening to the United States during the time of the Kennedy administration, an interesting diplomatic probing that fizzled out as each, perhaps somewhat disappointed by the lack of immediate success, turned to other matters.

The Soviet Union, equally concerned not to put all its Middle Eastern eggs in the Egyptian basket, had developed close ties with the Syrian Ba'thist regime, brought to power by military coup in 1966. Such was the immediate background to one of the turning points in the events leading to the Six Day War.

On 13 May 1967 the Soviet government informed Nasser that Israel was concentrating troops in the north, almost certainly in preparation for a major attack against Syria. This triggered Nasser's request for the partial removal of the UN troops (UNEF) that had patrolled Egypt's border with Israel since the Suez War. It is generally agreed that the Soviet action was intended to give some respite to the Syrian government, sorely pressed by domestic disputes and openly threatened with retaliatory measures from Israel.

That the Soviet signal to Nasser played an important role in the events leading to war is beyond dispute, but was the Soviet action in mid-May the point of no return? A more decisive date was over a week later, on 22 May, when Nasser announced the closing of the Gulf of Aqaba. Nasser's demanding, and obtaining, the removal of UNEF forces did not give Israel a casus belli. Announcing a blockade did (even if the blockade was not effective or was not even seriously intended—points that could be argued). Moreover, one week after the announced blockade Nasser upped the ante again when he announced before the Egyptian National Assembly: "The issue today is not the question of Aqaba, or the Strait of Tiran, or UNEF. The issue is the rights of the people of Palestine, the aggression against Palestine that took place in 1948, with the help of Britain and the United States. . . ."[6]

[6] Al Ahram 30 May 1967 as cited in Nadav Safran, *From War to War: The Arab-Israeli Confrontation, 1948-1967* (New York, 1969), p. 270.

Many more bits and pieces of evidence could be added:

1. The appearance of indecisiveness on the part of Levi Esh-kol's government in Israel
2. The American response after mid-May which Nasser could have interpreted as an eagerness to avoid war
3. Nasser was perhaps trapped by his own tactical successes (being thereafter no longer able to control—and unwilling to disappoint—the enthusiasm raised within the Arab world).

One common theme unites all these points. They place the primary initiative within the Middle East.

Finally, Israel started hostilities on June 6, surprising the Arabs and the world. Almost everyone outside the Israeli government expected a few more tortured twists and turns of diplomacy before hostilities or even (as a few remaining optimists believed) a negotiated settlement. The Israeli action, in short, was a surprising unilateral regional initiative, just as Nasser's earlier steps had been. In the diplomacy leading up to the June 1967 war the Soviet Union can be charged with dangerous brinksmanship. They contributed to the crisis but never controlled it.

Historians will argue for years to come over the exact mix of causes and responsibilities leading to the June war, but the most serious scholarship on the subject already approaches consensus on two critical points:

1. A complex of actions and reactions characterized developments. The idea of a single master planner seems hopelessly simplistic.
2. Regional initiatives outweighed those from outside throughout the crisis and, most important, at the crucial turning points.

NIXON, 1970

What, then, of the 1970 Jordan crisis and President Nixon's allegation that King Husayn was in danger of being "over-

thrown by a Soviet-inspired insurrection"? Again, the only
adequate interpretation must emphasize the continuing inter-
play of regional and great power actions. Regional actions,
however, predominated.

The immediate crisis was clearly triggered—and deliberately—from within the Middle East, not by an established
government but by a small, radical group of the Palestinian
Liberation Organization (PLO) that was attempting to impose a more assertive policy. This was the Popular Front for
the Liberation of Palestine (PFLP) led by George Habash.

Other strictly regional concerns provided the broader background to the Jordan crisis.

1. The long-standing animosity between the Jordanian dynasty and the Palestinian leadership (of almost all per-
   suasions) within the PLO, which can be traced back to
   earlier quarrels between King Husayn's grandfather, Abdullah, and the majority of Palestinian leaders.

2. The Jordanian dynasty's fragile legitimacy within the Arab
   world. Distrusted for its pro-Western ties, suspected (with
   reason) of a willingness to negotiate with Israel, and never
   forgiven for having been the one Arab state to profit
   from the first Arab-Israeli war in 1948 (by later annexing
   the West Bank), the Hashimite Kingdom of Jordan survived in large measure through a nimble manipulation of
   negative balances: the existing state was less distasteful to
   its enemies than the likely alternatives.

3. The post-June 1967 war capture of the PLO by Yasir
   Arafat's al-Fatah and other smaller but even more radical
   groups—such as the PFLP—created a situation in which
   the PLO was no longer the docile instrument of the Arab
   states but a growing power in the region.

4. The continuing struggle over personalities and policies
   within the PLO.

5. Nasser's acceptance that his war of attrition against Israel
   (begun spring 1969) was too dangerous to sustain. It
   had brought deep-penetration Israeli air strikes against

Egypt, which then led to Nasser's desperate appeal for Soviet missile and air cover, arriving in spring 1970.

6. The commitment of Soviet military power directly in the area increased the likelihood of a great power confrontation which neither the U.S. nor the Soviet Union wished, but neither was willing to abandon its regional clients.

7. The Israeli dilemma (yet another example of Israel's military "Midas touch," especially after 1967) of having inflicted a military defeat on Egypt in the war of attrition only to find that victory brought increased insecurity in the form of a Soviet military presence on its borders.

Out of these problems facing Egypt, Israel, the United States, and the Soviet Union emerged a mutual interest in de-escalation which resulted—after tortuous negotiations—in the 7 August 1970 Egyptian-Israeli cease-fire. The United States had served as the principal outside mediator, but behind the scenes support from the Soviet Union had been evident.

Jordan and several other Arab states backed Nasser's démarche. Syria, Iraq, and the PLO were among the opponents. As with every Arab effort at a negotiated settlement with Israel, the August 1970 cease-fire brought the threat of a bitter division in Arab ranks. The cease-fire was viewed by the PLO, and even more by the PFLP, as a dangerous prelude to a negotiated settlement of the Arab-Israeli confrontation at the expense of the Palestinians. The PLO feared becoming the victims of Soviet-American detente and Egyptian fatigue. The PFLP reacted with hijackings that brought three commercial airplanes to a desert field near Amman, Jordan.[7] The PFLP had clearly gained its immediate aims. World attention was riveted on the Palestinians. The point that Palestinians must not be ignored in the Arab-Israeli settlement had been forcefully made. Moreover, all Arabs—Nasser, the Saudis, and

[7] Another plane was hijacked, taken to Cairo, and destroyed. An attempt against an El Al plane was foiled. The three planes in Jordan were later destroyed, the passengers taken as hostages to points in Amman and eventually released.

others—were put under pressure to make their diplomacy match their rhetoric (of unqualified support for the Palestinian cause).

By these dramatic, militarily meaningless hijackings a mere handful of men and women had jeopardized a great-power-sponsored easing of Arab-Israeli tensions, leading perhaps eventually to a quiet, behind-the-scenes settlement.

King Husayn was most immediately threatened. The hijacked planes were on his territory, in a defiant PFLP flouting of his authority. Any move by him against the PLO (for the PFLP had easily forced the hand of the larger organization) would risk his losing all Arab support, no small matter for a dynasty that had always teetered precariously between pariah status and grudging acceptance within the Arab world.

PLO military units throughout Jordan were flaunting their strength, and the Jordanian army bristled in reaction. To the hardcore supporters of the Hashimite dynasty, overwhelmingly from the old Transjordan a less developed society closer to its bedouin roots, the whole affair was degenerating into a PLO takeover of Jordan. This pro-Hashimite core, concentrated in the Jordanian army leadership, wanted action. Otherwise, not even loyalty to Husayn was indefinitely assured. Facing the immediate prospect of losing control over his own army Husayn judged military intervention by Syria or Iraq (which had nearly 20,000 troops in Jordan[8] ostensibly as part of the joint Arab defensive effort against Israel) less threatening. In mid-September he authorized action against the PLO forces in Jordan. There followed a brief, but vicious, fratricidal war that came to be called "Black September" in Palestinian accounts.

Husayn's regular army was prevailing against the less well equipped and less thoroughly trained PLO forces when the Syrian army intervened from across Jordan's northern border. Husayn frantically appealed for help to Britain and the United

[8] William B. Quandt, *Decade of Decisions: American Policy toward the Arab-Israeli Conflict, 1967-1976* (University of California Press, 1977), p. 111. Kissinger gives the figure of 17,000, Henry Kissinger, *White House Years* (Boston, 1979), p. 595.

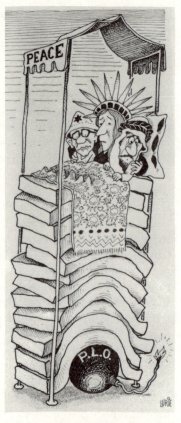

15. Even the weakest player in the Middle East political game can often upset the plans of the most powerful (Ranan Lurie. Reprinted with permission from *Foreign Policy* 28, Fall 1977. Copyright 1977 by the Carnegie Endowment for International Peace).

States, but questions of timing and terrain made it clear that only Israeli military intervention would prove effective. Thus was born the U.S. plan for direct Israeli military involvement. Even this, the beleaguered Husayn was prepared to accept in extremis, but he preferred U.S. and British participation or—another alternative suggested—Israeli moves directly into Syria. The Israeli government, intent on keeping Jordan from falling into the hands of the PLO or Syria, responded positively to the U.S. proposal.

As it happened, open Israeli military moves toward the north in preparation for intervention were sufficient to give the Syrian government pause. When Husayn, assured of outside support, finally committed his air force against the Syrian troops in northern Jordan, the Syrian air force[9] did not intervene. Soon Syrian forces began to withdraw. The crisis was over.

What is the best interpretation of this crisis? To argue that it was Soviet-inspired, or for that matter American-inspired, ignores too many facts. That the crisis was deliberately initiated by the PFLP is undisputed. Thereafter, all parties got involved in a dangerous game of guesses and gestures. That Syria would not have intervened if faced with a categorical Soviet veto can be accepted. This, however, in no way demonstrates that the Soviets were encouraging the Syrians to move or that the Soviets had control over Syrian actions.

Other interpretations are more plausible. The original Syrian military intervention was crudely masked as the entry of PLO military units, Syrian army insignia on the tanks having been hastily painted over with PLO markings. Had the Syrian authorities convinced the Soviets that a limited escalation would be the best way to keep all options open? This is a possibility.

Neither the Syrians nor the Soviets wanted to see the PLO crushed, but whether the Soviets sought to overthrow King Husayn is questionable. Assuming Soviet wariness about regional tensions getting out of control—the lesson they drew from the War of Attrition—they probably were reluctant to risk the cataclysm that Husayn's fall would bring.

Limited support for the PLO and Syria might well have appeared a good gamble to the Soviets. The Soviets had long sought to get Western acceptance of Soviet standing in the Middle East. This the United States had continued to resist. Even the Egyptian-Israeli cease-fire was a U.S. plan. The Soviet Union was not invited to co-sponsor the idea.[10] By sup-

---

[9] Hafiz al-Asad, President of Syria since 1971, was then Minister of Defense and Commander in Chief of the air force. Opposing the Syrian intervention in Jordan from the beginning, his refusal to use the Syrian air force obliged his rivals in the Syrian government to abandon the venture.

[10] Raising an interesting legal and diplomatic point concerning the Soviet-Egyptian violations of the cease-fire by continuing the move of missiles into

porting limited resistance to the American plan, the Soviets might be able to make the point that no regional settlement was possible without them. Moreover, if the Soviets could provoke the United States or Israel to make threatening moves against King Husayn's enemies, without having the crisis get out of hand, the regional isolation of all three—Israel, Jordan, and the United States—would be increased. The Soviets could present themselves as the Arabs' only true friend against a bullying Israel backed by an imperialist United States manipulating such puppets as Jordan.

Such an interpretation is consistent with the several Soviet statements throughout the crisis calling for calm and non-intervention on the part of outsiders. These statements were hypocritical, it is true; but they may well offer an accurate gauge of the limited wager the Soviets wished to gamble. The way the Soviets clearly signalled their intention not to raise the ante after Israeli preparatory moves seems to support this interpretation.

None of this is to argue that the Soviets played their cards well. Kissinger in his memoirs makes a powerful case to the contrary: "In every crisis a point is reached where one side must decide whether to clinch its gains or to gamble for more. If the Soviet Union had around September 10 pressed for the release of hostages and a cease-fire, the gain for the fedayeen would have been massive; the authority of the King would have been gravely weakened. Instability in Jordan would have been added to insecurity along the Suez Canal; Soviet prestige would have been demonstrated and reinforced. But by getting too greedy—by not helping to rein in their clients—the Soviets gave us the opportunity to restore the equilibrium before the balance of forces had been fundamentally changed."[11]

---

the cease-fire zone. "One might have wondered what obligation the Soviet Union had to respect the terms of an American-arranged cease-fire to which it had not been a party. The Soviet bid for a cooperative approach had been rebuffed in early June, and the United States had proceeded unilaterally. The Soviet Union was not violating any agreement to which it was a party." Quandt, *Decade of Decision*, p. 108.

[11] *White House Years*, p. 609.

Kissinger is suggesting that the Soviet Union drifted with the current. The image of the Soviet Union planning and "inspiring" developments does not offer nearly so satisfactory a framework for understanding the crisis. If the Soviet Union was not the master puppeteer in the Jordan crisis, what can be said of the United States? Did the United States pull the strings causing King Husayn and the Israelis to act as they did? Here, one is dealing with a more public record than with the Soviet Union and Syria. Although differences of interpretation abound there can be no argument about the basic points: neither King Husayn nor Israel was waiting to be prodded into action by outside forces. King Husayn, as always, played his fated role of the weak surrounded by stronger enemies. He sought British or American intervention rather than Israeli if possible, then urged an Israeli attack directly into Syria as second best, and finally was able to get the crisis stopped—just barely—short of an Israeli move across the Jordanian border. Although everyone knew what had transpired, appearances were saved. King Husayn could accept the formality of inter-Arab mediation, for his throne was safe and the PLO broken in Jordan.

The Israeli government as the dominant military power in the immediate region had only Soviet intervention to fear. The safest way to neutralize Soviet action was through an agreement with the United States. Under these circumstances, it would be difficult to decide which side—the U.S. or Israel—was courting the other more assiduously, but President Nixon long sought to resolve the issue without Israel and gave in on this point only when convinced that Israel was needed to make the military threat credible.

The question that never had to be answered in this crisis was whether the Israelis would have moved, even without U.S. support, rather than see Jordan fall into the hands of Syria and the PLO. Israeli action in June 1967, Israeli public statements concerning Jordan, and Israeli military strategy of countering all Arab efforts to change the status quo with an even stronger riposte, suggest that Israel would have acted alone if need be. The risk of Soviet intervention was great but remote. The risk of a radical Arab and PLO state on Israel's eastern border was immediate. Great powers having world-wide interests often forget that smaller states, when forced to choose, deal with their immediate problems first, trusting that the more awesome but remoter problems will not materialize. The United States and the Soviet Union were principals in the Jordan crisis, but most of the initiatives came from the region, and the region was manipulating the great powers at least as much as the other way round.

Other intriguing questions remain. The original fear of both King Husayn and those outsiders interested in his survival was of Iraqi intervention. Why did not the Iraqi troops already stationed in Jordan move? As early as 1 September Iraq had warned King Husayn against cracking down on the PLO units, and this was after an abortive Palestinian guerrilla attempt to assassinate the king, the second attempt of that year. What changed Iraqi orientation so radically between the first and the middle of September?

Another unanswered question concerns Syrian intentions. Did the Syrian government expect to overthrow Husayn without provoking an Israeli response? If not, then at what intermediate point did they intend to stop and conserve their gains?

Even posing these questions highlights the extent to which the region, far from manipulated by outside powers, was largely determining developments—for better or worse.

ZUMWALT, 1976

The interpretation of Middle Eastern politics given by Admiral Zumwalt is more open-ended: The Soviets are the "principal fomenters of trouble in the Middle East. . . . They not only keep Arab hatred of Israel burning high, but provide the Arab states with the wherewithal to turn their hatred into action." Admiral Zumwalt's is a common type of explanation which seeks out a single nefarious "fomenter" who manipulates everything. All others are denied political autonomy. The implication is that the Arabs cannot act politically unless acted upon. Such views are no more than variations of the "devil" or "hidden hand" theory. All would be well but for the malevolent actions of an outsider.

These ideas are by no means the monopoly of the Left or the Right, of hawks or doves. Those who see the Soviets maliciously sicking the Arabs on plucky, innocent Israel are matched by those who attribute all troubles in the Arab world to the intrusive presence of Israel backed by imperialism.

Alternatively, the rhetoric of Soviet spokesmen and of Arab radicals offers a mirror reflection of the Zumwalt/Johnson position: The United States deliberately keeps the Arabs divided for its own imperialist purposes.

Students of colonial history recognize the syndrome. Colonial officials and spokesmen were always to be found attributing colonial nationalism to outsiders. Without that outside influence "our natives" who had always been content would return to their contentment. The powerful (colonial powers or great powers) are reluctant to attribute as much autonomy and assertiveness to lesser political entities as to their rivals of roughly equal strength.

The fallacy of Admiral Zumwalt's reasoning can be readily demonstrated. The Arabs opposed Zionism in the last years of the Ottoman Empire, during the years of the British mandate, and in the period from 1948 to 1955—all in a period before the Soviet Union was a factor in the Arab world. An equal pattern of consistency could be shown for Zionist endeavors to establish a state in Palestine, and after 1948 to maintain the strength and independence of Israel. The Zionist, and later Israeli, leaders might appeal now to one and then to another outside power, but the consistency of their own political autonomy in striving for goals which they—not outsiders—had set matches that of the Palestinians and the Arabs.

In a word, one side won and the other lost. The many complex reasons for that provide the student of Middle Eastern international relations a significant case study. There is no need to obfuscate the matter by assuming—against all evidence—that outsiders were calling the tune. Those inclined to attribute long-lived regional conflicts to outside manipulation would do well to reflect on Machiavelli's maxim: "When once the people have taken arms against you, there will never be lacking foreigners to assist them."

(B) NINETEENTH-CENTURY EXAMPLES

Attributing regional troubles to the machinations of the great-power enemy is not a peculiar American failing. A review of great-power thinking concerning Eastern Question politics before 1914 demonstrates the trait to be well-nigh universal.

The nineteenth-century British official mind concerning Middle Eastern affairs offers a good example. Since nineteenth-century British diplomacy is often deemed to have possessed a sophistication and sensitivity to political nuance well beyond what today's super powers can muster, concentration on earlier British perceptions is especially pertinent.

HUNKAR ISKELESI

"I have always treated as wholly erroneous the belief entertained by some that Russia could act with what people call moderation in these matters or cease for one moment to aim at the subjugation of Turkey."[12] So wrote the British ambassador to the Ottoman Empire, Lord Ponsonby, in 1836, three years after the Russo-Ottoman treaty of Hunkar Iskelesi had increased Russian influence at Constantinople. Speaking of that same treaty soon after it had been signed, Lord Palmerston noted darkly that the obligation to consult meant "the Russian ambassador becomes the chief Cabinet Minister of the Sultan."[13]

With Hunkar Iskelesi the British penchant for seeing a Rus-

[12] FO 78/274 Ponsonby #52 24 April 1836, cited in H.W.V. Temperley, *England and the Near East: The Crimea* (London, 1936), p. 75.

[13] Cited in Jelavich, *Century of Russian Foreign Policy*, p. 86. The text of the treaty is found in Hurewitz, *Middle East and North Africa*, Vol. I, pp. 252-253.

sian hand at work behind the scenes in Eastern Question issues was firmly fixed. This "Russophobia"[14] came to be associated with the policies and personality of Lord Palmerston,
whose assertive, bumptious moralism in foreign affairs "earned
him the sobriquet of 'Lord Pumicestone' ";[15] but many individuals contributed to this mindset destined to become so deep-
rooted.

One of the most penetrating observers of the Eastern Question scene, Adolphus Slade, argued in a book published the
very year of Hunkar Iskelesi: "It is time seriously to look to
Russia, and not let slip the opportunity, now held out to us
through emancipated Greece, of making European Turkey a
partial counterpoise to her. Russia should be the watch-word
of the British cabinet. We want a Cato to ring it in the ears
of our politicians."[16]

Russia was an expanding power throughout the nineteenth
century. So, too, was Britain, and for that matter the United
States. Moreover, Russian and British expansion placed them
in direct confrontation. There was reason for both sides to
think in terms of "the great game," pitting the sea-borne empire of Britain against the land-based behemoth, Russia. This
is not in question, but were British statesmen correct in assuming that Russia was manipulating Middle Eastern affairs
as part of a long-term expansionist scheme?

The immediate background to Hunkar Iskelesi was noted
in Part I. The Greek struggle for independence forced a pain-
ful choice upon the governments of Tsar Alexandar I and his
successor Nicholas I. Should they support legitimate government against revolutionary nationalism or back Orthodox
Christians against infidel rule?

Step by step, Russia moved toward the latter choice, pro-

[14] See J. H. Gleason, *The Genesis of Russophobia in Great Britain* (Harvard
University Press, 1950; reprinted 1972), the pioneering study on the subject.

[15] Kenneth Bourne, *The Foreign Policy of Victorian England* (Oxford University Press, 1970), p. 45.

[16] *Records of Travels in Turkey, Greece, Etc.* (London, 1833), 2 vols.; I, pp.
430-431.

ceeding from ultimata to joint naval action with Britain and France (Navarino), to a unilateral declaration of war (1828), followed by great power conference diplomacy and eventually the creation of a small, independent Greek state. In 1829 the Tsar called a secret meeting of his principal advisers to consider whether Russia should work for an orderly dissolution of the Ottoman Empire or, instead, keep this weakened state in existence as a useful buffer. The Russian statesmen proposed the latter strategy, which Tsar Nicholas accepted.

Thus, Russia entered the 1830s disposed to keep the Ottoman Empire alive, a policy also favored by British statesmen. Even though neither rival understood what the other was up to or trusted the other, confrontation should have been avoidable. Each side could have worked toward the goal they shared even while enjoying the pleasure (so satisfying to statemen) of appearing to impose one's will upon others. No such sensible outcome resulted. Why?

Muhammad Ali's venture into Syria had triggered the crisis. The Egyptian army under Ibrahim Pasha overwhelmed the Ottoman forces. A frantic Sultan Mahmud II looked for help. Britain, occupied with pressing problems at home (the agitation of 1831-1832 leading to the great Reform Bill), temporized.

Britain even turned a deaf ear to Metternich's proposal for great power guarantees to the Ottoman Empire, although this surely would have made Hunkar Iskelesi unnecessary. With Ibrahim's army only 150 miles from Istanbul, Sultan Mahmud appealed to the old enemy for immediate military support. Tsar Nicholas agreed.

This brought Eastern Question multilateralism to full play. Britain and France moved to reverse the fait accompli that they could easily have avoided earlier, pressuring both the Ottomans and Muhammad Ali to reach a quick settlement and thus eliminate the need for a Russian military presence. Sultan Mahmud, buttressed by great power support, rejected Muhammad Ali's harsh terms; but later, on finding that Russian military support could not possibly arrive in time to save Istanbul should Ibrahim Pasha decide on a quick strike, had to back down. Muhammad Ali vacillated between his son's advice to march on the Ottoman capital, thereby presenting all with a fait accompli, and the more prudent course of settling for half a loaf in the hope of securing great power acquiescence.

It was in this context that Sultan Mahmud granted Muhammad Ali the province of Syria and the latter, carefully eying increased Anglo-French pressure, decided against going for more. Later that year the Russo-Ottoman treaty was negotiated and then signed (July 1833).

As for the British interpretation of Russian behavior several points appear beyond dispute:

1. The major initiatives came from the region—Muhammad Ali's invasion of Syria and Sultan Mahmud's appeals for help ending in his desperate call to Russia.
2. Britain had ample opportunity to act in concert with other European powers.
3. Sultan Mahmud surrendered nothing of substance in the treaty. The secret agreement to close the Straits to foreign warships upon activation of the alliance seemed ominous to the maritime powers but made the Ottoman Empire no more vulnerable. The treaty did provide the Ottomans their firmest guarantee against a dangerous Muhammad Ali. France had recently conquered the Ottoman province of Algeria and had a military mission in Muhammad Ali's Egypt. She could not be relied on. Britain was galvanized into action only *after* the Ottoman appeal to Russia (itself a demonstration that the desperate step was useful). European conference diplomacy, in which anything could happen, was no substitute for a great power ally answering an immediate need.[17]

[17] Twentieth-century equivalents of Sultan Mahmud II's gambit include: Nasser's resorting to Soviet military presence in Egypt to counter Israel's deep penetration raids in 1970, King Husayn's appeal to the United States and Britain against Syrian attack later that same year, Lebanese President Chamoun's call for American support against Nasserist forces in 1958, and Kuwait's requesting British support to parry an Iraqi invasion in 1961.

Accepting that the Russians did not initiate the crisis leading to this treaty and that earlier British inaction let developments get beyond their control, it can still be argued that the Russian government exploited almost too greedily the unforeseen opportunity. A Russian government expressing its interest in keeping the beleaguered Ottoman Empire intact might have been able to calm British apprehensions. The price paid for a less assertive diplomacy would probably have been the rewriting of the bilateral Russo-Ottoman treaty into a multilateral accord, which is just what took place later.[18]

THE SECOND SYRIAN CRISIS

A second confrontation between Sultan Mahmud II and Muhammad Ali took place before the end of the decade and with even more unfortunate military results for the Ottoman Empire. In April 1839 the Ottoman army crossed into Egyptian-controlled Syria, bound for Aleppo, only to be routed by Ibrahim Pasha's army in June. A few day later Sultan Mahmud II died (apparently without learning of the defeat and not, as is often alleged, from the shock that the dismal news caused), and soon after that the Ottoman grand admiral took most of the Ottoman fleet to Alexandria, joining forces with Muhammad Ali.

Surveying this string of Ottoman setbacks, the *London Times* concluded that there could be: . . . "no human so incredulous as to imagine that if Russia had in her heart desired to save the unfortunate Mahmoud from destruction, by rescuing him from his warlike demonstration against Egypt, he would have dared to resist her command."[19]

---

[18] Eastern Question history is filled with the diplomatic wreckages of unilateral great-power attempts at preemptive diplomacy. The ill-fated Soviet-Egyptian treaty of May 1971 (interestingly, following the Hunkar Iskelesi sequence of military aid in a time of peril and then later a long-term treaty) is a recent example. One might also question whether America's Camp David initiative will succeed unless other powers are involved in underwriting a comprehensive Arab-Israeli settlement.

[19] *London Times* 25 July 1839, cited in Gleason, *Russophobia in Great Britain*, p. 243.

Lord Ponsonby, still British ambassador in Constantinople, was convinced that the Tsar's government encouraged the Sultan toward war with Muhammad Ali as a design to increase Ottoman dependence on Russia. Yet, inconsistently, Ponsonby also nudged the Sultan to the same end.

Not everyone went to the extremes of the *Times* and Lord Ponsonby, but British thinking did tend to assume a Russian masterplan at work. Where did the initiatives causing this crisis come from?

Sultan Mahmud II took this desperate gamble, motivated, seemingly, by consuming obsession to bring Muhammad Ali to heel. Mahmud realized that the Ottoman Empire was in mortal danger as long as a strong Muhammad Ali could combine a regional military threat with tempting diplomatic démarches to the great powers. No outside goal was needed to spur Sultan Mahmud into action. Mahmud had long sought firm support from the powers for action against Muhammad Ali, but then sent his army into Syria *after* such efforts had failed. A major aspect of the sustained Ottoman campaign to win British support against Muhammad Ali was the Anglo-Ottoman treaty of Balta Liman (August 1838).

Historians occasionally categorize the treaty as Britain's imposing classical economic liberalism upon an Ottoman governing elite too unsophisticated to appreciate that they would be ruined by the theories of Adam Smith. Such an interpretation is, however, one-sided. To the Ottomans the treaty was a way of lining up British diplomatic support. Moreover, the terms of the treaty, if they could be imposed on Muhammad Ali, would destroy the Egyptian pasha's state monopolies.

The Ottoman campaign for support from the powers, especially from Palmerston's government, continued into the spring of 1839, but by then the British government had made clear that, while prepared to protect the sultan against further encroachments from Muhammad Ali, Britain's overriding interest was stability and the status quo. Neither Britain nor Russia was prepared to underwrite an assertive campaign by Sultan Mahmud to regain Syria. Ironically, the prudent estimate in London that precipitate Ottoman action might well strengthen the hand of Russia was matched by a similar cautious estimate in St. Petersburg that Britain stood to gain.

The one thing the rival European powers could agree upon was that a Middle Eastern status quo best guaranteed safety. This lesson had already been imposed upon Muhammad Ali in 1838. If Sultan Mahmud yearned to redress Ottoman losses to Muhammad Ali, the latter was just as eager to consolidate his gains. Throughout the spring of 1838 Muhammad Ali made noises about declaring his independence from Ottoman rule, and in May he announced the intention publicly.

For his pains Muhammad Ali got both British and Russian naval preparations, categorical warnings from both powers, and a veritable concert of Europe position against such a dramatic change. Even Egypt's strongest supporter, France, felt obliged to go along with this European consensus. In July Muhammad Ali withdrew the proposal while—in best Eastern Question fashion—leaving the door to ultimate Egyptian independence slightly ajar.

Europe's quashing of Muhammad Ali's bid for independence was a boon for the beleagured Ottoman Empire; but it was clear that Europe would just as strongly resist Ottoman suggestions for a change at Muhammad Ali's expense. Sultan Mahmud II thus found himself in a situation much like that facing President Sadat of Egypt 134 years later. He could be reasonably assured of outside support against a turn for the worse, but could line up no outside help to improve a situation that he found intolerable. His decision, like that of President Sadat in planning the October war, was to surprise everyone with military action.

This second Syrian crisis, begun with troop movements in April 1839 and moving quickly to a seemingly disastrous outcome for the Ottoman Empire two months later, continued thereafter with more diplomatic than military maneuvers for almost two more years. During that hectic period the outside power alignment changed, with France, not Russia, playing the loner's role by backing Muhammad Ali against a great power determination to support the Ottoman Empire.

The period also witnessed the promulgation of the Hatt-ı-Şerif of Gulhane (November 1839), the first of three great nineteenth-century Ottoman constitutional documents to be forged in the white heat of international crisis. When the issue was finally settled in mid-1841, Muhammad Ali had suffered a diplomatic defeat as crushing as his earlier military victory. He was ousted from Syria and left with only the hereditary governorship of Egypt.

This complicated episode demonstrated the intrusive power of Europe in Middle Eastern affairs, but from beginning to end, the major initiatives came from the region. The European powers reacted. Raw power lay with Europe, but the closest approximation to long-range planning was to be found in Cairo or Constantinople—not London, Paris, or St. Petersburg.

THE CRIMEAN WAR

The diplomatic blundering that led to the Crimean War can also be examined to test the idea of outside powers manipulating regional clients. In this case there can be no doubt that most of the initiatives came from the great powers. A listing of the often bizarre incidents that brought on the Crimean War illustrates the overwhelmingly European dimension of the diplomatic crisis:

1. The push-comes-to-shove between Napoleon III and Tsar Nicholas I over the holy places
2. The massive misunderstanding arising from the Tsar's conversations with British Ambassador Seymour
3. The crudely inept Menshikov mission to Istanbul
4. Austria's surprising stand against Russia which only four years earlier had helped the newly crowned Emperor Francis Joseph suppress the Hungarian revolt[20]

[20] The prophecy of the Austrian minister, Schwarzenberg, that Austria would one day astound the world with its ingratitude toward Russia has become famous, cited in most studies of diplomacy.

5. Gunboat diplomacy with British and French fleets approaching the Dardanelles (to restrain Russia) or moving back (to restrain the Ottomans) with, however, the diplomatic and naval maneuvers poorly synchronized
6. The "great elchi" Stratford de Redcliffe hurrying back to his ambassadorial post in Istanbul in order to assure, largely on his own authority—or so many have alleged—that the Ottoman would hold firm even at the risk of war.

All this seems to leave very little room for regional initiatives. One historian has even argued: "The real stake in the Crimean War was not Turkey. It was central Europe; that is to say, Germany and Italy."[21] Another historian archly notes, "War having been declared, the question was to find a battleground for it."[22]

Admittedly, the Middle East was more led than leading in the diplomacy that produced the Crimean War; but even in this case certain Ottoman initiatives deserve attention. The first concerns the Ottoman response to the Vienna Note of July 1853, a concerted European effort to cool the crisis. By this time, the Ottomans had rejected the crudely provocative demands of the Russian emissary, Menshikov; Russia had responded by sending its army to occupy the Ottoman principalities (Moldavia and Wallachia); and the British and French had moved their fleets close to the Dardanelles. None of the European powers wanted war, but Russia, Britain, and France had clumsily placed their military in positions from which "honorable" disengagement would be difficult.

A conference of ambassadors in Vienna was arranged to find a way out. The Russian ambassador refused to attend, pleading no instructions from his government; the Ottomans were not invited (consistent with the one-sided way the great powers applied the Eastern Question rules); but representa-

[21] A.J.P. Taylor, *The Struggle for Mastery in Europe, 1848-1918* (Oxford University Press, 1954), p. 61.
[22] Rene Albrecht-Carre, *A Diplomatic History of Europe Since the Congress of Vienna* (New York, 1958), p. 89.

tives of Austria, Britain, France, and Prussia found a formula for settlement. This was accepted by the Russian government.

The Ottomans, however, proposed significant changes which conceded Russia's professed concerns about Ottoman Orthodox Christians but presented the concessions as between the Sultan and his subjects, not the Ottoman Empire and Russia. Russia rejected the Ottoman proposal out of hand and, in the process, interpreted the Vienna Note as clearly giving Russia the right to intervene on behalf of Ottoman Orthodox subjects. The Vienna effort at achieving a balanced, even deliberately vague statement capable of getting all sides to withdraw gracefully, was undermined.[23]

The Ottomans could present a strong case for countering the Vienna Note with their own, quite different proposal. They had remained calm even after Russian forces had occupied the Principalities. The Ottoman counter-proposals had, in fact, reached the ambassadors working at Vienna *before* the Vienna Note was completed. Moreover, the Ottomans had sent this statement[24] with the understanding that they would not be pressed to make further concessions. To have their démarche so casually set aside raised fears that the Sublime Porte might well eventually be "negotiated" into complete defeat.

In terms of elementary justice the Ottoman position was unassailable, but in the context of 1853 (in which the Sublime Porte neither had nor was believed entitled to have much diplomatic maneuverability) their decision was noteworthy. With

[23] The episode calls to mind a more recent concerted effort at finding an acceptable formula for negotiated settlement—UN Security Council Resolution 242 of November 1967 attempted to set out in broad lines both Israeli and Arab rights and duties. Always interpreted differently by the several parties and occasionally criticized as unnecessarily vague, Resolution 242 still offers a useful point of departure for serious negotiation. Those who consistently fault diplomatic statements that "paper over" real differences are at best only half right. Concerted diplomatic initiatives such as the Vienna Note or Resolution 242 are to be judged for their usefulness as "pump primers," not as draft treaties.

[24] Which European diplomats unfortunately labelled a "Turkish ultimatum"—an unbelievably loose usage in that age of precise diplomatic language.

a judicious mix of further conciliatory words, trimming, dissimulation, and even deceit (just the tactics Europeans accused them of using) the Ottomans could have achieved a settlement restoring the status quo. Instead, they knowingly adopted a different course.

A second Ottoman initiative was to present an ultimatum in early October demanding Russian evacuation of the Principalities within two weeks, and when that deadline passed the Ottomans began military actions even before a formal declaration of war. Then, in November the Ottomans sent a naval squadron into the Black Sea, where it was annihilated by the vastly superior Russian fleet at Sinope on November 30. To the already overheated British and French public opinion this became the "massacre of Sinope," and it proved to be the additional incident required to set off general war.

Even after Ottoman-Russian hostilities in late October the Tsar, by then much less impetuous than earlier, was disposed to accept four-power mediation. If the Ottoman government really sought a settlement, then it made no sense to send inadequate naval units into the Black Sea in search of the superior Russian forces. Sinope was indeed a massacre in the sense that the charge of the Light Brigade was a massacre, but there was clearly nothing contrary to the laws of war in the Russian action.

These several Ottoman initiatives that contributed to the descent into war have sometimes been explained by a "master puppeteer" theory of outside great power manipulation. In this case, the presumed culprit was not Russia, but Britain or more exactly Britain's powerful ambassador to the Ottoman Empire, Stratford de Redcliffe, whose paternalistic identification with Ottoman reform and intense Russophobia impelled him, so it is argued, to keep Ottoman forces lined up against a negotiated settlement.

This theory, once so popular, was convincingly challenged by the British historian, Harold Temperley, in his *England and the Near East: The Crimea* (1936). Since then, serious students have backed away from casting the long-tenured British ambassador to the Ottoman Empire in the role of self-appointed eminence grise. A stubborn tendency does persist, however, to look for credit or blame almost exclusively among the European actors.

Temperley and others have emphasized such important issues as:

1. Acute rivalries within the British cabinet
2. The influence of an aroused, Russophobe British public opinion
3. Napoleon III's search for glory and acceptance by the crowned heads of Europe
4. The confusing combination of willfulness and vacillation that characterized Tsar Nicholas.[25]

Yet, most Western scholars on the Crimean War seen unable to consider the possibility of a coherent Ottoman policy not beholden to any outside power. Even less would the usual Western scholarly treatment pay attention to the possibility of Ottoman bureaucratic infighting, but the Ottoman government, just as the British government, was divided between those favoring a firm stand against Russia and those supporting conciliatory diplomacy. Moreover, the Ottoman political elite were so anti-Russian that prudent compromise would have been domestically difficult, if not indeed dangerous. Autocratic empires have their problems with public opinion.

Stratford de Redcliffe *was* influential and he was certainly a diplomat who made his presence felt. Even so, the evidence

[25] "Most dangerous of all was the fact that the Tsar really did not know what he wanted from Turkey or how to get it. Canvassing the various possibilities for action before the Menshikov mission, he ended up determined to settle issues with Turkey, though not sure what the issues were; insistent on getting reparations and guarantees, though unable to define them or assess their worth; ready for strong measures and confident Turkey would collapse under pressure, though convinced the status quo was still desirable and anxious about the final outcome. In short, Nicholas was ready to open up and solve the Eastern Question without believing that a really good solution was available." Paul Schroeder, *Austria, Great Britain, and the Crimean War: The Destruction of the European Concert* (Cornell University Press, 1972).

presented by Temperley remains convincing. While Stratford's very presence in Istanbul made it easy for outsiders to assume that he was pulling strings to produce an unyielding Ottoman policy, the record shows that he worked faithfully to implement his government's policy of seeking a negotiated settlement.

A more plausible interpretation is that the Ottoman government, in the best Eastern Question tradition of the weak manipulating the strong, shrewdly used Stratford for their policy purposes. Stratford has been convincingly shown to have been "a diplomat of determination rather than skill, a lion rather than a fox."[26] There may have been more Ottoman manipulation of British policy than the contrary.

Great power mutual misperceptions undeniably set the stage for the Crimean War, but the history of how the powers stumbled into war is not complete without due attention to the role played by the Ottoman Empire. Fourteen years earlier Sultan Mahmud II had gambled by sending Ottoman forces against Muhammad Ali. The result was immediate military disaster but ultimate political victory. In 1853 the Ottoman Empire had brighter prospects of success in choosing to present its adversary and its potential allies with a fait accompli.

THE EASTERN CRISIS, 1875-1878

The three years of turmoil, beginning with the revolts against Ottoman rule in Herzegovina and Bosnia and ending with the Congress of Berlin, would seem to offer an exception to the pattern previously sketched. During these years the great powers realized that regional initiatives set the stage. European statesmen understood that the crisis was triggered by insurrection

---

[26] W. E. Mosse, "The Return of Reschid Pasha; An Incident in the Career of Lord Stratford de Radcliffe," *English Historical Review*, lxviii (1953). See also Lynn M. Case, "A Duel of Giants in Old Stamboul: Stratford versus Thouvenel," *Journal of Modern History*, XXI (1963). Both articles treat incidents of diplomatic maneuvering after the outbreak of the Crimean War, but they are nevertheless useful examples of Stratford's persistent modus operandi.

within the Ottoman Balkans. Moreover, the first European effort to arrange a settlement, the Andrassy Note of December 1875, was not frustrated by great power rivalries. The insurgents in Bosnia and Herzegovina themselves rejected the Andrassy proposal.

The next year—1876—brought a Bulgarian insurrection against Ottoman rule and a harsh response by Ottoman irregulars, the notorioous bashi-bazuks. This provoked, it will be recalled, Gladstone's pamphlet on *The Bulgarian Horrors and the East*. British public attention was not on presumed great power machinations but on the idea that the Ottoman government was the source of all the difficulties. Ironically, such a British reaction took place at a time when actual Russian machinations in the Middle East were clear, indeed much more so than in previous Eastern Question crises. Pan-Slavism had become a significant political force in Russia. The demand that all Slavs still under Ottoman rule be liberated challenged those Russian statesmen who would have preferred a less interventionist foreign policy.

An ardent pan-Slavist, Count Nicholas Ignatiev, was then serving as Russian ambassador to the Porte. If ever there was a would-be master puppeteer, it was Ignatiev. He had become so enmeshed in efforts to manipulate Ottoman policy by working with Sultan Abdul Aziz and his grand vizier, Mahmud Nedim, that the latter was sarcastically referred to by the populace as "Nedimoff." The Russian Ambassador himself was dubbed "Sultan Ignatiev."[27]

Had British public opinion chosen to see a Russian hand behind Middle Eastern events during these months, more evidence—and not just speculation—was at hand. In July 1876 (or two months before Mr. Gladstone's pamphlet) Serbia declared war on the Ottoman Empire. A Russian general, Chernayev, was appointed commander of the Serbian army; hundreds of pan-Slav Russians volunteered for military service with

[27] Roderic H. Davison, *Reform in the Ottoman Empire, 1856-1875*, p. 283.

the Serbs; and some 3 million rubles was raised in Russia for the cause.[28]

British policy and British public opinion did eventually swing violently to the other end of the political spectrum. When in April 1877 Russia declared war on the Ottoman Empire, a period of Anglo-Russian brinksmanship ensued. Three different times from mid-1877 to early 1878 the British fleet was ordered to the Dardanelles, and in April 1878 Disraeli summoned 7,000 British Indian troops to Malta.[29] Henceforth, the issue was not alleged Ottoman misgovernment in the Middle East. It was, instead, as Queen Victoria and Disraeli insisted whether there was to be a British or a Russian supremacy in the world.[30]

The great power confrontation was settled without war in the Congress of Berlin (June-July 1878). There the Ottoman Empire and the lesser powers of the Middle East were given scant attention. It was a great power settlement of great power issues. All the rest, including the hapless Ottoman Empire, were deemed expendable.

The question here is how the Eastern Crisis related to the master puppeteer motif. The crisis illustrates several points of general applicability:

1. What might be labelled the law of great power preemptive bidding prevails. As long as the contending great powers are treating the Middle Eastern crisis with cir-

[28] Shaw and Shaw, *Ottoman Empire and Modern Turkey*, Vol. II, p. 165. M. S. Anderson, *The Eastern Question 1774-1923: a Study in International Relations* (London, 1966).

[29] A totally inadequate military gesture which can, accordingly, best be interpreted as using troops for diplomatic signalling. One might see a similarity with President Carter's 1980 decision to create a rapid deployment force for the Persian Gulf following the Soviet invasion of Afghanistan.

[30] G. D. Clayton, *Britain and the Eastern Question: From Missolonghi to Gallipoli* (University of London Press, 1971), p. 139. A. P. Thorton, "Imperial Frontiers in the Levant, 1870-1900," *For the File on Empire* (London, 1968), p. 231.

cumspection, the politicians and the public of the several great powers concentrate on the Middle Eastern scene itself (e.g. Gladstone's *Bulgarian Horrors*, Russian pan-Slavism). When, however, any great power enters the fray, the rival great power quickly reinterprets the Middle Eastern crisis in great power terms.

2. The proclivity of an outside power to concentrate on regional initiatives, while giving less emphasis to the presumption of outside manipulation, is directly proportional to the importance of domestic public opinion. A Britain concerned about the *Bulgarian Horrors* or a Russia caught up in pan-Slavism will look for "good guys" and "bad guys" in the Middle East itself, just as several different European powers did earlier in support of the Greek war of independence and just as powers were later to divide over Zionism.

3. To the extent that great power foreign ministries act unimpeded by domestic public opinion, attention remains devoted more to the great power balance and less to the regional issues. This would seem to be the case equally in autocratic and democratic political systems. The foreign policy professionals serving in the area (the "old hands" or, in post World War II lingo, the area specialists) present a more area-oriented analysis, but these contributions are usually (a) ignored in halcyon times and (b) shaped in times of crisis to fit assumptions prevailing among the concerned great power's governing elite.

4. In states sensitive to domestic public opinion (and thus especially the democratic states) a difference in perception and interpretation of whether a Middle East crisis is generated from within the area or by an outside manipulator usually results in a hesitant foreign policy. This perhaps seems trivially obvious. The equally important opposite case is not so often considered: When the public and diplomatic professionals *both* see an outside ma-

229

nipulator the resulting foreign policy will be strongly, at times even violently, assertive and confrontational.

THE CONTINUING GAME WITH NEW PLAYERS

Britain emerged from the Eastern Crisis with a deepened suspicion of Russia. Britain also emerged with Cyprus, reluctantly granted by the Sultan in return for a general British commitment to help maintain the integrity of remaining Ottoman territories in Asia. Seemingly at the end of the 1870s, Anglo-Russian rivalry in the Middle East was destined to grow in virulence. In fact, developments already underway would dampen the fires of Anglo-Russian rivalry. As British strategic thinking increasingly concentrated on the Suez Canal, the fate of Constantinople or even the Ottoman Empire itself came to appear less crucial.

Then, after the 1882 occupation of Egypt Britain found its principal rival in the Middle East to be an aggrieved France (which had forfeited the opportunity for joint Anglo-French action against Egypt). Thereafter, British insistence—with considerable truth—that the occupation of Egypt had been unintended matched by a more hypocritical British reluctance to leave Egypt fueled a fierce diplomatic struggle with France that saw the two come to the brink of war in 1898 (the Fashoda Incident). Only with the 1904 Entente Cordiale (yet another division of Middle Eastern territory to settle European accounts—a free hand for France in Morocco and the same for Britain in Egypt) was Anglo-French bitterness in the Middle East eased.

By then Britain had reason to fear the naval and commercial rivalry of a post-Bismarck Germany beginning to claim concessions beyond Europe (which the Iron Chancellor had had the good sense to avoid). With this newly perceived threat came new fears that Germany might assume the role of master puppeteer in the Middle East. The best example of this new-found phobia was the much exaggerated concern about the so-called "Berlin to Baghdad railway."

The first and second Moroccan crises (1905-1906 and 1911) are also relevant in this context as showing the persistent great power double standard in its dealings with the Middle East. It is true that Germany was, indeed, manipulating Morocco for its own purposes. German policy in these two crises was also crudely provocative, but before sympathy is extended toward a France being bullied by Germany, it is well to remember that the arrangement Germany was challenging—for its own imperial purposes, to be sure—was European acquiescence in France's plan to absorb Morocco.

The great power incapacity to see the regional dimension of such crises calls to mind the way in which British statesmen never understood Ottoman disapproval of the opportunistic way in which Britain got control of Cyprus. Seen in this light, the British occupation of Egypt—only four years later—wrecked the possibility of friendly Anglo-Ottoman relations. It would have been more appropriate if Sultan Abdul Hamid, rather than Lord Salisbury had made the statement about backing the wrong horse.

By the beginning of the twentieth century Britain had come to see Germany, not Russia, as the threat to British imperial interests in the Middle East and elsewhere. German economic and political penetration into the area, which only a few years earlier British statesmen had seen as a useful counterweight to Russian or French ambitions, was thenceforth viewed with alarm. The Eastern Question went on. Britain was not unmindful of regional developments, but a certain disposition to see a German hand behind Middle Eastern matters also insinuated itself into British thinking.

For a great power to assume that a rival great power is pulling the Middle Eastern strings is a trait common to both centuries of Eastern Question history. When Anthony Eden cabled Eisenhower on the eve of the 1956 Suez Crisis, "There is no doubt in our minds that Nasser, whether he likes it or

HIS MASTER'S VOICE.

The Kaiser (*to Turkey, reassuringly*). "Leave everything to me. All you've got to do is to explode."
Turkey. "Yes, I quite see that. But where shall *I* be when it's all over?"

16. Outsiders often see the Middle Eastern government
as merely a weapon in the hands of a great power rival.
The reality is not so simple (*Punch*, 1914).

not, is now effectively in Russian hands . . . ,"[31] he was in the
Palmerston tradition. Equally, President Eisenhower, in proposing the Eisenhower Doctrine, said: "Russia's rulers have
long sought to dominate the Middle East. This was true of
the Czars it is true of the Bolsheviks. . . . The reason for Russia's interest in the Middle East is solely that of power poli-

[31] Anthony Eden, *The Suez Crisis of 1956* (reprinted from *Full Circle: The
Memoirs of Anthony Eden* (Boston, Beacon Press Paperback, 1960), p. 135.

232

tics." He showed that a new player could learn the oldest of Eastern Question rules.

II. EASTERN QUESTION SYSTEMIC DURABILITY: AN AGENDA FOR FUTURE RESEARCH

Many other examples of Eastern Question systemic durability spanning the last two centuries could be cited. What follows may be seen as a partial listing of topics intended to show how thinking of modern Middle Eastern international politics as a long-lived, ongoing system can provide much needed clarity.

THE OUTSIDE MANIPULATOR

Middle Eastern readers and "old Middle East hands" were probably surprised that Part III began with a discussion of how great powers tend to attribute Middle Eastern politics to the machinations of other great powers. It is more common to attribute such "devil theories" to Middle Eastern mentality. Middle Easterners *do* link major political developments within the region to the presumed behind-the-scenes actions of a great power. Such a mentality seems to have prevailed ever since the Eastern Question system became established. Interestingly, however, this pervasive Middle Eastern attitude has rarely been studied in a systematic way.

The evidence to document that such an attitude exists, while accessible, has been largely ignored. Much lies tucked away in the breezier memoirs and accounts of old-time Western residents in the area. Much more is to be found in the often ephemeral slogans, tracts, newspapers and speeches of Middle Easterners, past and present. The data which demonstrate this pervasive Middle Eastern attitude are often imprecise or bombastic or fuzzily oracular or demonstrably at variance with the facts. Such data are moreover, often supercilious if not scurrilous. Fastidious historians usually avoid this dubious documentation, preferring the seemingly purer evidence of well-written official dispatches or of well-bound books. Perhaps largely for this reason, neither the present reality nor the historical development of this marked Middle Eastern tendency to depict politics in conspiratorial terms has been adequately studied.

An interesting twentieth-century example of such thinking is the persistent Zionist assumption that Britain was "really" supporting the Palestinian Arabs and trying to abandon its commitment to the Jewish National Home, matched by the equally persistent Arab assumption that Britain "really" remained committed to Zionism throughout the Mandate period in order to keep the Arabs divided and weak. Neither side has found it easy to accept that the British political establishment was divided on the issue, awkwardly searching a way to reconcile the irreconcilable.

A nineteenth-century example: the only satisfactory interpretation explaining Britain's occupation of Egypt is that Gladstone's government let itself be dragged along by events. Moreover, Britain in the first several years after 1882 was more inclined to evacuate Egypt than to remain. Such evidence did not stop several generations of Egyptian scholars and polemicists from finding a long-range British plot to dominate Egypt.

Equally illustrative of this mindset is the way throughout the last two centuries certain statesmen or regimes have been categorized as completely in the clutches of one or another outside power. The Ottoman grand vizier satirized as "Nedimoff" or the Tunisian statesman given the sobriquet "al-Inglizi"[32] have their twentieth-century equivalents.

[32] On "Nedimoff" see above, p. 227. The mid-nineteenth-century Tunisian minister, Hasan al-Murali, was—in the words of the British consul—so strongly pro-British "that he has obtained the sobriquet of 'the Englishman' at the Bey's Court." British Consul Reade in his reporting naively overlooked that the sobriquet had a sting. See L. Carl Brown, *The Tunisia of Ahmad Bey*, 1837-1855 (Princeton University Press, 1974), pp. 251-253.

Of course, many Middle Easterners have been closely associated with one or another of the great powers from the beginnings of the Eastern Question to this day. Not a few have been in the pay of one or another outside power, and several of the more enterprising have been in the pay of more than one outside power. It is equally true that the outside powers have relentlessly sought out individuals or governments to support, overtly and covertly. Even so, Middle Eastern political actors tend to exaggerate both the power and consistency of purpose of the presumed outside manipulator. The myths of the master puppeteer and of the outside manipulator are complementary. Neither Middle Eastern political actors nor outsiders concerned with the Middle East adequately appreciate the power to influence events available to even the weakest players in the Eastern Question game.

THE ARMS NEXUS

Ever since Selim III inaugurated a cautious program of Westernizing the Ottoman army in the 1790s Middle Eastern rulers have bargained, begged, wheedled, and threatened for Western arms and Western military training. For almost two centuries Middle Eastern leaders have assumed that arms and training imported from the West can cure all political ills. This attitude has prevailed whether Middle Eastern leaders have been radical or reactionary, whether the government in question sought to hold together a beleagured establishment or to construct a new, revolutionary polity.

Outside powers have also accepted that arms transfers, with the concomitant battery of military training missions and technical advisers, provide the linchpin for a sound Middle Eastern policy. One of the most important turning points in modern Middle Eastern diplomatic history was an arms deal. This was the so-called Czech-Egyptian (actually Soviet-Egyptian) arms agreement of 1955 which made Nasser the idol of Arab masses. Those discomfited by the Soviet-Egyptian agreement (Israel, the United States, Britain, and France—each for different reasons) then began actions which contributed to the stormy diplomacy of 1955-1956 ending with the Suez War. This arms agreement of 1955 was in the Eastern Question tradition. Nasser had previously taken soundings about obtaining arms from the United States and other Western powers but had been disappointed.

In any case, Egypt's policy aims did not accord with those of the West. The latter sought to maintain an informal Western hegemony in the region, barring the Soviet Union. The Egyptian leadership sought to escape this Western security network. Equally, the Western desire to settle the Arab-Israeli confrontation and turn the attention of the Middle Eastern states toward joint defense against the Soviet Union totally reversed Egyptian strategic priorities.

Over a century earlier, Ottoman Sultan Mahmud II faced a not dissimilar situation. Seeking arms and military training in the 1830s, Mahmud II could hardly turn to France, which was closely tied to the sultan's most dangerous enemy, Muhammad Ali. Britain, as France's major rival, was more acceptable, although British philhellenism of the previous decade was bitterly remembered. Arrangements were worked out between Britain and the Ottoman Empire in the years 1835-1838, but in implementation they amounted to very little.

It was against this background that the Ottomans turned to Prussia, and among the Prussian officers sent on this early military advisory mission was a young lieutenant destined to achieve fame as Field-Marshal Helmuth von Moltke. Thus began an Ottoman-German connection in military matters never completely broken thereafter.

From the great power perspective the two cases separated some 120 years in time are quite different. Nasser, by giving this opening to the Soviets, was increasing great power rivalries in the region. He was heating up the cold war. Mahmud II's calling upon Prussia (and also Austria) provided no such radical intensification of great power rivalries. From the Middle Eastern perspective the two cases are similar. Both Nasser and Mahmud II were attempting to hedge their bets, to play the game of divide-that-ye-may-not-be-ruled. To Nasser offering the Soviet Union a larger role in the Middle East was not destabilizing, as the West maintained. An enhanced Soviet position in the Middle East would partially offset the Western capacity to work its will. Mahmud II, in a different time and facing different circumstances, was attempting to achieve essentially the same result.

While Mahmud II was negotiating arms and military aid arrangements with several different European powers, Ahmad Bey of Tunisia was hesitating between accepting a British or French military mission. A British colonel, responding to an imprecise Tunisian invitation, actually arrived in Tunis in 1838. Both the colonel and the British consul in Tunis saw this as the beginning of a British-led military training mission. Ahmad Bey had second thoughts and adopted the Eastern Question tactic of the weak regional ruler facing great power pressure. He stalled. After sixteen months the British colonel gave up in disgust and left Tunis. A year later Ahmad Bey had worked out an agreement with France for a military advisory mission.

Why did Ahmad Bey let military ties with Britain wither away and then seek such ties with France, who invaded neighboring Algeria in 1830? Part of the answer may have been Ahmad Bey's infatuation with the country that produced Napoleon, but surely the decisive difference was Tunisian awareness of great power balances. Britain was supporting the central Ottoman Empire, which, having restored direct administration over Tripolitania in 1835, seemed intent on doing the same in Tunisia. France, even though a dangerously close great power neighbor following the French conquest of Algeria, was eager to maintain Tunisia's de facto independence.

The tightrope act of attending to military modernization while paying due obeisance to great power considerations was exemplified in the period of Young Turk rule just before the First World War. In 1913 a German military mission under General Liman von Sanders was appointed to modernize the

Ottoman army, but this move toward Germany was matched by a British naval mission under Admiral Limpus to modernize the Ottoman navy.

Recent Egyptian history offers another example of Eastern Question arms diplomacy. In July 1972 President Sadat asked for the withdrawal of the huge Soviet military mission. This was Sadat's gambit in a strategy to cut Egypt's dependence on the Soviet Union while luring the United States into playing a mediating role in a possible Arab-Israeli settlement, a strategy that began to bear fruit only after the October 1973 war.

Sadat was able to make this move without fear of Egyptian domestic reaction largely because the Egyptian military and political establishment had come to resent the Soviet presence. This evokes another theme as old as the first Western military mission to the Middle East. The Middle Eastern political leadership may accept as an article of faith the need for alien military technology but they soon bristle at the sight, day after day, of alien military advisers. Rarely have the alien military advisers themselves been able to establish good working relations with those whom they have been sent to train. The complaints that made their way into the memoirs of young Lieutenant von Moltke and the shrill criticism filling the archives of the French military mission to Tunisia have a strikingly contemporary ring.[33] The staff of von Sanders and Admiral Limpus felt, it seems, the same way, and one may confidently speculate that the views of the Soviet military mission hardly differed.

One might counter that the British-led Arab Legion (until

---

[33] Moltke wrote: "The colonels gave us precedence, the officers were still tolerably polite, but the ordinary man would not present arms to us, and the women and children from time to time followed us with curses. The soldier obeyed but did not salute." Cited in Lewis, *Emergence of Modern Turkey*, p. 81. One Captain Daumas of the French military mission to Tunisia wrote with acerbity: "Without doubt these young men are adroit like monkeys. They are satisfied to imitate me the way that animal might, and they do not try to grasp either the plan or the purpose of all these exercises." Cited in Brown, *Tunisia of Ahmad Bey*, p. 271.

the dismissal of Glubb Pasha in 1956) was an effective fighting force, with good relations between the few British officers, on the one hand, and the Arab officers and men, on the other. This was not, however, a foreign military advisory group obliged to work outside the indigenous chain of command. The foreign advisor is expected to produce changes that can be implemented only by the command structure. The foreign advisor who gives his advice and then shrugs his shoulder in indifference as to whether the advice is implemented achieves little, but the foreign advisor who "goes to the top" to get things done provokes the kind of antipathy all foreign military advisory missions have faced.

Given these inescapable structural difficulties it is amazing that great powers have continued to rely so heavily on such missions. The triumph perhaps of hope and bureaucratic inertia over realism and historical experience? Finally, the sheer volume of Middle Eastern commitment to arms transfer and building imposing military machines stands out as a persistent theme since the earliest days of the Eastern Question. To attribute the enormous military expenditures in today's Middle East[34] to uniquely twentieth-century developments, such as the vast oil wealth in the Middle East or the long-standing Arab-Israeli confrontation, is only partially correct. More than any other single factor it was military expenditures that pushed nineteenth-century Egypt, Tunisia, and the Ottoman Empire into state bankruptcy. The other side of the coin is that the occasional present-day Western critics of their own govern-

---

[34] A tabulation of defense expenditure as a percentage of a country's gross national produce (GNP) for the years 1978-1979 revealed that at least six of the top ten defense spenders in the entire world were Middle Eastern states. Israel led the list spending 31.1 percent of total GNP in 1979. Other Middle Eastern states included Syria (22.1 percent), Saudi Arabia (15 percent), and Iraq (10 percent). Iran in the last year of the Shah's rule spent 10.9 percent (1978). These figures are taken from the International Institute for Strategic Studies, *The Military Balance*, for the years 1978 and 1979. Slightly different military expenditure estimates are found in *World Military Expenditures and Arms Transfers, 1970-1979*, published by the U.S. Arms Control and Disarmament Agency.

ments for engaging in these arms transfers have had no more impact on getting these arms transfers stopped or slowed down than their nineteenth-century predecessors.

The fateful arms link between the Middle East and the West since the beginning of the Eastern Question represents a compelling example of systemic continuity that awaits its author. Many writers have called attention to the nineteenth-century record or to that of the twentieth century, but few have stressed the continuity. Many have deplored the tendency of Middle Eastern rulers to clutch at ambitious arms policies as a way of resolving all problems, and many have scored the Western tendency to send increasing numbers of arms and military technicians to the area, but few have noted the interrelatedness of these two tendencies. From the beginning of the Eastern Question to this day critics have scoffed at the incapacity of the host military institutions to absorb Western military technology. Critics attacking the Western penchant for building a Middle Eastern foreign policy on arms transfers and military advisory missions have been around for just as long. What seems to be lacking is an appreciation of the way in which it all fits together.

THE ARAB-ISRAELI CONFRONTATION IN THE EASTERN QUESTION PERSPECTIVE

The Arab-Israeli confrontation is a problem about which we have heard so much for so long that completely new thinking becomes difficult. Let us, however, try to look afresh at this issue that has bedeviled the world since 1948.

The four Arab-Israeli wars—of 1948, 1956, 1967, and 1973—all ended quickly. Only the first was a matter of months, and even that was broken up by intervening cease-fires. The other three were all less than a month with the shortest being the 1967 Six Day War. All were stopped by international diplomatic intervention. Moreover, the parties themselves based their military strategy on assumptions concerning not whether but when outside intervention would occur. In all four wars

240

the outside intervention proved capable of stopping the shooting, usually rather quickly, but in the period following each of the four wars the same outside intervention could not bring the contending parties to peace. Instead, the fragile instability of cease-fires (intended to be only temporary pending a final settlement) became the norm until broken by yet another spell of fighting.

Why were the wars short? Why, more precisely, were they planned as and expected to be short wars by the parties in conflict? Why was international intervention successful in fostering a cease-fire, but unsuccessful in orchestrating moves from cease-fire to permanent settlement?

The dispute, itself, partakes of many universal themes to be found in human conflict elsewhere—such as two different peoples struggling for control of the same territory—but the Arab-Israeli conflict has its own characteristic pattern which is a natural outgrowth of the Eastern Question system. Indeed, the Arab-Israeli confrontation represents the Eastern Question system in its most developed form.

There is, first, the multilateral nature of the confrontation. Several regional states were directly involved in all of these wars, except for the Suez War, which was between Israel (in collusion with Britain and France) and Egypt. Even the Suez War brought concern and behind-the-scenes maneuvers by other Arab states. Without the enhanced standing Nasser gained from the Suez War, the dramatic events of 1958 (union of Egypt and Syria to form the U.A.R., Lebanese civil war leading to U.S. military intervention, and the overthrow of the Hashimite dynasty in Iraq) might not have occurred.

In all four wars not only were several great powers involved, but their interests only partially overlapped with the goals of the regional powers. There existed two simultaneous confrontational situations—the regional and the international. The two were different but at the same time closely intertwined. It was not that a regional confrontation, by getting out of hand, attracted the great powers. Rather, the regional and great power confrontations developed in close symbiosis.

241

17. Presidents Carter and Sadat and Prime Minister Begin at the signing of the March 1979 Egyptian-Israeli peace treaty (*Wideworld Photos*).

Those involved acted with both the regional and great power dimension in mind.

President Sadat's daring gamble, in cooperation with Asad of Syria, to start a war, the military prospects of which were decidedly bleak in *order to stimulate outside diplomatic intervention* that could be turned to Egypt's advantage stands out as the clearest example of the close links binding together domestic, regional and international concerns.

Nasser's actions on the eve of the June 1967 war can possibly be explained as a faulty reading—based on his experience during the Suez Crisis—of his ability to use great power pressures as a means of frustrating a regional adversary. The Egyptian-Israeli "war of attrition" in 1969-1970 offers the different pattern of a sustained period of low-level military action, not a short war. Nasser feared the domestic and regional loss of standing that would come from accepting the best peace he could get after Israel's overwhelming victory in the 1967 war. The Soviet Union supported his painstaking rebuilding of the Egyptian military, but the realistic prospect of "another round" was years in the future. Nor was it at all sure that Soviet support would ever extend that far. A war of attrition with Israel could exact considerable penalties on the latter (limited but still appreciable casualties for a country whose small population dictated a strategy avoiding extended war or long-term military mobilization). It was the only feasible military strategy available to Egypt for the foreseeable future.

Israel made essentially the same calculation and refused to be sucked into such a war. The "deep penetration raids" were Israel's answer. Nasser's appeal for Soviet military aid, the positive Soviet response, the increased U.S. efforts—in the form of the Rogers initiatives—to keep the regional pot from boiling over all followed in quick succession.

The Sadat strategy since the October 1973 war (actually since the ouster of Soviet military advisers in July 1972) led eventually to another variation on the dominant theme—the Egyptian-Israeli peace treaty of March 1979. Instead of the familiar pattern of wars stopped by outside intervention and effective cease-fires but no progress thereafter toward peace treaties, this time an Egyptian-Israeli peace treaty resulted in March 1979, almost five and one-half years after the war.

Yet, in other ways the maneuvers that led to this first peace treaty between Israel and an Arab state were vintage Eastern Question diplomacy. These included:

1. Sustained efforts at conference diplomacy (Geneva peace talks and the resulting concept of the "Geneva formula")
2. Efforts by politically weak regional actors to disrupt developments going against their perceived interests (such as the major PLO raid into Israel in March 1978)
3. Kaleidoscopic regional responses to Sadat's breaking of Arab ranks by negotiating with Israel (expulsion of Egypt

from the Arab League, bid for Arab leadership on the part of Iraq's Saddam Husayn)
4. Readjustments of regional international alignments, such as the increasing success of the PLO at the UN and with Western Europe
5. Use of fait-accompli steps consistent with tactical virtuosity and zero-sum mentality but possibly contrary to long-term strategic requirements. Examples are of Israel's settlements policy in the occupied territories, the virtual annexation of the Golan Heights in 1981, and the invasion of Lebanon in 1982 (all jeopardizing good relations with Egypt and prospects for negotiated settlement with other Arabs)

Developments leading to Egyptian-Israeli peace show their Eastern Question roots in the use of outside, great power mediation. From shuttle diplomacy to Camp David, the role of the United States and (perhaps even more a factor) the way in which the regional parties used the United States to achieve their aims provides the key to understanding how the Egyptian-Israeli peace treaty was attained.

No better indicator of this outside mediator function—insisted on by the regional powers themselves—can be found than the following: In November 1977 Sadat surprised the Israelis and the world by agreeing to come to Israel, thus starting the process of direct negotiations between Israel and an Arab state. This is what the Israelis had been championing for years as the best way to a peaceful settlement—direct, face-to-face negotiations without cumbersome arrangements for third-party mediation or sponsorship. Yet, within days after Sadat's visit to Israel, Begin flew to Washington to discuss Israeli peace proposals with the American government!

In several other ways the Arab-Israeli confrontation reveals an underlying Eastern Question pattern. From the beginning of Zionism and Arabism both sides have appealed to Western (and, later, world) public opinion. From the beginning the West (and, later, the world) has responded in highly charged emotional terms to the confrontation, just as was the case a century earlier with the Greek War of independence. Thus, Zionist success in getting the UN General Assembly to vote for partition in November 1947 is to be classified—from the Eastern Question perspective—with PLO leader Yasir Arafat's triumphant reception before that same U.N. General Assembly in November 1974. In both cases the regional party appealed successfully to the international forum which responded for several reasons only partially linked to regional issues.

The Arab-Israeli confrontation offers several examples of fait-accompli politics—precipitate action to present the regional opponent(s) and the outside world (both friend and foe) with a new situation which cannot readily be undone. These would include:

1. The Anglo-French-Israeli collusion for the Suez War
2. The Egyptian and Syrian launching of the October 1973 war
3. Israel's pre-emptive strike in June 1967
4. The Egyptian-Soviet "cheating" on placement of missiles following the 1970 cease-fire agreement
5. The PFLP hijackings of that same year which led to the Jordanian crisis
6. The Israeli policy of piecemeal settlement in the Arab territories occupied since the June 1967 war
7. The 1982 Israeli invasion of Lebanon

All of these characteristics illustrative of the Arab-Israeli confrontation have nineteenth-century antecedents. The following might be noted:

1. The Greek War of independence as an example of a regionally weak party using great power interventions to right the balance and achieve its aims
2. Sultan Mahmud II's beginning a disastrous war against Muhammad Ali but nevertheless, by way of great power intervention, coming out the winner

3. Weak regional actors—Druze, Maronites, and Muslim groups—contributing to the two Syrian crises, pitting Egypt against the Ottoman Empire in the 1830s
4. The disturbances in Lebanon during the years 1858-1860, which ended disastrously militarily for the Christians but provoked European intervention, leading to a de facto Lebanese autonomy
5. The synchronic confrontation of great powers and of regional powers in a way that was both different and closely interrelated. Throughout the nineteenth century the great powers were at loggerheads over perceived geopolitical interests—Constantinople, Suez, the Berlin to Baghdad railway. The concurrent regional interests touched on the same issues but for quite different reasons, e.g., an Ottoman Empire seeking support now from Russia and later from Britain against expansionist Muhammad Ali; or a Tunisia pushed into a pro-French stance to fend off Ottoman pressures; an Egyptian ruler, Tawfiq, relying on outside (British) support to put down the local 'Urabi Pasha revolt; Sultan Abdul Hamid falling back on a combination of pan-Islam and closer ties to Germany (comparable to Nasser's later combination of pan-Arabism and closer ties to the Soviet Union).

No issue in modern Middle Eastern history has stimulated more attention than the Arab-Israeli confrontation. It is a unique diplomatic problem. Yet, an important dimension of the Arab-Israeli confrontation is best elucidated by reference to the Eastern Question system. Moreover, with attention drawn to "the game" instead of the players, it is easier to be both more objective and, paradoxical as this might seem, more sympathetic to the actors directly involved.

FROM CONCERT OF EUROPE TO UN

In the time period covered by this book the world has moved from a European-centered great power system (Concert of

Europe) to a global international system (first the League of Nations and then the United Nations). A study of how these two international relations systems influenced the Middle East and were, in turn, influenced by the Middle East would need to consider the points noted below.

Both the Concert of Europe and the United Nations (plus the earlier League of Nations) grew out of forces and ideas not directly connected with the Middle East. Both, however, became intimately involved in the Middle East. The Concert of Europe used the Middle East—longer and more consistently than any other part of the world—as an arena for carefully circumscribed competition and conflict. The several European powers would take positions for or against Middle Eastern forces, according to how they perceived them to affect their interests within the framework of the European balance of power. It was not simply a matter of Europe manipulating the Middle East. Many initiatives and many successful efforts at manipulation came from weaker parties within the Middle East. Even so, the European-imposed system had three major principles that penalized the Middle East:

1. Conflict and competition was to be contained in the Middle East and not permitted to spread to Europe (the Crimean War being the great example of a breakdown in the system)
2. The ultimate settlement of any specific competition or conflict was to be achieved through collective European consultation—the nineteenth-century conference or congress pattern
3. Any disturbance of the European balance of power was to be righted by appropriate compensations. The Middle East was obliged to provide the compensations.

The League of Nations represented to some extent a repudiation of the Concert system. The notion of an exclusively European club was rejected. So, too, under Woodrow Wilson's influence was the very idea of the balance of power as a regulating mechanism. On the other hand, the mandates system was an adaptation of the older idea of European control and tutelage. Although the nineteenth-century view of compensation was not explicitly recognized, the mandated territories were divided up among the European victors very much in accordance with earlier Eurocentric concepts of balance and bargaining. Moreover, the Permanent Mandates Commission of the League may be seen as an echo of the earlier Concert system with its provisions for group review and consensus on these territorial arrangements beyond Europe.

The United Nations brought an even more decided break with Eurocentrism. Two of the five permanent members of the Security Council—the United States and China—were non-European powers, and rotating representation on the Security Council for other UN members from all over the world was accepted. The UN was not, however, envisaged as a world parliament or even less a world government. The creation of a strong Security Council in which the five permanent members had a veto power institutionalized great power control. The UN did evolve into a genuinely world-wide organization in other ways (unlike the League), a development stimulated by the interaction of superpower competition and rising Third World consciousness. This resulted in greater power, or at least greater diplomatic visibility, for the General Assembly, UNESCO, the secretariat-general, and other UN agencies at the expense of the Security Council.

The situation as it exists today is complicated, unsettled and easily misunderstood. Those critics—usually from the Third World—who complain that the great powers and even more the superpowers really control international politics are only half correct at best. Those latter-day Lord Salisburys who disdainfully regard the small powers at the UN as so many pesky mosquitoes distracting the important powers from their task of managing world affairs also misperceive the way the system is developing.

Such a broad subject goes beyond the scope of this book, but these pages have indicated that the Middle East has been, of all non-Western regions, the most important testing ground in the historical evolution of international politics from the Concert of Europe to the United Nations. The intimate ties between the Concert of Europe and the Eastern Question system figured prominently in Part One of this book.

As for the League of Nations, it was not so powerful as the earlier Concert or the later UN. It did not last so long as either. Institutionalization of the League was considerably more developed than that of the Concert (which had no staff and no charter, but did have fairly well-elaborated rules implicitly accepted by its members), but less so than the UN. The League represented, as an international relations system, an important but short transitional phase, perhaps as significant in its failures as its successes.

These several limitations duly noted, the Middle Eastern part in the League's brief history was considerable. The evolution of the mandates system itself was significantly shaped by the tortuous negotiations over the fate of the Fertile Crescent. Britain's championing of Sharif Husayn and his sons gave this leading imperial power a vested interest in the newly emerging principle of great power stewardship instead of old-fashioned imperialist colony collecting. This, as was shown in Part Two, both mollified liberal sentiment at home and worked to undercut French claims in the region.

The King-Crane Commission of 1919—that very Wilsonian gesture which, when contrasted with the style of a Metternich or Castlereagh, shows how much international diplomacy was changing—also respresented a linkage between the rules of great power diplomacy and the Middle East. Simply stated, the King-Crane Commission was brought into existence as follows: Britain and France could not agree on the terms for dividing up the Fertile Crescent. Wilson proposed an Allied commission to determine the wishes of the people. Neither Britain nor France could afford to reject this proposal out of hand. That would have been too brazen, leaving the implication that the people of the Fertile Crescent had no standing in the case. Instead, Britain and France accepted the idea but kept finding excuses for delaying implementation.

249

Finally, an exclusively American commission briefly toured the area and found—to no one's surprise—that political spokesmen of the Fertile Crescent preferred independence, would accept an American mandate as second best, a British mandate after that but definitely not French control. They also strongly opposed the idea of a Jewish national home in Palestine. The recommendations of the Commission were ignored in the final settlement, but like the mandate system itself the King-Crane Commission represented another step toward recognizing the self-determination of peoples as a guiding principle of international diplomacy (however difficult that might be to implement as nineteenth-century Eastern Question history so clearly demonstrated).[35]

The Permanent Mandates Commission of the League did not really impede operations of the mandatory powers either in the Middle East or elsewhere. It should hardly have been expected that it would, given the membership of that body— representatives from European states that also had important imperial holdings. The systemic continuity with earlier Eastern Question history is, nevertheless, evident. Each mandatory power had to report annually to the Commission, justifying actions taken to representatives who claimed the right to defend an agreed-upon international relations system.

A case in point was the action of the Permanent Mandates Commission in raising questions about minority rights in Iraq before agreeing to the termination of the mandate there, questions that appeared to have been appropriate in the light of the later 1933 action of the Iraqi army against the Assyrian Christian minority in northern Iraq (the Assyrian massacres).[36]

[35] The most thorough work on the Commission is Harry N. Howard, *The King-Crane Commission: An American Inquiry Into the Middle East* (Beirut, 1963).

[36] The Assyrians (Nestorian Christians) had fled from Turkey and Iran during the First World War and were settled by the British in Northern Iraq, where many of their young men served as auxiliaries in the British military, assignments hardly calculated to endear them to the Iraqis. The general schol-

One of the last acts of the dying League's Permanent Mandates Commission was to withhold its approval of Britain's 1939 White Paper, which, if implemented, would have halted Jewish immigration after five years and left a permanent Jewish minority in an ultimately independent Palestine.

The Palestine problem, of considerable importance to the League of Nations, has dominated United Nations activities in the Middle East. Indeed, the Middle East—especially Palestine—has stimulated more different kinds of UN action than any other part of the world. Many UN activities now taken for granted as part of the international organization's modus operandi began in the Middle East.

The list of such arrangements intertwining the UN with Middle Eastern diplomatic problems begins with the United Nations Special Committee on Palestine (UNSCOP) created in May 1947, whose majority report proposing the partition of Palestine into separate Jewish and Arab states was approved by the General Assembly in November of that year.

In the 34 years since 1947, the UN has created and used (in many cases used several times in response to different crises) the following assortment of approaches to Middle Eastern problems:

1. Cease-fire resolutions
2. Mediation services
3. Multinational military truce supervision
4. Refugee administration
5. Hearing and judging complaints on truce and related violations
6. Initiating general guidelines for settlement of conflicts
7. Use of permanent or ad hoc UN officials to facilitate acceptance by Middle Eastern antagonists of UN guide-

---

arly consensus that whatever the provocations from the Assyrian side might have been, the action of the Iraqi army was inexcusable has been challenged by Khaldun S. Husri in a carefully documented article "The Assyrian Affair of 1933," *International Journal of Middle Eastern Studies*, Part I in Vol. 2 (April 1974), and Part II in Vol. 3 (June 1974).

lines for settlement (from Ralph Bunche to Gunnar Jar-
ring, plus—since at least the term of Dag Hammar-
skjöld—a significant role for the UN secretary general
himself).

A thorough account of these various UN activities in or
concerned with the Middle East would provide a useful study,
especially if approached from the perspective of the earlier
League and Concert of Europe experience.[37]
No, these structural changes from the time of the Concert
of Europe to the present age of the UN have not changed the
basic facts of world politics. The superpowers still have a veto,
explicit in the Security Council, implicit in world affairs, whether
within the UN framework or not. An examination of the UN,
in itself, would no more adequately explain Eastern Question
international relations since 1945 than exclusive attention to
the working of the Concert of Europe would make sense of
the Eastern Question throughout the nineteenth century.
  Even so, given the concern throughout this book with systems, it seems appropriate to conclude Part Three with the
suggestion that among the benefits of studying the Eastern
Question as an international relations system may be the insights such an approach offers to the emergence of the UN as
an even larger international relations system.

[37] The impressive study by Rosalyn Higgins, *United Nations Peacekeeping
1946-1967: Documents and Commentary* (3 vols., Oxford University Press,
1969, 1970, and 1980), devotes one entire volume to UN activities concerned with the Middle East. Fred J. Khouri, *The Arab-Israeli Dilemma* (Second Edition, Syracuse University Press, 1976), concentrates on the UN dimension of the subject.

CONCLUSION

CONCLUSION

THIS book has suggested one way of interpreting international politics in the Middle East. There are other ways as well. One approach would be to concentrate on the fragility of most Middle Eastern states. The limited political institutionalization as well as the limited political legitimacy of all but a few Middle Eastern states stand out as significant characteristics. A lack of consensus on the very purpose and scope of politics is widespread. Today, the Middle East—seemingly even more than other parts of the world—offers a discordant struggle between romantic religio-political nostalgia and vaguely defined but strongly felt aspirations for revolutionary change.

The disjunctive results of the Middle Eastern oil boom is another important theme. Seldom in history has such a rapid reversal of economic fortunes taken place so quickly. Most Middle Eastern oil resources are located in sparsely inhabited countries which, until the discovery of oil, were the most underdeveloped parts of the Middle East itself.

A century ago Cairo and Istanbul represented cultural worlds farther removed from, say, Riyadh or Abu Dhabi than New York or London ever were from Dodge City or the Australian outback. This raises questions of how much change can such societies absorb in so short a time.

Leaving aside the more qualitative aspects of change—always difficult to measure—a few statistics tell the story of disjunctive change:[1] Saudi Arabia has only some 10 inhabitants per square mile, and that is accepting a very generous estimate of total Saudi population. In Egypt's Nile valley, by contrast,

---

[1] All statistics cited in this conclusion are conservative estimates drawn from several sources, especially the annual publications of *The Military Balance*, by the International Institute of Strategic Studies, and *World Military Expenditures and Arms Transfers, 1970-1979*, by the U.S. Arms Control and Disarmament Agency.

there are roughly 3,000 inhabitants per square mile. Another striking contrast; the per capita GNP of Egypt is approximately $400 per year, that of Saudi Arabia about $7,600. The figures go even higher for other oil-rich, thinly populated states: $18,600 in Kuwait, $19,800 in the United Arab Emirates. Over 90 percent of the total Arab oil revenues go to Arab states whose combined populations make up less than 10 percent of the total Arab world.

Today, the Arabian peninsula exerts an influence in the Middle East and in the world that would have been unimaginable before the First World War and not seriously considered likely even after the Second World War. This surprising new power also brings a precarious vulnerability. The black gold of the Arabian peninsula insures that these states will not be permitted—by either the region or the outside world—to proceed at their own chosen pace. A dangerous imbalance between economic strength and politico-military weakness faces these rudimentarily institutionalized, thinly populated oil states.

The more populous and politically stronger oil-producing Middle Eastern states—such as Iraq and Algeria—have a better chance of controlling their destinies, but they, too, are exposed because of their oil wealth to a combination of threats and temptations. Unevenly distributed Middle Eastern oil wealth at the time of a world energy crisis has clearly given Middle Eastern politics a distinctive cachet.

Yet another way to gauge international politics in the Middle East would be as follows: The Middle East boasts no great powers. There has not been a great power in the Middle East since the Ottoman Empire became the sick man of Europe. The Middle East, as defined in this book, is a region with only two mid-sized states—Egypt and Turkey—some dozen small states ranging in population from over 2 million to almost 20 million and then a number of mini-states such as the United Arab Emirates (860,000) and Qatar (200,000). With a total population of roughly 180 million, the Middle East is considerably less populous than Black Africa or South America, dramatically less than the Indian subcontinent or China.

CONCLUSION

Yet, this region of the Middle East—with no great powers among its many states, having only a modest population and quite limited natural resources (save oil)—provided the arena less than a decade ago for the second largest tank battle in world history. This was the conflict in the Sinai Desert between Egypt and Israel during the October 1973 War.[2]

Most Middle Eastern states spend enormous sums on armaments. Israel devotes over 30 percent of its gross national product to defense expenditures, Syria over 20 percent, and Iraq over 10 percent. Saudi Arabia in 1980 is estimated to have spent over $2,500 per person on defense in that single year. One Middle Eastern state—Israel—already possesses a nuclear capacity. The area recently witnessed the world's first preemptive strike against an enemy's nuclear potential. This was the Israeli air attack destroying the Iraqi nuclear facility at Baghdad on 7 June 1981.

The militarization of the Middle East as measured by expenditures, sophistication of military hardware, numbers in the armed forces, and influence of military establishments on the body politic can only be described as awesome. This is a major theme of Middle Eastern politics that cries out for attention.

* * *

Clearly, this book offers only one way of interpreting international politics in the modern Middle East. The picture is not complete without attention to these other themes—fragile states and a confusion of political ideologies, the disjunctive impact of Middle Eastern oil wealth, and the grotesque quest for military might by so many states of the region.

Yet, the idea of a continuing Eastern Question system does perhaps provide the best framework for studying international politics in the Middle East. The many other significant char-

[2] The first being between the Nazis and the Soviets during the Second World War.

257

acteristics of modern Middle Eastern political life can be linked to the Eastern Question system. In most cases, such characteristics can be shown to have grown naturally out of earlier Eastern Question experience. Even new developments fit the Eastern Question pattern.

The fragility of Middle Eastern states and the confusion of political ideologies, for example, are well explained in Eastern Question terms. A hitherto self-sufficient cultural area—that of the Ottoman political world which, in its turn, built on Western Asian imperial experience going back to earliest times— began to come apart some two centuries ago under the impact of the West. Ever since, efforts to pick up the pieces and fit them into a new pattern have been made by different regional political figures, all such efforts being matched by sustained outside attempts to control developments.

The present Middle Eastern armaments mania is unprecedented in scale, but the deadly fit between outside powers providing arms and advisers while trying to line up Middle Eastern states in great power strategic games is as old as the Eastern Question. So, too, is the compulsive—even if often self-destructive—penchant of Middle Eastern political figures for playing the armaments game.

Nothing in the Middle Eastern past quite matches the way in which oil has disrupted the region while making it of crucial interest to the rest of the world, but even the story of Middle Eastern oil follows well-worn Eastern Question trails. Ever since the beginning of the Eastern Question the great powers have acted on the assumption that the Middle East possesses a strategic interest appreciably greater than other regions.

Today's belief that the industrial nations must have uninterrupted access to Middle Eastern oil is in the tradition of British (and Western) thinking concerning the Suez Canal and protecting the lifeline to India or Russian (and Western) assumptions about the importance of Istanbul and the Straits.

Today's historians see a consistent pattern of "worst case" thinking on the part of nineteenth-century European statesmen concerned with the Straits, Suez, and related Middle Eastern problems. Will later historians arrive at similar appraisals concerning the perceived strategic (not economic but strategic) importance of Middle Eastern oil? Does one great power or great power bloc have plans to seize the Middle East and deny Middle Eastern oil to others? The questions themselves indicate the continuing structural similarity of Middle Eastern international politics even into this age of an oil rich Middle East facing an energy starved world.

By viewing other issues—whether the Middle Eastern arms race, oil and the Middle East, the many problems of political development, the search for acceptable political ideologies, or the Arab-Israeli confrontation—within the framework of the Eastern Question system one can better appreciate how deeply rooted they are in the Middle Eastern political soil.

✳ ✳ ✳

The scope (and thus also the limits) of the Eastern Question system as an organizing and explanatory device has been presented in the metaphor of games. Giving attention to the game and its rules—as in this book—can perhaps usefully complement the tendency in most writing on the subject to concentrate on the players and the immediate contest, whether it be diplomatic history writing of past crises or accounts of the present diplomatic scene. Study of the game and its rules does not, however, eliminate the need carefully to examine the performance of individual players at any particular time.

This suggests a useful short agenda for summing up in these final pages. First, accepting that the rules of the Eastern Question game may have changed over the last two centuries we must ask in what ways. Even more important, if significant changes of rules have occurred often, then the utility of the games metaphor in explaining Middle Eastern international politics is called into question. This book has argued that Eastern Question rules changes have been minimal, that the Eastern Question system does provide an especially stable constant factor around which many variables can be organized. This thesis has been presented in different ways and from different perspectives throughout the book. One last overview is in order.

Second, only with a good working knowledge of the nature of the game can one evaluate the performance of present-day players. Of course, to know the game is not to predict the outcome of future contests. The intervention of an unexpected event, the brilliant performance of one player, the ineptitude of another can tilt the balance of forces. Even so, knowledge of the game and of past performances removes much of the guesswork. One is able to estimate the strategies likely to be used. One knows which moves are likely to fail and which have a good chance of success. Within these limits a few concluding remarks are offered on current Middle Eastern international politics in the light of the Eastern Question.

CHANGES IN THE RULES OF
THE EASTERN QUESTION GAME?

Part One demonstrated that instead of a single, beleaguered Middle Eastern state facing a number of aggressive European powers throughout the nineteenth century there was a multiplicity of political units on the Middle Eastern side as well. Since the end of the Ottoman Empire the multiplicity of Middle Eastern political units has been obvious. Here, then, is a similarity of rules and characteristics binding together the nineteenth- and twentieth-century Eastern Question experience—the multiplicity of Middle Eastern political units. As for the players in that political game, rather more change is to be noted. The nineteenth-century political units were classified in Part One as established states (including states in all but name—those possessing their own bureaucracies and armies) and would-be states. The former included, first and most important, the central Ottoman Empire plus Egypt, Tunisia, and as a marginal case Lebanon after 1860. The latter were divided into warlords, national liberation movements and religio-political movements.

This century offers many more Middle Eastern states. Warlordism, on the other hand, no longer exists as a significant political phenomenon. Ali Pasha of Janina or Jazzar Pasha in Syria-Palestine have no real equivalents in this century. States have become so much more centralized that the challenge of the periphery against the center has become unlikely. Even the ruling elites that lack effective political legitimacy are more likely to be challenged, and often toppled, by other centralized groups (especially the military).

The nature of religio-political movements has changed as well from the nineteenth to the twentieth century. Again, the increase of centralizing state power makes the difference. The more important religio-political movements of the nineteenth century (Wahhabiyya, Sudanese Mahdiyya, and Sanusiyya) organized the countryside either to pose an explicit threat to the urban-based state (Wahhabiyya and Mahdiyya) or to assert a hinterland autonomy vis-à-vis central government (Sanusiyya).

Religio-political movements in this century not only have moved to the cities (e.g., the Salafiyya) but also appeared for a time to be in the process of becoming neutralized by secularizing forces. The Ataturk experience provided the most dramatic case, but tendencies in the same direction, even if falling well short of Ataturk's bold initiatives, could be witnessed in most Middle Eastern states.

Yet, as early as 1928, with the founding in Egypt of the Muslim Brethren, the Middle East began to witness the political potential of Muslim religio-political movements based in the cities, using modern methods of organization and grafting alien, modern political ideas to fundamentalist, anti-establishment programs. In the last few years the importance of such Muslim fundamentalist religio-political groups has increased. So, too, has the nervous concern of most Middle Eastern governments.

The extent to which religious movements have made in-

261

roads on the secular state (and not the reverse, as almost all observers were predicting roughly a generation ago) can be seen in all Middle Eastern religious communities. The Muslim Brethren and other religio-political fundamentalists in Egypt and Syria, the fundamentalist Gush Emunim in Israel, Maronite efforts to create a Christian Zion in Lebanon, the upsurge of Shiʻi consciousness and political activity in that same country, and the religious-reactionary National Salvation Party in Turkey are examples.

Given these many contradictory changes, students of modern Middle Eastern history now ask if the long-term trend in the area is toward increased secularism or increased use of religion as basis for political organization. Both possibilities have one characteristic in common: they have emerged in an age of increased political centralization.

Throughout this century the remaining category—national liberation movements—became even more significant, not just domestically but in international politics as well, than in the nineteenth century. In addition to many nationalist movements that led the decolonization struggle (such as the Algerian FLN), there have been others, some now crushed, others dormant, some having achieved their goals, others still very much in the fight with the outcome undecided. A summary rollcall reveals the variety—the PLO, the Kurdish struggles against Iraq, the successful overthrow of the imamate in Yemen, the abortive Southern Sudanese struggle against the government of Khartoum, the overthrow of monarchies in Egypt (1952), Iraq (1958), and Libya (1969), and the radical guerrilla movements in Southern Arabia. These different movements also obey the modern logic of state-building and political centralization.

Tribes, warlords, religio-political prophets crying in the wilderness have largely given way to centralizing organizers of political power.[3] The resulting Middle Eastern political life

[3] National liberation movements, such as the FLN or the PLO, may rely on the sanctuary provided by the hinterland in resisting establishment governments, but political success for such movements comes only by their or-

has given the Eastern Question system greater consistency. As noted in Part One, the efforts of a warlord or a hinterland religio-political leader could fade away in the next generation, leaving hardly a trace. Centrally organized state systems are not so easily removed from the scene. Even if subjected to numerous coups, these states usually remain in existence and continue to figure in the ongoing Eastern Question game.

Has there perhaps been a major change in the nature and number of great power players in the Eastern Question game from the nineteenth to the twentieth centuries? In some ways it would appear that great power alignments in the Middle East have shifted from multilateralism (the Concert of Europe) to bilateralism (polarized around the two superpowers, the U.S. and the U.S.S.R.). It is worth noting that the very term—the great powers—is hardly used today except in describing earlier periods, and the term—superpower—was not even coined until after the Second World War.

Although much evidence can be marshalled to suggest a shift toward superpower bilateralism in the Middle East, the counterargument for continued multilateralism seems more nearly correct. It was shown, for example, in Part One that the Eastern Question system, even in the period before the First World War, often had two principal European antagonists, with the other European powers taking less assertive positions. A certain clustering around the two front runners is unexceptional within the framework of Eastern Question multilateralism.

Part Two traced the unsuccessful efforts of a single outside power (Britain or the United States or the Soviet Union) to establish hegemony in the Middle East, and it was shown that such an ambitious goal has to date eluded all powers. The hegemonic effort itself provoked regional efforts to bring in counterbalancing outside powers. Part Two concentrated on reactions from within the region to hegemonic drives, but it

---

ganizing support in what has come to be called the modern sector, that is the urban dominated core.

263

can be shown that outside responses to such Middle Eastern sirens have never been lacking.

Part Two also mentioned the considerable multilateral jockeying for position among outside powers interested in the Middle East during the period from roughly 1930 until the mid-fifties. If great power multilateralism has given way to superpower bilateralism in the Middle East, then it has done so only in the last quarter century. What, then, about this last quarter century?

British and French influence seemed unlikely to be restored after Suez, and throughout the sixties British governments even carried out the withdrawal from Britain's last Middle Eastern bastions, in the Persian Gulf and southern Arabia. The Soviets and Americans moved in to fill the void. The 1955 Soviet-Egyptian arms deal and the 1957 Eisenhower Doctrine—what might be called the opening and closing curtains on the Suez crisis—epitomized the beginning of a new era.

Seemingly, superpower bilateralism had pushed multilateral great power politics aside in the Middle East, but a review of earlier Eastern Question history reveals apparent bipolarizing moves later reversed by the tenacious durability of structural multilateralism (Table I in Part One and Table V in Part Two presented these cycles). Does the period since 1956 of apparent superpower bilateralism show signs of a muted great power multilateralism? France offers an interesting case study. The French secret agreement with Israel to take action against Nasser set in motion the chain of events leading to the Suez Crisis.

Then, a few years later de Gaulle's policy of mending fences with the Arab world (probably in germ from the time he came to power, but put into operation following Algerian independence in 1962) caused France to move away from Israel. French actions in the period beginning before the outbreak of the June 1967 war and continuing to this day also challenged the would-be monolithic Western policy toward the Middle East led by the United States. De Gaulle's independent policies have been continued by his successors.[4]

[4] DeGaulle consistently sought to reverse superpower bilateralism globally

Since the Israeli invasion of Lebanon in June 1982, French diplomatic initiatives, in association with Egypt, have been prominent. Although seemingly overshadowed at the time by the imposing American role, the French démarche may eventually prove to have been an important development. The participation of French (and Italian) troops along with those from the United States in the policing of Beirut is also noteworthy.

In the past few years the European Economic Community has been showing a will to stake out a position on the Arab-Israeli issue independent of Washington and more favorably disposed to the Palestinians. On the same Arab-Israeli issue, the mediating role of smaller outside powers such as Austria and Rumania should be recorded. Yugoslavia now seems to be taking a less prominent position in Middle Eastern affairs than during the long period of Tito's rule, but that earlier history stands as a reminder that middle-sized outside states did have influence even in the heyday of the Cold War.

Outside powers beyond the traditional Eastern Question limits of Europe (plus, later, North America) have demonstrated a newly awakened interest in the Middle East since 1956, the beginning of presumed superpower dominance. China's modest challenge to the Soviets in various countries of the Middle East should be noted for the record. India's relative success in blunting Pakistan's appeal for Arab support on the basis of Islamic solidarity is an often overlooked aspect of Middle Eastern international politics that has existed since the partition of the Indian subcontinent in 1947. Nehru's strong support for Nasser during the Suez crisis represented a high point of this sustained Indian policy.

In the same way, the growing rapproachement between Pakistan and Saudi Arabia is best evaluated in terms of the long-standing Indo-Pakistan bidding for Arab support. The Indian-Pakistani rivalry in the Middle East offers an interesting example of old-style Eastern Question politics picked up by new players.

---

and not just in the Middle East. It is, however, relevant that he found opportunities for advancing such aims in the Middle East.

As the most dramatically successful new economic power on the world stage, Japan has thus far played a remarkably effaced political role in the Middle East. This policy orientation is in line with Japan's generally restrained foreign policy throughout the world. Looking ahead, however, one can predict an increasing Japanese role in Middle Eastern politics. Japan's critical need for Middle Eastern oil and the oil-rich Arab states' eagerness for a rapid infusion of high technology make for a blending of interests that neither side is likely to ignore. Japan's position in the Middle East today can be roughly compared to that of the United States in the twenties and thirties—a strong and growing economic role and minimal political aims combining to make the Japanese acceptable to virtually all Middle Eastern political groups.

Most important of all as a counter to presumed superpower dominance of the Middle East during the last quarter century has been the striking role of Middle Easterners themselves on the world scene. Such figures as Nasser, Ben Bella, Yasser Arafat, Sadat, King Husayn, King Faisal, and Qaddafi, plus many Israelis (Ben Gurion, Abba Eban, Moshe Dayan, Golda Meir, and Begin) have left their mark on international history since c.1956. It is not simply that the Middle East produces charismatic political figures in abundance. Global recognition of so many Middle Easterners (many having had imposing symbolic value in many parts of the world) demonstrates an outside interest in the Middle East that goes well beyond the great powers to embrace the remoter corners of the Third World. Nor should the thoroughly multilateral dimension of UN activities in the Middle East (briefly noted in Part Three) be overlooked.

The period 1956-1981 brought a move toward superpower bilateralism, but this now seems to have peaked and is in process of receding to the more normal pattern of multilateralism. Even this period witnessed more multilateral maneuverings by outside powers than is usually assumed.

This misreading of recent Middle Eastern international politics (assuming the above argument is accepted) is not unprecedented. Great powers operating in the Middle East do occasionally fall victim to bilateral myopia. In 1878, at the peak of the Eastern Crisis, Queen Victoria and her prime minister, Lord Beaconsfield, were in agreement that the true issue was whether Britain or Russia should be supreme in the world. That seems whimsically wrong-headed now. A century from now the present bilateral squaring off of the superpowers in the Middle East may appear equally so.

One mutation in the working of the Eastern Question system over the past two centuries is clear: the principal focal points of Eastern Question competition (in terms of both political units and specific territories) have changed considerably over time. It was noted, for example, in Part Two, that the Fertile Crescent in the twentieth century has played the dominant Eastern Question role assumed by the Balkans in the nineteenth. On the other hand, the European portions of the former Ottoman Empire have dropped out of the Eastern Question system. The Arabian peninsula and the Persian Gulf, something of a backwater in the nineteenth century, now share a leading role in Eastern Question politics with the Fertile Crescent.

The embattled political elites of the Ottoman Empire were in the eye of the Eastern Question storm throughout the nineteenth century. Turkey, the core successor state to the Ottoman Empire, has enjoyed greater freedom from the lures and snares of Eastern Question politics and has used that freedom to sharply reduce its stake in the Eastern Question game. Ataturk's decision to cut Turkey's intimate political ties with the Arab world forced a major systemic change.

Turkey's international position and its foreign policy can still be elucidated in Eastern Question terms. Twentieth-century examples of old style Eastern Question politics would include: Turkey's wresting of Alexandretta (Hatay) from French-controlled Syria in the thirties, Turkey's fence-sitting tactics during the Second World War, the crude Soviet pressures against Turkey immediately after that war (evoking memories of the Menshikov mission to Istanbul before the

Crimean War almost a century earlier), Turkey's role in the Baghdad Pact, co-operation between Turkey and the United States in pressuring left-leaning Syria in the mid-fifties, and the 1974 Turkish military intervention in Cyprus (a clear case of limited fait-accompli politics to reverse the earlier Greek fait accompli gambit). Nevertheless, these significant examples of Eastern Question continuity in Turkish diplomacy must not obscure the systemic change begun by Ataturk and continuing to this day.

The one state that has remained at the center of Eastern Question activity throughout both centuries is Egypt. These contrasting examples—Egypt and Turkey—illustrate an aspect of the Eastern Question system. In its kaleidoscopic complexity the system does tend to have a self-sustaining momentum. It is difficult for any single player to change the nature of the game or even to succeed in dropping out—difficult, but not impossible. Republican Turkey could take its distance from Eastern Question politics. Egypt has not done so. The distinctive Middle Eastern diplomatic culture predisposes a limited range of choices, but it never completely forecloses a creative breakthrough.

It does seem justified to confirm the conclusion that was implicit throughout this book. The rules of the Eastern Question game have been remarkably stable, strikingly so when set alongside the many revolutionary changes the Middle East has experienced over the past two centuries.

PRESENT POLICY OPTIONS IN THE LIGHT OF EASTERN QUESTION EXPERIENCE

Politics is the art of the possible, and forces reducing the scope of the possible in foreign policy are always formidable. In addition to the obvious limitations fixed by the finite power of any state there are the constrictions imposed by what a statesman's own constituency will permit. The first obstacle clearly affects all states—or would-be states—setting up a scale of rankings that can be to some extent quantified (e.g., military force levels, economic resources, population, technology, geostrategic factors). The second obstacle is equally universal.

Autocracies have difficulties, as do democracies, in satisfying their respective publics. The nature and number of that public may vary from state to state, linkages between government and people may be stable and well institutionalized or sporadic and haphazard, but in one way or another the problem of a government's gaining the acceptance of its own constituency cannot be conjured away.

Statesmen not only are bound by limits of physical power and public opinion; they are also hemmed in by prevailing perceptions. Nothing is more difficult for political leaders, conditioned by the assumptions, traditions, and prejudices of their following, than to think the unthinkable.

Logical scenarios for improved international relations can be drafted with embarrassing ease. They may, however, fail the test of making sense to the flesh-and-blood players involved in the immediate diplomatic game. At the same time, logical scenarios have the virtue of insinuating new ideas into a diplomatic situation that may be bogged down in old patterns of thought and action. The remarks which follow attempt to strike a balance between the reality of established procedures and thinking the unthinkable.

The first lines in this book emphasized the coherence of the Middle Eastern international relations system but added the warning that this was no cause for comfort. The Eastern Question system demonstrates a high degree of stability (the rules of the game are not easily changed) and predictability as compared to other international relations systems. This enhances the tactical advantage gained by those who master the system. Yet, Eastern Question politics, for all its systemic stability and predictability, exacts a high cost from those involved—significant economic resources consumed on military requirements, persistent inter-group violence, penetration of Middle Eastern political life by outside influences, all of which curtail needed political and economic development.

Although the immediate tactical goal of the political players involved must be to reap the gains that come from playing the existing Eastern Question game well, the net result of everyone's so acting is the maintenance of a system that is not beneficial. Since the game itself has become dangerous for the players, the strategic goal of each player should be to so restructure the game that the present penalties imposed on virtually all can be removed or at least reduced.

Policy projections must not, however, be based on the assumption of unilateral self-abnegation by one of the participants. No state or other political force involved in the existing Eastern Question game will surrender immediate assets as a first step toward eventually achieving greater gains for all. How, then, can the players in the Eastern Question game break out of this confining circle?

A review of Eastern Question history to date offers one strong systemic characteristic: no outside state has been able to dominate and organize the Middle East, squeezing out thereby outside claimants for power and influence. No outside state appears likely to be able to do so in the foreseeable future. Any state making the attempt is likely soon to reach a point at which further investment of diplomatic capital provides a very poor return. Britain's Ottoman policy and the following British Arab policy, on the one hand, and the Middle Eastern diplomacy of Dulles or of Kissinger and his several successors, on the other, all converge to expose the limitations of pre-emptive politics in the Eastern Question context.

A corollary of the above is that an outside state, not being easily excluded from the Eastern Question game, can usually manage to maintain a minimal position at limited risk and expenditure. Stated differently, a relatively uncommitted or excluded outside power can often achieve quick diplomatic gains by adopting a more assertive Middle Eastern policy, but a point is soon reached at which easy winnings fade and new initiatives tend to bring more liabilities than assets.

Accordingly, it would seem that the safest policy for any outside power to adopt would be to move prudently toward

'DON'T YOU THINK IT'S TIME WE PUT A STOP TO THIS?'

18. No single outside power seems to organize the Middle East,
but great power rivals seldom cooperate for long in "damage control"
(By permission of Gib Crockett, *The Washington Star*, 1970).

that point of commitment in the Middle East at which easy
victories cease, to resist the temptation of seeking to eject great
power rivals and to settle instead for informal adversary alliances with these rivals. A few examples culled from earlier
discussions in this book suggest the possibilities:

1. Britain's Canning, dealing with the Russians and the
   Ottomans in the diplomatic crisis resulting in Greek independence, cooperated with the rival (Russia) while
   pressuring the regional client (Ottoman Empire) to make
   unavoidable concessions in time to be useful. Had Can-

271

ning lived longer (he died two months before the battle of Navarino), the Ottoman-Russian war might have been avoided.

2. Bismarck's successful foreign policy was based on leaving the Eastern Question game for others to play. In the process, he skillfully deflected potential challenges to German interests in Europe toward the Middle East, where they could be played out with a net loss in strength of Germany's rivals at no risk to Germany.

3. The American Truman Doctrine (1947) succeeded because it responded to clearly expressed regional interests. The Eisenhower doctrine (1957) failed in attempting to impose an American-initiated policy on the Middle East in terms that did not accord with clearly expressed regional interests. The Carter Doctrine (1980) repeated the error.

4. The Soviets achieved immediate gains in the Middle East with the 1955 Egyptian-Soviet arms deal because that step responded to clearly expressed regional interests. Later Soviet efforts to use Egypt as the vanguard of a more assertive policy in the Middle East failed. Egyptian leadership no longer saw a clear fit between their interests and those of the Soviets.

5. Syria's breaking away from Egypt in 1961 after three years together in the United Arab Republic caused no international crisis because neither the United States nor the Soviet Union was disposed to see the situation as critical.

6. Gaullist policies in the Middle East that came into full operation in 1962 after France lost Algeria, the last possession of its once impressive Arab empire, reveal the potential of outside powers to regain influence after apparently disastrous losses. In the Eastern Question game neither the victories nor the losses of outside powers are as impressive as they might appear.

7. The immediate American response to the October 1973 war achieved impressive gains because Kissinger could

demonstrate to all, friend and foe, the advantages of dealing with the United States. Later, more assertive policies
openly aimed at reducing Soviet influence met the expected Soviet response, increasing the commitments of
both superpowers without a concommitant increase in
the maneuverability of either. The tactic of coopting one's
enemy as practiced by George Canning earlier was not
used consistently, after a promising beginning.

8. The Camp David process and the Egyptian-Israeli peace
treaty of March 1979 were major achievements, but from
the standpoint of superpower diplomacy in the Middle
East the following reservations should be noted: The
United States responded to regional initiatives (which is
a sound approach) but later claimed exclusive great power
sponsorship of the process without gaining adequate
control over the regional parties to make the claim stick
(which is not sound). The U.S. underwrote the Egyptian-Israeli peace treaty on terms that (a) were costly to
the United States, (b) largely left the initiative with the
regional parties, and (c) created a situation in which a
major responsibility for failure would be borne by the
United States. Later steps toward Arab-Israeli peace are
likely only if the United states relinquishes in part at least
its self-assumed role as the exclusive mediator between
Israel and the Arabs. The Egyptian-Israeli peace treaty,
when compared with the many dismal failures to resolve
the Arab-Israeli confrontation since 1948, stands out as
a triumph of promising new thinking. The Camp David
initiative can also be seen more as a monument to American persistence and lavish expenditure of major diplomatic resources than to finesse. A great power—even more
a superpower—by pouring almost limitless resources into
a specific diplomatic campaign can sometimes beat the
odds and achieve success. Such approaches cannot be the
norm. No great power has that much diplomatic capital
to expend. It is also important to consider the possible

long-term liabilities picked up in winning at great price an unexpected success.

In the same way, a review of Eastern Question history reveals that no state from within the Middle East has been able to establish a regional predominance. No state appears likely to be able to do so in the foreseeable future. The Ottomans could not shore up established power. Nor could two ambitious rulers of Egypt separated over a century in time, Muhammad Ali and Gamal Abdul Nasser, sustain their new power. Even less luck attended Hashimite efforts throughout the first half of this century to organize the Fertile Crescent and Arabia.

Could it not then be suggested that regional powers, like outside powers, usually would find more circumspect foreign policies to be the better part of wisdom? Certainly, the record of those who opted out of the Eastern Question system or at least cut back their commitments has been noteworthy. The principal example remains the Turkey of Ataturk's creation. Sadat's scaling down of Nasserist ambitions is also to be noted, but Sadat, in moving his country so dramatically from one superpower sponsor to another, did not completely escape the Eastern Question.

One might well ask if the logic of limited commitment applies equally to smaller regional entities. The plight of Lebanon immediately comes to mind. In a sense Lebanon can be viewed as a casualty of the Eastern Question in its most virulent contemporary form, that of the still unresolved Arab-Israeli confrontation. In retrospect, it can be suggested that Lebanon's leaders over the past decades might have given more attention to insisting on a de facto neutrality of the weak against both the blandishments of her fellow Arab states and the threats or enticements coming from Israel. A Lebanon insisting on absolutely no violations of its border by either the PLO or Israel while publicly always drawing the attention of Israel and the world community to the still unresolved Palestinian problem might have escaped the brutality of civil war and of foreign invasions. To state the matter thus is, admittedly, to ask for almost superhuman political leadership from a vulnerable country. Realistically, it is probably more accurate to point out that continuation of the Eastern Question system is likely to produce other Lebanons, just as it earlier produced a Palestinian problem that still resists settlement.

Israel, certainly a small state in terms of territory and population, has under the Begin government shown increasing signs of seeking regional predominance in informal alliance with an outside superpower, the United States. Taking note of Israel's preemptive strike against the Baghdad nuclear facility, the de facto annexation of the Golan Heights, the continued settlements in the West Bank, and the Israeli invasion in Lebanon beginning in June 1982, the historian might conclude that the Middle East has not seen such a sustained mix of military assertiveness and diplomatic faits accomplis since Muhammad Ali sent Egyptian troops into Syria a century and a half ago.

19. "Menachem! Open the *@#* Tunnel!!!" (By permission of Bill Garner, *The Memphis Commercial-Appeal*, 1982).

Can Israel make such an activist policy succeed? Such ambitions rest on a tiny demographic base (Israelis account for 2 percent of the Middle East population). Moreover, Menachem Begin as much as Muhammad Ali must consider the outside world, not just regional power balances. His actions have largely eroded outside support for Israel except in the United States. Even there, existing Israeli policies are being seriously questioned. For all its regional strength, Israel's diplomatic fortunes are now in the hands of a single outside power, the United States, as much as Muhammad Ali was obliged to take Britain into account. One might well question whether regional predominance gained at the price of being obliged to rely on the whim of a single outside power is the best possible diplomatic posture for a small state. Israel, like the great powers, might be advised to explore the possibilities of adversary alliances within the region as well as a less assertive foreign policy.

If the above argument drawing on Eastern Question history is accepted, then it is to the interest equally of regional or outside powers to seek more limited Middle Eastern diplomatic commitments. This raises the question of whether such action by one or even several players in today's Eastern Question game would suffice to bring about systemic change. The most honest answer, again in the light of experience, is that it probably would not. The Eastern Question thrived with Bismarck sitting on the sidelines. The Eastern Question reached an especially intensive phase in Egypt and the Fertile Crescent after Ataturk had sent Turkey off in search of other goals.

Even so, the example of several states with clear Middle Eastern interests pursuing these interests in a more restrained manner might prove contagious. This is not to suggest that statesmen, East or West, usually esteem unilateral acts of self-abnegation by others. They do, however, often begin to wonder if the other party is not being devilishly clever. Then, possibly the process of emulation can begin.

Moreover, it is to be hoped that if the present-day participants become more aware of the long-lived Eastern Question system and realize more fully its constraints they might become more interested in effecting useful rule changes.

* * *

This book has sought to explain the distinctive Middle Eastern approach to international politics, to describe its origins and its later developments, to demonstrate how it works, and to illustrate its stubborn durability.

It is to be hoped that the book can be of use to those seeking to understand international politics in the modern Middle East or even to those who might wish not just to understand but to change the rules of the Eastern Question game.

THE DISTINCTIVE MIDDLE
EASTERN DIPLOMATIC CULTURE:
A BIBLIOGRAPHICAL ESSAY

WORKS on the international politics of the modern Middle East may be roughly divided into two broad groups. There is, first, the enormous body of writings on the Eastern Question as traditionally defined (that is, from the late eighteenth century to the end of the Ottoman Empire after World War One, which approach the subject from a markedly Eurocentric perspective). The second group includes the many books and articles treating Middle Eastern international politics since World War One.

Traditional Eastern Question historiography is well developed and defined. This has been a recognized topic in diplomatic history for over a century. Public records and private papers have been sifted by several generations of scholars. The reader has available a rich diversity of broad interpretative accounts presented by different historians in this century and the previous century. Scores of articles and monographs produced over the past several generations clarify many of the fine points.

The difficulties, however, for purposes of this book are two. Traditional Eastern Question historiography tells only half the story, stopping with the end of the Ottoman Empire. Even for that earlier period the traditional Eastern Question has always been a topic in European history. The Middle East itself has been regarded more nearly as an arena for European diplomatic jousting, Middle Eastern political figures being studied only to the extent that their actions are seen as having set in motion European responses. That interestingly different policy orientations among Middle Eastern statesmen might have existed is largely discounted, the question of how Middle

Easterners themselves viewed their international situation equally so.

Certain more recent Eastern Question scholarship attempts to right this imbalance and to see that the topic in its multilateral complexity involved Europeans and Middle Easterners with equal intensity. Such scholarship appreciates rather better that the Eastern Question game had players on both sides—Europe and the Middle East.

As a general rule, however, the Middle Eastern side of the traditional Eastern Question is not so well developed. Moreover, Middle Eastern documentary sources for modern diplomatic history are only beginning to be systematically tapped. Giving the Middle East the full treatment it deserves thus remains difficult. Anyone, for example, with access to a good library could uncover a wealth of fact and interpretation on, say, Gladstone and the Eastern Question. One could obtain a reasonably good sense of not only what Mr. Gladstone did but how he felt about the issues. What if one tried to do the same for someone whose role in Eastern Question history was equally central—Sultan Abdul Hamid II? The available books and articles would provide a very sketchy picture, indeed, largely tendentious as to his deeds and almost nothing about his ideas.

The second group of writings, treating Middle Eastern international politics since the First World War, lacks the coherence of traditional Eastern Question historiography. Indeed, it would be incorrect to speak of a single theme organizing Middle Eastern diplomatic history since the First World War, in the way that the conventional, Eurocentric Eastern Question approach did for the earlier period.

On the other hand, these works offer one advantage over traditional Eastern Question historiography. Generally, writing on this later period is more concerned with the Middle East as a subject of importance in its own right. Although the tendency to see Middle Eastern diplomacy through the eyes of outsiders is by no means laid to rest, the improvement over what might be called standard Eastern Question writing is palpable.

Yet, much of this writing that treats events since the First World War lacks a genuinely regional outlook. Instead, in line with the Western proclivity for national history there is a tendency to concentrate on a single people or a politically organized group, usually a juridically recognized state. Egypt, Israel and Turkey are favored with the most coverage.

A related problem for this post-Ottoman period is that scholars have reached no agreement concerning the boundaries of the Middle East. Accordingly, even those few works that would seek to offer a region-wide coverage of post-Ottoman diplomatic history define the Middle East differently.

Moreover, writings on post-Ottoman Middle Eastern international relations tend to concentrate on Middle Eastern relations with a single outside power. Several works treat Britain and the Middle East, the United States and the Middle East, and, especially for the period since the 1950s, the Soviet Union and the Middle East. Few works give sufficient attention to the kaleidoscopic interaction of many Middle Eastern political units and many outside political units.

The rather poor fit between Eastern Question historical coverage for the nineteenth century and the different approaches to Middle Eastern international relations in the twentieth century reduces the possibility of comparison between pre-Ottoman and post-Ottoman Middle Eastern international relations—on the basis of existing literature.

This means that the reader interested in testing the thesis presented in this book will need to pick and choose among different scholarly traditions, not being distressed in finding that certain issues treated exhaustively in these works may be of marginal importance to the subject of this book while issues central to the concerns treated here are scarcely dealt with at all.

Having noted these limitations, however, one should emphasize the positive side of the historiographical ledger. There is more scholarly writing on modern Middle Eastern diplomatic history than many realize. The best is of the highest quality. Many older works that may now appear to be somewhat off target in their general approach remain excellent contributions, not only in their careful documentation but in their scope and methodology. Even what these books omit offer clues to those who would explore the always changing styles and outlooks in historical writing.

Altogether, the entire corpus of literature relevant to the Eastern Question system is the work of several successive generations, of different "national" schools, and of varying theoretical orientations ranging from old-fashioned, viewed-from-the-top diplomatic historical narration to Marxist revisionism and from self-confident colonialist history to assertive anticolonialism. The dialectic of these many scholarly battles—even if often the battles are poorly joined—has refined our knowledge of modern Middle Eastern international relations.

While useful new scholarly construction of modern Middle Eastern international relations is waiting to be done many of the more important parts of the needed new interpretative edifice are already at hand. They have been painstakingly put together by earlier scholars pursuing other purposes. These useful works need now only to be identified and put to somewhat different use.

BIBLIOGRAPHIES: A good, working bibliography for both the nineteenth- and the twentieth-century phases of the Eastern Question is to be found in the valuable bibliographical notes that conclude the editor's commentary on each of the documents in J. C. Hurewitz, *The Middle East and North Africa in World Politics* (Vol. I, 1535-1914; Vol. II, 1914-1945; Vol. III in preparation). Hurewitz's definition of the Middle East and North Africa embraces all of Ottoman Afro-Asia (and its successor states), adding as well Morocco, Iran and Afghanistan.

The best annotated bibliography for the period 1774-1923 is in M. S. Anderson, *The Eastern Question*.

Good bibliographies that emphasize the recent period, with greater attention as well to social science literature are: Ann Schulz, *International and Regional Politics in the Middle East and North Africa: A Guide to Information Sources;* Ann Gordon

Drabek and Wilfrid Knapp, *The Politics of African and Middle Eastern States: An Annotated Bibliography* (limited material on each subsection under the rubric "External Relations"); Clement M. Henry with Jeffrey Wolff and Steven Heydemann, *Politics and International Relations in the Middle East: An Annotated Bibliography*.

A number of general surveys on the modern Middle East offer extensive bibliographies but without annotation. None of these books is mentioned, because such lists that neither describe nor evaluate the many works cited are of little help. Indeed, they can at times cause the serious student to seek out superficial accounts bearing intriguing titles while overlooking the more solid contributions available.

On the other hand, several good annotated bibliographies that cover a single country or part of the Middle East as defined in this book do deserve attention. Among these must be included Stanford J. Shaw and Ezel Kural Shaw, *History of the Ottoman Empire and Modern Turkey*, covering the years 1808-1975. Their very detailed bibliography may accordingly be favorably compared with that of Anderson for the period to the end of the Ottoman Empire. The bibliography on the period of Republican Turkey is equally thorough. The Shaws are concerned with much more than diplomatic history, but their bibliography does give this subject its due.

William R. Polk, *The Arab World* (this is the 4th edition of the book earlier entitled *The United States and the Arab World*) has a good, general annotated bibliography, with considerable attention given to international relations. The companion volume in this series on the Maghrib is Charles F. Gallagher, *The United States and North Africa*. The annotated bibliography is very good, but even shorter than that of Polk on the Arab East.

The bibliography in P. J. Vatikiotis, *The Modern History of Egypt*, offers a good introductory coverage of that important subject. For Israel, the thorough bibliography in Noah Lucas, *The Modern History of Israel*, is recommended. The bibliography is arranged so one can readily locate those works treating international relations.

Bibliographies abound on the subject of Palestine, Israel, and the Arab-Israeli confrontation. The following (which cover much more than the strictly international relations aspects of the subject but are arranged to facilitate easy reference) may be mentioned: Walid Khalidi and Jill Khadduri (eds.), *Palestine and the Arab-Israeli Conflict: An Annotated Bibliography*, and Ronald M. DeVore, *The Arab-Israeli Conflict: A Historical, Political, Social and Military Bibliography*.

DIPLOMATIC AND PUBLIC DOCUMENTS: For this subject the basic reference is Hurewitz, *Middle East and North Africa in World Politics*, already mentioned. This two-volume (eventually three) work is a greatly augmented second edition of his earlier work entitled *Diplomacy in the Near and Middle East*. The new edition should be consulted if possible.

M. S. Anderson has assembled a small group of documents in a little book (181 pages) entitled *The Great Powers and the Near East, 1774-1923*. The short excerpts from both public documents and scholarly studies provide an excellent companion volume to his *The Eastern Question*.

Very useful for UN activities in the Middle East is the three-volume work edited by Rosalyn Higgins, *United Nations Peacekeeping: Documents and Commentary*. The entire first volume is devoted to the Middle East.

Attention is also called to Muhammad Khalil (ed.), *The Arab States and the Arab League: A Documentary Record* (2 vols.). The second volume is concerned with inter-Arab and international politics from the time of the First World War on.

A convenient collection of both public documents and numerous readings is the three-volume *The Arab-Israeli Conflict* (1974), edited by John Norton Moore.

General information on the various official governmental publications, including diplomatic papers, which deal with the Middle East along with other world areas can be found in such basic reference handbooks as Helen J. Poulton, *The Historian's Handbook* (Chapter II).

JOURNALS: Recent articles on one aspect or another of this subject appear in a broad range of scholarly and public affairs journals, among which the most important are *Foreign Affairs, Foreign Policy, Middle East Journal, Middle Eastern Studies* (especially for high-quality, detailed articles on modern Middle Eastern historical subjects, including many on diplomatic history), *Orbis* and *World Politics*.

The best way to locate scholarly articles that may be too recent to appear in standard bibliographical lists is by reference to the *Middle East Journal*, which contains in every issue (published quarterly) a territorially and topically arranged "Bibliography of Periodical Literature." This quarterly bibliographical service has the added advantage of including journal articles from Arab countries, Israel and Turkey, as well as Europe and America.

The *Middle East Journal* is also the most thorough in reporting—and usually reviewing—new books on Middle Eastern subjects. In the narrower field of Middle Eastern international relations the review coverage of new books is rivalled only by *Foreign Affairs*. The regular reader of both the *Middle East Journal* and *Foreign Affairs* is unlikely to miss the notice of any serious new work on Middle Eastern international relations.

The Middle East Studies Association (the major North American scholarly society of those from all disciplines concerned with the Middle East) sponsors the *International Journal of Middle Eastern Studies*. Its articles and reviews are of high quality, but since it covers the Middle East during the entire Islamic period (with attention to languages and literatures as well as history and the social sciences), articles and reviews on Middle Eastern international politics are limited.

GENERAL WORKS: The standard general work covering the entire period from the beginning of the Eastern Question to the present is that of George Lenczowski, *The Middle East in World Affairs* (now in its fourth edition). Part One of the book offers a historical overview from the dawn of the Eastern Question to after the First World War. Thereafter, the book

285

treats separately the diplomatic history of each of the Middle Eastern countries (the Middle East being defined by Lenczowski to include Egypt, Arab Asia, Israel, Turkey, Iran, and Afghanistan, but excluding Sudan and the Maghrib). The last section of the book addresses several broad themes such as strategic waterways, Arab unity, and the Great Powers and the Middle East.

General surveys on the period from the beginning of the Eastern Question to the First World War are more abundant than for the period thereafter. This is not surprising, given the long-established acceptance of the traditional Eastern Question as a topic in European diplomatic history as contrasted with the considerable confusion that reigns concerning how to classify the diplomatic history of the Afro-Asian successor states to the Ottoman Empire.

For the period up to the end of the First World War, pride of place for general surveys should go to Anderson's *The Eastern Question*, which takes advantage of recent scholarship (the book was published in 1966), is thorough and fair. Moreover, although Anderson chooses to stay within the Eurocentric framework of Eastern Question historiography, he has taken note of the more important works presenting the Middle East side of these diplomatic entanglements.

The much older work by J.A.R. Marriott, *The Eastern Question* (1st edition, 1917; and 4th edition, 1940), remains of interest. Marriott, to his credit, does set the stage with considerable background on the Ottoman Empire. Chapters III, IV, and V are entitled respectively "The Advent of the Ottomans," "The Ottoman Empire: Its Zenith, 1453-1566," and "The Decadence of the Ottoman Empire." Even so, these chapters are useful now only to illustrate prevailing European views of the Ottomans early in this century. More recent works by Ottomanists (of which a few are noted later) offer sounder interpretations. After his Chapter V, Marriott takes a strongly Eurocentric line.

Although in the narrow sense of the term Marriott's *Eastern Question* has been superseded by that of Anderson, the former

286

retains certain strengths, including the self-confident judgments typical of an earlier school of British narrative history, an especially effective use of citations from European contemporaries of the events being related, and—all in all—a good example of old-fashioned diplomatic history emphasizing the role of leading statesmen. Much the same can be said for the French historical equivalent of Marriott, Edouard Driault's *La Question d'Orient* (8 editions between 1898 and 1920).

Another often cited general survey is that of William Miller, *The Ottoman Empire and Its Successors, 1801-1927*, a book that went through four editions between 1913 and 1936. Miller's work is especially strong on Greece and to a lesser extent the Balkans. His treatment of diplomatic events concerning Ottoman Africa and Asia is less sure. Throughout, Miller tells his story with superciliousness and heavy irony at the expense of the Ottomans and, indeed, all non-Europeans. Given the existence of more balanced accounts, the book can now be recommended only as a good case study in European inability or unwillingness (or both) to see the Eastern Question through Ottoman or other Middle Eastern eyes.

Britain and the Eastern Question: Missolonghi to Gallipoli, by G. D. Clayton, is an interesting little book. Part of the *London History Studies* series designed for students, Clayton's work is clear and a pleasure to read. Telling the story mainly in terms of representative British statesmen—Canning, Palmerston, Gladstone, Disraeli, and Salisbury—the author succeeds in giving his subject a strong organizational framework. He is also good in being able both to present different viewpoints and to offer his own sharply etched appraisals. The one weakness in what would otherwise be a gem of a students' survey is a consistent slighting of the Middle Eastern dimension. In its rampant Eurocentrism, the book is rather like European works that were written a half century ago.

A stimulating general study that places the Eastern Question within the somewhat different framework of British/Russian rivalry from the Levant to India is David Gillard, *The Struggle for Asia, 1828-1914: A Study in British and Russian*

Imperialism (1977). Selected parts of several standard historical surveys or reference works can provide useful interpretative and narrative detail that may be used to flesh out or to challenge the argument presented in this book. For example, the chapter by Dankwart Rustow, "The Political Impact of the West," in Vol. I of the *Cambridge History of Islam*, addresses broad themes of interest here.

Nor should the many chapters in the appropriate volumes of the *New Cambridge Modern History* be overlooked. The following are worth mentioning: Volume 9: Chapter 19 "The Near East and the Ottoman Empire, 1798-1830," by C. W. Crawley, plus parts of Chapter 25 "International Relations, 1815-1830," by the same author. Volume 10: parts of Chapter 10, "The System of Alliances and the Balance of Power," by Gordon Craig; Chapter 16, "The Mediterranean," by C. W. Crawley; and Chapter 18, "The Crimean War," by Agatha Ramm and B. H. Sumner. Volume 11: Chapter 12, "Austria-Hungary, Turkey, and the Balkans," by W. N. Medlicott; Chapter 20, "International Relations," by A.J.P. Taylor; and Chapter 21, "Rivalries in the Mediterranean, the Middle East and Egypt," by A. P. Thornton. Volume 12: parts of Chapter 5, "Diplomatic History, 1900-1912," by J.P.T. Bury; parts of Chapter 6, "The Approach of the War of 1914," by J.M.K. Vyvyan; and Chapter 10, "The Middle East 1900-1945," by Elie Kedourie.

Readers might find it stimulating—if not always totally satisfying—to sample certain of the better survey works on modern European diplomatic history to see their treatment of nineteenth- and twentieth-century Middle Eastern issues, and then to match this exploration with a sampling of surveys covering the modern Middle East. One can, for example, work through appropriate portions of A.J.P. Taylor's brilliant and opinionated *The Struggle for Mastery in Europe*; the solid, thorough study, *Britain in Europe, 1789-1914*, by R. W. Seton-Watson (author of the excellent *Disraeli, Gladstone, and the Eastern Question*); Barbara Jelavich's *A Century of Russian For-*

eign Policy; or Rene Albrecht-Carrie's *A Diplomatic History of Europe Since the Congress of Vienna.*

Then, one could turn to such works treating the Middle Eastern perspective as William Yale, *The Near East: A Modern History* (which gives considerable attention to international relations); William R. Polk, *The Arab World*; volume II of Shaw and Shaw, *History of the Ottoman Empire and Modern Turkey*; Bernard Lewis, *The Emergence of Modern Turkey*; Niyazi Berkes, *The Development of Secularism in Turkey*; P. J. Vatikiotis, *The Modern History of Egypt*; K. S. Salibi, *The Modern History of Lebanon*; Abdullah Laroui, *The History of the Maghrib: An Interpretive Essay*; and Jamil M. Abun-Nasr, *A History of the Maghrib.*

Comparing books on European diplomatic history that slight the Middle East or tend to treat the Middle East only as an "arena" for Europe's diplomatic duels with books on the Middle East that slight the diplomatic dimension should at least sensitize the reader to different perspectives and the need for a new scholarly orientation.

Another useful way to get a good overview of the subject—although again somewhat indirectly—is by reference to the best general survey of Balkan history: *The Balkans Since 1453*, by L. S. Stavrianos. This is a thorough and readable large book (845 pages of text, plus a 73-page bibliographical essay), with most of the strengths and few of the weaknesses of American college textbooks. A good history of the Balkans cannot be Eurocentric in the sense that conventional Eastern Question history written from the viewpoint of London, Paris, Vienna, or Moscow is likely to become. It is also not quite Middle Eastern, either. The resulting view, somewhat removed from both the European and Middle Eastern power centers, offers worthwhile insights.

As already mentioned, narrative histories of the post-Ottoman Eastern Question are not to be expected since to conventional historians the Eastern Question came to an end with the fall of the Ottoman Empire. Nor has any new scholarly consensus emerged on just how to classify and study the international relations of the post-Ottoman Middle East, comparable to the well-grooved idea of the Eastern Question from c.1774 to 1923.

Even Islamicists and Middle Eastern specialists (who would be more inclined to continue viewing the area as a coherent entity) have tended to go along with classifications that implicitly discount the notion of a single political culture embracing today's many different sovereign states that were once part of the Ottoman Empire. For example, the best general studies of the Ottoman Empire in its last century or more of existence (such as Berkes, *Development of Secularism in Turkey*; Lewis, *Emergence of Modern Turkey*; and Shaw and Shaw, *Ottoman Empire and Modern Turkey*) treat only Turkey after the First World War.

In the modern history of the Arab world there is, on the other hand, a decided tendency to downplay the Ottoman heritage and to push Arabism much farther back in time than the historical record would warrant. Moreover, in all cases the strong Western bias for depicting the nation-state as the basic unit of political history strengthens the tendency to avoid the region-wide approach.

Nevertheless, several good narrative accounts of diplomatic history in part of the region (as defined in this book) for part of the time since the First World War can be cited. Arnold J. Toynbee's now quite old *The Islamic World Since the Peace Settlement* (1927) stands up very well after over a half-century, giving a detailed account of those turbulent first few years after World War One in both the Middle East and North Africa.

The book by Howard M. Sachar, *Europe Leaves the Middle East, 1936-1954*, concentrates, as the title indicates, on the European/Middle Eastern involvement during these years. Sachar has produced a good survey of international politics in Egypt, the Fertile Crescent, and Turkey for these critical years, with somewhat greater attention given to the problem of Palestine. His earlier work, *The Emergence of the Middle East: 1914-1924*, is also to be noted.

Two solid books by George Kirk deserve notice. They are

The Middle East in the War (i.e., the Second World War) and *The Middle East: 1945-1950.*

Perhaps one of the best short surveys and interpretative works for the first half of the twentieth century is Elizabeth Monroe, *Britain's Moment in the Middle East, 1914-1971.* As the title indicates, Ms. Monroe delineates the British role, but, since Britain's standing in the Middle East was so great, her book serves larger purposes as well. It is also one of the more readable books on the subject.

Two other excellent books that adopt a narrative historical framework for the short period they treat and also emphasize the multilateral nature of international politics are Malcolm Kerr, *The Arab Cold War: Gamal Abd Al-Nasir and His Rivals, 1958-1970,* and Patrick Seale, *The Struggle for Syria: A Study of Post-War Arab Politics, 1945-1958.*

Two broad general surveys that link the nineteenth and twentieth centuries (indeed, they look farther back into history) are Richard Allen, *Imperialism and Nationalism in the Fertile Crescent: Sources and Prospects of the Arab-Israeli Conflict,* and Peter Mansfield, *The Arabs.* As well written overviews, they can be recommended to the non-specialist.

The Elusive Peace: The Middle East in the Twentieth Century, by William R. Polk, is a little book (less than 200 pages of text) that is highly recommended. Author of *The Arab World,* Polk knows the Middle East and he knows international politics.

Several works on the Arab-Israeli confrontation emphasize the complex intertwining of international and regional policies. Lawrence J. Whetten's *The Canal War: Four-Power Conflict in the Middle East* concentrates on the period between the June 1967 and October 1973 wars. His concluding chapter, "On the Roles of Great and Small Powers in Regional Confrontations," is especially relevant to the subject of this book.

Peter Mangold's *Superpower Intervention in the Middle East* is good on events of the seventies, depicting a Soviet Union that has been perhaps more circumspect than the United States in the Middle East. *The Middle East: Nations, Superpowers, and*

Wars (1973), by Yair Evron, uses a systemic approach to the study of the Arab-Israeli confrontation between 1948 and the early seventies.

Nadav Safran's *From War to War: The Arab-Israeli Confrontation, 1948-1967* (1969), is a good blend of social science analysis and interpretation with historical narrative. Chapters II, "The Pattern of Inter-Arab Relations and the Arab-Israeli Conflict," and III, "The Big Powers and the Middle East," are especially recommended.

A short book which effectively tackles a broad subject is *Conflict in the Middle East*, by P. J. Vatikiotis. The first two parts treat "Arab Aspects of Political Conflict" (with a subsection on the role of the great powers). These are followed by an analysis of the June 1967 War and its aftermath.

Conflict in the Middle East offers a thoughtful study of what can be called—in terms we have used—the Middle Eastern diplomatic culture, properly emphasizing both regional and international components of that culture.

THE TRADITIONAL MIDDLE EASTERN POLITICAL CULTURE: Conventional Eastern Question writing generally does a good job in explicating the common core of political assumptions that Europeans shared as they played the Eastern Question game. The way rising forces of nationalism, Romanticism, liberalism, imperialism, and the industrial revolution clashed with older ideas and institutions to shape a distinctive modern European approach to international politics has been exhaustively studied. Scholars differ on the weight to be given to this or that factor, but one can readily follow these debates by consulting reliable general accounts.

By contrast, Middle Eastern political assumptions have not been so thoroughly studied. Moreover, what is known about how Middle Easterners in modern times have viewed politics does not usually find its way into the Eastern Question literature. It is, instead, in the works of Islamicists and Middle Eastern specialists, most of whom devote little attention to diplomatic history.

Yet, the Middle Eastern side of the Eastern Question diplomatic history cannot be told by reference only to the dynamic new factor of an intrusive West. Equal attention must be given to the traditional Middle Eastern political culture which took the shock of those new ideas and institutions, temptations, and threats, coming first from the West. The following writings on this broad subject might be suggested: the first two chapters of Albert Hourani's *Arabic Thought in the Liberal Age, 1798-1939*—entitled "The Islamic State" and "The Ottoman Empire"—offer a good introduction to traditional Middle Eastern/Islamic political thought and practice on the eve of modern times. An excellent statement concentrating more on the earlier developments in Muslim political experience but still relevant as background is the article "Politics and War," by Bernard Lewis, in Joseph Schacht and C. E. Bosworth (eds.), *The Legacy of Islam* (2nd Edition).

An especially good, and conveniently concise, general interpretation of the Ottoman world is the little book by Norman Itzkowitz, *Ottoman Empire and Islamic Tradition*. The final chapter, "Ottoman Consciousness," neatly sums up the Ottoman world view. Also recommended is Chapter 3, "The Islamic Intellectual Heritage of the Young Ottomans," in the book by Şerif Mardin, *The Genesis of Young Ottoman Thought: A Study in the Modernization of Turkish Political Elites*.

Chapter Four, "Government and Administration in the Arab Provinces," in H.A.R. Gibb and Harold Bowen, *Islamic Society and the West* (vol. I, part I), offers a very bleak interpretation of pre-modern political life in the Fertile Crescent and of governmental relations with the subjects. *Islamic Society and the West* (which appeared in two separate books labelled as Parts One and Two of Vol. 1) was an ambitious, encyclopaedic effort to sum up what was then known about the Ottoman Middle East on the eve of the "impact of the West." Although several of the interpretations advanced have been challenged by later scholars, the work remains of value, but perhaps more as a reference to be consulted than as an integral study to be read in its entirety. A dense work filled with Turkish and Arabic technical terms, *Islamic Society and the West*, is somewhat forbidding to the neophyte. Those profiting from chapter four cited above will probably also be attracted to Chapter I, "The Ottoman Empire and the Sacred Law," and Chapter II, "Caliphate and Sultanate."

More sanguine interpretations of government's relations with the governed in the Ottoman political world are to be found in Stanford J. Shaw, "The Ottoman View of the Balkans," in Barbara Jelavich and Charles Jelavich (eds.), *The Balkans in Transition* (Shaw provides a good study of the Ottoman theory and practice of provincial administration in general) or in Albert H. Hourani, "Ottoman Reform and the Politics of Notables," in William R. Polk and Richard L. Chambers (eds.), *Beginnings of Modernization in the Middle East.*

On the Tunisian variant of Ottoman political culture, one might note Part One, "The Traditional Political Culture," of my *The Tunisia of Ahmad Bey, 1837-1855*, especially chapters II, "The Political Class," III, "The Web of Government," and V, ". . . And the Ruled."

Anyone seeking to get a feel for relations between government and the governed in the traditional Ottoman world should certainly read the novel *The Bridge on the Drina*, by Ivo Andric. Treating what is now Yugoslavia from early Ottoman times onward, the novel in its description of villagers' relations to the Ottoman authorities could—many specialists would agree—just as easily have been set in the Fertile Crescent or other Ottoman lands. *The Bridge on the Drina* is also a superb literary achievement.

The Changing Middle East, the Same Eastern Question System: While emphasizing the systemic durability of the Eastern Question pattern of international politics, this book on several occasions pointed out that the Middle East itself has experienced revolutionary change since the Eastern Question began. Moreover, in the past several decades the Middle East has been changing at a quickening pace.

Of course, the West (and for that matter the rest of the world) has changed radically as well since the beginning of the Eastern Question. The basic contours of Western change in modern times have been thoroughly studied, and the broad outlines of the findings of scholars (with all their different views) are available in standard works.

It is not quite so easy for those who, lacking specialized knowledge, would wish to obtain a good overview of historical developments in the modern Middle East during roughly the past two centuries. The few general works that exist do not yet rest on the same solid foundation of literally thousands of earlier books and articles produced by generations of scholars. Even the best must, for this reason, be much more tentative than their equivalents in Western history. To compound the problem, many general reference works and textbooks that include the Middle East as part of larger subjects often draw on outdated or distorted sources concerning modern Middle Eastern history.

An exhaustive bibliographical account of what is known concerning modern Middle Eastern history, or even modern Middle Eastern political history (that is, including but not confined to diplomatic history), would take us too far afield. Yet, one does need a sense not only of the traditional Middle Eastern political culture but also of the still rapidly changing modern Middle East in order fully to understand Eastern Question politics. This gets us into what scholars, depending on fluctuating intellectual styles, have dubbed the impact of the West or modernization studies or political development. Only a few such works will be cited by way of illustration.

Bernard Lewis's *The Middle East and the West* is perhaps the best overview. The chapter titles of his little book effectively convey his subject—'Sketches for a Historical Portrait," "The Impact of the West," "The Quest for Freedom," "Patriotism and Nationalism," "The Revolt of Islam," and "The Middle East in International Affairs" (pertinent to the Eastern Question as system). The article cited earlier by Dankwart Rustow, "The Political Impact of the West," should be included in this rubric as well.

Three other books already cited more than once have the advantage of demonstrating the stages of change over several generations in the Ottoman Empire and later the Republic of Turkey. They are Lewis, *Emergence of Modern Turkey*, Berkes, *Development of Secularism in Turkey*, and Shaw and Shaw, *History of the Ottoman Empire and Republican Turkey*. Vatikiotis, *The Modern History of Egypt* does the same for that country, and my *Tunisia of Ahmad Bey* traces Tunisia's early modernization phase.

My chapter "The Tunisian Path to Modernization" in Menahem Milson (ed.), *Society and Political Structure in the Arab World* attempts to trace comparatively the broad lines of political development in Tunisia from the early nineteenth century to the present.

The history of changing ideas and ideology is perhaps the best developed field in modern Middle Eastern history. The most important single work is Albert Hourani, *Arabic Thought in the Liberal Age*. Among the many others that might be mentioned are Nadav Safran, *Egypt in Search of Political Community*; Hisham Sharabi, *Arab Intellectuals and the West: The Formative Years, 1875-1914*; and two covering North Africa— Elbaki Hermassi, *Leadership and National Development in North Africa* (especially Chapter I, "The Historical Traditions of the Maghribi State," and Chapter II, "Colonial Domination; Social Change and Underdevelopment") and Clement Henry Moore, *Politics in North Africa* (Chapter I, "Precolonial Political Systems," and Chapter II, "The Colonial Dialectic").

Other good works on changing ideas and ideology are Şerif Mardin, *The Genesis of Young Ottoman Thought*; Ibrahim Abu-Lughod, *Arab Rediscovery of Europe*; Jamal Mohammed Ahmed, *The Intellectual Origins of Egyptian Nationalism*; and a good account of such change traced through the intellectual odyssey of a single key figure, *The Making of an Arab Nationalist: Ottomanism and Arabism in the Life and Thought of Satiʿ Al-Husri*, by William L. Cleveland. *Arab Nationalism: An Anthology*, edited by Sylvia G. Haim, also treats changing political ideas. It is a good representative selection of Arab political thinkers, and Haim's long (72 pages) introduction is especially lucid.

Zionism if it was not in quite the same sense "Westernization" (although that was involved, as Eastern European Jewry absorbed ideas from Western Europe) did certainly include the "nationalization" and "politicization" of religious ideas that had previously been otherworldly and apolitical. To this extent, the Zionist roots are comparable to the roots of Turkish and Arab nationalism. The early chapters of Walter Laqueur, *A History of Zionism*, and of Amos Elon, *The Israelis: Founders and Sons*, can be recommended. Both are very readable. Laqueur's is much longer (over 600 pages), while Elon's is shorter (over 400 pages) and more impressionistic. Elon's biography of Theodor Herzl is also highly recommended.

The economic history of the modern Middle East, while less well advanced than that of intellectual history, is progressing rapidly. Two general introductions which elucidate the economic challenge posed by Europe are recommended: Charles Issawi, *The Economic History of the Middle East: 1800-1914* (a selection of reading with commentary by the editor), and Issawi's *An Economic History of the Middle East and North Africa*, which surveys the last two centuries.

Institutional history of the modern Middle East is perhaps least developed of all, but this is now fortunately provoking the interest of present-day scholars. Several works have been written on the intrusion of modern, Western educational systems. See, as a general synthesis of the subject, Joseph S. Szyliowicz, *Education and Modernization in the Middle East*. Two short chapter-length essays on specific countries, Tunisia and Egypt, appear written by the present author and Malcolm Kerr respectively in *Education and Political Development*, edited by James S. Coleman. A splendid, detailed study of bureaucratic change is *Bureaucratic Reform in the Ottoman Empire: The Sublime Porte, 1789-1922*, by Carter V. Findley.

The above few works must be seen as only a sampler of work available on modernization or Westernization or political development of the modern Middle East, but it may suffice to underline yet again the caveat that that old saw about *plus ça change plus c'est la meme chose* applies only to the Eastern

Question international relations system, not to overall political life in the modern Middle East.

DIPLOMACY AS A PROFESSION: The post-Napoleonic era brought, as is well known, the elaborate institutionalization of European diplomatic practice. This began thereafter slowly to influence the Ottomans, who could no longer afford to ignore European ways.

The clash of two different diplomatic systems, that of Europe and that of the Middle East, has been the theme of this book, but the concern here has been largely with power, perceptions, and the unconsciously accepted, implicit rules of the game.

Another very fruitful approach would be to examine the rise and development in the Middle East of diplomacy as a profession. The European idea, for example, of resident ambassadors was not accepted by the Ottoman Empire until the nineteenth century. Nor did a specific bureaucratic office that could be called a foreign ministry exist before the impact of the West. Background on this fascinating story can be found in Norman Itzkowitz and Max Mote, *Mubadele: An Ottoman-Russian Exchange of Ambassadors* (excellent for setting out the Ottoman assumptions and practices concerning negotiations with Europe just at the time when the Eastern Question was beginning), plus two articles by Carter V. Findley, "The Legacy of Tradition to Reform: Origins of the Ottoman Foreign Ministry," and "The Reform Under Selim III and Mahmud II," both in the *International Journal of Middle Eastern Studies*, I, no. 4 (October 1970), and III, no. 4 (October 1972), respectively, as well as the stimulating discussion (with excellent bibliographical notes) by Thomas Naff, "Ottoman Diplomatic Relations with Europe in the Eighteenth Century: Patterns and Trends," in Thomas Naff and Roger Owen (eds.), *Studies in Eighteenth Century Islamic History*.

No similar institutionalization of professional diplomacy took place in nineteenth-century Egypt or Tunisia (at this point the formal, legal position of each being part of the Ottoman Empire did make a significant difference). Even so, the Egyptian and Tunisian political elites, while not going so far as to develop resident ambassadors, were responding and adjusting to Western ways of diplomacy. Evidence of these developments can be found tucked away here and there in the works on modern Egypt and Tunisia, but the careful study of the rise of diplomacy as a profession in Egypt and Tunisia (and a fortiori the rest of the Middle East) awaits its author. Such studies can build on the trailblazing efforts on the central Ottoman Empire cited above.

FOREIGN POLICY IN MODERN MIDDLE EASTERN STATES: Perhaps the next step in tracing the rise of diplomacy as a profession in the Middle East will come in response to the useful work now underway by social scientists treating contemporary foreign policymaking in different Middle Eastern states. Indeed, if historians and social scientists could collaborate in this area of work, one might well be able to offer more refined answers to such elusive questions as whether there is an Egyptian or Turkish or Israeli or Tunisian or Arab approach to foreign policy and international relations.

An interesting pioneering work is R. D. McLaurin, Mohammed Mughisuddin and Abraham R. Wagner, *Foreign Policy Making in the Middle East: Domestic Influences on Policy in Egypt, Iraq, Israel, and Syria*. The several substantial volumes by Michael Brecher deserve special attention, for they offer the rich detail of narrative diplomatic history at its best while seeking to classify and analyze the foreign policy decision making process in Israel. His works include: *The Foreign Policy System of Israel: Setting, Images, Process* (1972), *Decisions in Israel's Foreign Policy* (1975), and *Decisions in Crisis: Israel, 1967 and 1973* (1980). It is to be hoped that Brecher's students or others influenced by his work will adapt his promising approach to other countries of the Middle East. One comparable study which is very sound is A. I. Dawisha, *Egypt in the Arab World: The Elements of Foreign Policy*.

For Turkish foreign policy the works of Edward Weisband, *Turkish Foreign Policy, 1943-1945: Small State Diplomacy and Great Power Politics* (a good case study especially appropriate to the overall themes of this book) and Kemal H. Karpat (ed.), *Turkey's Foreign Policy in Transition: 1950-1974*, can be consulted.

I. William Zartman's chapter "North African Foreign Policy," in L. Carl Brown (ed.), *State and Society in Independent North Africa* (1966) is recommended.

A useful new book is *Middle East Foreign Policy: Issues and Processes* (1982) by R. D. McLaurin, Don Peretz and Lewis W. Snider. It offers separate chapters on foreign policy making in Egypt, Iraq, Israel, Saudi Arbia and Syria.

THE MIDDLE EAST AND INDIVIDUAL OUTSIDE POWERS: As noted, much of the literature treats relations between a single outside power and one or more countries of the Middle East. Although such an approach risks overlooking the kaleidoscopic pattern of relations among many Middle Eastern and outside powers that has existed since the Eastern Question began, these books are not to be ignored. Some of the very best works are of this genre.

THE UNITED STATES AND THE MIDDLE EAST: Material on the early period is to be found in James A. Field, Jr., *America and the Mediterranean World, 1776-1882* (which contains an excellent annotated bibliography). John A. DeNovo wrote *American Interests and Policies in the Middle East, 1900-1939*, as he notes in his preface, when he realized that there was no book about U.S. relations with the Middle East equivalent to what Samuel F. Bemis had done for Latin America and A. W. Griswold for the Far East.

Robert W. Stookey, *America and the Arab States: An Uneasy Encounter*, offers a solid historical overview. The articles in the special American bicentennial issue of the *Middle East Journal* (summer 1976) are all devoted to various aspects of American relations with the Middle East.

John S. Badeau's *The American Approach to the Arab World* is more a thoughtful extended essay than an in-depth history, but, coming from a man of his wide Middle Eastern experience (missionary, university educator, charitable foundation director, and U.S. ambassador to Egypt in the Kennedy administration), it is especially valuable for just this reason.

Part 7 of Polk's *The Arab World* treats the United States and the Arab world from earliest beginnings through the period of the Carter administration. His annotated bibliography contains one section on "United States interests in the Middle East."

A work of many authors is *The Middle East and the United States: Perceptions and Policies* (1980) edited by Haim Shaked and Itamar Rabinovich. The seventeen different contributions range over the historical background, present-day strategic concerns, oil and economics, plus such usefully different studies as the Soviet perspective of the U.S. role in the Middle East as well as the European economic community and the United States in the Arab world. The book offers, thus, useful diversity. Most of the contributions are of high quality.

A commendable case study dealing with one crucial ten year period is *Decade of Decisions: American Policy Toward the Arab-Israeli Conflict, 1967-1976*, by William B. Quandt.

For American-Israeli relations one should consult Nadav Safran's impressive *Israel the Embattled Ally: The Shaping of American-Israeli Relations and the Creation and Transformation of Israel Through Three Decades of Middle East Crises and Wars* (1978).

On American-Turkish relations since the period of intensive involvement following the Second World War one could begin with the fine historical study by Bruce R. Kuniholm, *The Origins of the Cold War in the Near East: Great Power Conflict and Diplomacy in Iran, Turkey, and Greece*. This neatly sets the stage from the American perspective for *Troubled Alliance: Turkish-American Problems in Historical Perspective, 1945-1971*, by George S. Harris.

BRITAIN AND THE MIDDLE EAST: There are many good works to choose from, so long have the British been concerned with the Middle East. The best single short work is the often cited Elizabeth Monroe's *Britain's Moment in the Middle East*, with a very useful annotated bibliography. John

Marlowe's *Arab Nationalism and British Imperialism* is also highly recommended. It is readable and sound, with a healthy dash of anti-establishment thinking. Sir Reader Bullard's *Britain and the Middle East* is a reliable and sympathetic account by a long-time British diplomat who served in a number of Middle Eastern posts. A thorough historical treatment is also provided in *Empire by Treaty: Britain and the Middle East in the Twentieth Century*, by M. A. Fitzsimons.

A major theme that runs throughout most of Elie Kedourie's many highly regarded works is British relations with the Middle East. His *In the Anglo-Arab Labyrinth* (which largely supersedes his earlier *England and the Middle East*) is to be numbered among the most thorough and stimulating works on the complex British Middle Eastern diplomacy during the First World War and immediately after. All three of his books collecting separate articles and essays—*The Chatham House Version*, *Arabic Political Memoirs*, and *Islam in the Modern World*—contain material relevant to the subject of Britain and the Middle East. "The Chatham House Version" in the book by that title is, for example, a severe indictment of what Kedourie considers the misguided "establishment" view of Britain's Middle Eastern policy as personified and preached by the likes of Arnold J. Toynbee, H.A.R. Gibb, and others connected with the Royal Institute of International Affairs. (One is reminded of American attacks on the "Eastern establishment" as epitomized in the Council on Foreign Relations, although the American attack comes from the Left, that of Kedourie from the Right.)

Briton Cooper Busch has written three solid studies of British Middle Eastern policy that offer detailed coverage from the last years of the 19th Century to the 1920s. They are *Britain and the Persian Gulf, 1894-1914, Britain, India, and the Arabs, 1914-1921,* and *Mudros to Lausanne, 1918-1923*.

The works of J. B. Kelly cover much of British connections with Arabia. See his *Britain and the Perisan Gulf, 1795-1880* and also his *Arabia, the Gulf, and the West*, which treat the period from the phasing out of Britain's position in the Gulf until the time of publication (1980).

The official participants in Britain's moment in the Middle East were often good observers who wrote their memoirs (much more often than their American peers). The best of these published memoirs provide a precious, first-hand sense both of what the British did and what they thought they were doing. For details see the bibliography in Elizabeth Monroe's *Britain's Moment in the Middle East*. Let it suffice here to record one of the most readable of such memoirs, a book that is often amusing and always penetrating—*Bright Levant*, by Lawrence Grafftey-Smith. The autobiography covers Middle Eastern developments from 1914 to 1947, especially in Egypt and Arabia.

FRANCE AND THE MIDDLE EAST: Strangely, in view of France's long, intense connection with the Middle East (especially when defined, as in this book, to include North Africa), it is difficult to cite works that deal directly with Franco-Middle Eastern relations. The story of French interests, perceptions, and actions is, in large measure, to be found in works that treat the Middle East within the framework of larger subjects such as many of those cited under general works or books such as Jacques Chastenet, *Histoire de la Troisième République*, Henri Brunschwig; *French Colonialism, 1871-1914: Myths and Realities*; Stephen H. Roberts, *The History of French Colonial Policy, 1870-1925*; or A. Pingaud, *Histoire Diplomatique de la France Pendant la Grande Guerre*.

The older work by Henry H. Cumming, *Franco-British Rivalry in the Post-War Near East: The Decline of French Influence*, carries the story only through the Treaty of Lausanne. Clear and accurate but not especially penetrating, it may be considered superseded by later works treating the post-war settlement.

More substantial is *Britain, France, and the Arab Middle East, 1914-1920* (1969), by Jukka Nevakivi. Highly recommended as well is the clearly presented narrative analysis by Jan Karl Tanenbaum, "France and the Arab Middle East, 1914-1920," in *Transactions of the American Philosophical Society*, Vol. 68, Part 7 (October 1978), with a useful bibliographical listing.

The Climax of French Imperial Expansion, 1914-1924 (1981), by Christopher M. Andrew and A. S. Kanya-Forstner, is a solid study giving considerable attention to the Middle East set within the framework of overall French imperial history. Covering a slightly earlier period is William I. Shorrock's *French Imperialism in the Middle East: The Failure of Policy in Syria and Lebanon, 1900-1914*. The narrowly defined subtitle best describes the author's purpose. John P. Spagnolo's *France and Ottoman Lebanon, 1861-1914*, offers a solid case study of French policies, goals and actions.

The little book by Ann Williams, *Britain and France in the Middle East and North Africa, 1914-1967*, is a readable general survey (a scant 154 pages of text) for those years that has the advantage of covering the same "Middle East" as does this book. One might also look with profit at the older *The Mediterranean in Politics* (1938), by Elizabeth Monroe, for this book gives considerable attention to French policy.

The voluminous work by Jean Ganiage, *Les Origines du Protectorat français en Tunisie, 1861-1881*, is a detailed study of French and European diplomacy, thorough and penetrating in its coverage of the European side but marred by misperceptions and distortions of the Tunisian polity.

A recent work gives more of a historical overview of French policies in the Middle East (or, more precisely, the Arab world) than the title would indicate. This is *La Politique Arabe de la France: De De Gaulle à Pompidou* (1973), by Paul Balta and Claudine Rulleau. In the process of outlining, and supporting, the Gaullist turn toward the Arab world, the authors evoke the past as well as past French perceptions (not, of course, the same thing). The first chapter, for example, is entitled "De Charlemagne à la colonisation," just the sort of metahistorical sweeping of the centuries that staid academic historians scorn (but also sometimes envy). The authors are a husband and wife journalistic team.

GERMANY AND THE MIDDLE EAST: Four useful works

may be cited. Two cover the period of the First World War. They are Ulrich Trumpener, *Germany and the Ottoman Empire, 1914-1918*, and Frank G. Weber, *Eagles on the Crescent: Germany, Austria, and the Diplomacy of the Turkish Alliance, 1914-1918*. The third is an excellent study of Nazi Germany and the Middle East—Lukasz Hirszowicz, *The Third Reich and the Arab East*. Weber has written another study treating World War Two diplomacy, entitled *The Evasive Neutral: Germany, Britain, and the Quest for a Turkish Alliance*. A recent article based on considerable archival research—Francis Nicosia, "Arab Nationalism and National socialist Germany, 1933-1939: Ideological and Strategic Incompatibility," *International Journal of Middle East Studies* (November 1980)—argues persuasively that Hitler Germany in the 1930s had scant ideological or strategic motivation to challenge Britain in the Middle East by supporting Arabism.

RUSSIA/SOVIET UNION AND THE MIDDLE EAST: For the period of Tsarist Russia one should consult Barbara Jelavich, *A Century of Russian Foreign Policy, 1814-1914*, and also Ivo J. Lederer (ed.), *Russian Foreign Policy: Essays in Historical Perspective*, which is a group scholarly effort to examine the extent to which there has or has not been a continuity in pre- and post-1917 Russian foreign policy.

As for Soviet policy in the Middle East since the Second World War, and especially since the fifties, there has been an explosion of studies in English alone, not to mention other languages. The review article by Hannes Adomeit, "Soviet Policy in the Middle East: Problems of Analysis," *Soviet Studies* (April 1975) critically evaluates many works that appeared before that date.

The more useful works include Yaacov Ro'i (ed.), *From Encroachment to Involvement: A Documentary Study of Soviet Policy in the Middle East, 1945-1973*, a blend of documentation and interpretative commentary concentrating on the 1955 Soviet-Egyptian arms deal, the 1970 crisis in Jordan and Egypt's expulsion of the Soviets in 1972. Ro'i has edited another good book, *The Limits to Soviet Power in the Middle East* (1979).

A work of several authors is Michael Confino and Shimon Shamir (eds.), *The USSR and the Middle East* (1973).

The depth of solid coverage since the fifties is also demonstrated in the following three works, listed in order of chronological coverage: Oles M. Smolansky, *The Soviet Union and the Arab East Under Khrushchev* (for the years 1958-1965); Alvin Z. Rubinstein, *Red Star on the Nile: The Soviet-Egyptian Influence Relationship Since the June War* (which carries the story to shortly after the October 1973 War); and Robert O. Freedman, *Soviet Policy Toward the Middle East Since 1970* (the second edition covers developments through 1977).

Another good book on Soviet-Egyptian relations is *Soviet Foreign Policy Towards Egypt*, by Karen Dawisha. Galia Golan's *Yom Kippur and After: The Soviet Union and the Middle East Crisis*, is an excellent study of the Soviet policies in that war and the immediate aftermath. A perceptive and very readable study of a somewhat longer time period is *La Politique Soviétique au Moyen-Orient, 1955-1975*, by Hélène Carrère d'Encausse.

R. D. McLaurin, *The Middle East in Soviet Policy*, is to be numbered among those works that emphasize the limitations imposed by the area on Soviet policy. A cogent short statement that also notes the several regional obstacles to Soviet maneuverability is that of John C. Campbell, "The Soviet Union in the Middle East," *Middle East Journal*, 32, 1 (winter 1978).

In the Direction of the Persian Gulf: The Soviet Union and the Persian Gulf, by A. Yodfat and M. Abir, is a convenient short study (134 pages of text) that provides a brief historical background to the subject and then traces developments through 1976. Also treating Soviet policy in the Arabian peninsula is *The USSR in Arabia: The Development of Soviet Policies and Attitudes Towards the Countries of the Arabian Peninsula* (1971), by Stephen Page. This study is based largely on Soviet press and radio broadcasts.

A useful brief historical survey of Soviet views and policies toward Zionism, Palestine, and Israel is Ivar Spector's "The

Soviet Union and the Palestine Conflict," in Ibrahim Abu-Lughod, *The Transformation of Palestine* (1971).

THE MIDDLE EAST AS A DISTINCTIVE INTERNATIONAL RELATIONS SYSTEM: Two articles by political scientists may be mentioned: "The Middle East as a Subordinate International System," by Leonard Binder, first appeared in *World Politics*, April 1958 (it was included in Binder's collected essays published in book form six years later under the title *The Ideological Revolution in the Middle East*). It is a significant pioneering statement. Binder's strength is his mastery both of the discipline of political science and of Middle Eastern studies.

A more recent effort is "The Middle East: A Subordinate System in Global Politics," by Tareq Y. Ismael in the book he edited, *The Middle East in World Politics* (1974). Then, for a dissenting view one might note the brief but devastating criticism contained in Fouad Ajami's review "The Middle East: Important for the Wrong Reasons," in the *Journal of International Affairs*, 29, no. 1 (spring 1975). This was a special issue devoted to "An Era of Negotiations," and it contains several articles relevant to the subject of this book. The general study by Louis Cantori and Steven Spiegel, *International Politics of Regions: A Comparative Approach*, may also be noted.

GENERAL THEORIES, IDEAS, AND INSIGHTS: This book has argued for an interdisciplinary approach to the study of modern Middle Eastern international politics. A blending of conventional diplomatic history as developed in the West and usually largely concerned with the West, study of the Middle East as a subject in its own right, and study of international relations in general—all this together can enhance our understanding of the Eastern Question system and the distinctive Middle Eastern political culture shaped by that system.

In the process of planning this book, the author came across a number of fruitful theories, ideas, and insights. The sources of these are listed below in the belief that they may be of interest. Social scientists specializing in international relations may well find the list whimsically eclectic, but perhaps they will relish an outsider's view of their discipline. Those engaged in study of the Middle East—burdened by the demands of difficult languages and a relatively underdeveloped scholarly field and thus having limited time for "outside reading"—may find these suggested short-cuts helpful.

Two good books on games theory are highly recommended. They are Thomas C. Schelling, *The Strategy of Conflict*, and Anatol Rapoport, *Strategy and Conscience* (which incorporates much of his earlier *Fights, Games, and Debates*).

An excellent little book written in what might be considered a modernized equivalent of the age-old genre of advice for princes, is Roger Fisher's *International Conflict for Beginners*. In commonsensical, completely non-technical language Fisher offers a sharply etched picture of what diplomacy is all about. Disarmingly simple in style, this is a learned and stimulating book. A bonus for those interested in Middle Eastern politics, in a short appendix Fisher takes the Arab-Israeli confrontation (vintage 1969) as an example of how his maxims might be utilized to achieve a negotiated settlement.

Paul W. Schroeder's "Alliances, 1815-1945: Weapons of Power and Tools of Management," in Klaus Knorr (ed.), *Historical Dimensions of National Security Problems* argues that alliances are often created not for "capability-aggregation" but as "pacts of restraint," that is, a means by which enemies can keep a watch on each other. Coral Bell's *The Conventions of Crisis: A Study in Diplomatic Management* puts forward the same idea somewhat differently in speaking of "adverse partnership." "That is," she writes,"successful management of adversary crises helps create an adverse partnership, and this in turn makes the successful management of future crises more likely" (p. 51). A simple idea, really, but of profound importance in understanding, and evaluating, so much great power diplomacy in the Middle East from Canning's inspired management of Russia during the Greek crisis to the on-again, off-again U.S./Soviet detente in the recent Middle East.

Robert O. Keohane's review article, "Lilliputians' Dilemmas: Small States in International Politics," in *International Organization* (spring 1969), is a useful bibliographical note on the subject crucial to any study of the kaleidoscopic Eastern Question system. Among Keohane's refreshing strengths is an ability to convey important ideas in simple images. Note the following comment on would-be "management" of small states by great powers: " 'Keeping the lid on' is an appropriate metaphor: if the lid flies off, the force of the explosion may be roughly proportional to the effort expended in keeping it on" (p. 306). Keohane also coined the usage "Al Capone alliance" in which "remaining a faithful ally protects one not against the mythical outside threat but rather against the great-power ally itself, just as, by paying 'protection money' to Capone's gang in Chicago, businessmen protected themselves not against other gangs but against Capone's own thugs" (p. 302). This theme offers interesting possibilities—tracing the circumspect way Middle Eastern polities since the beginning of the Eastern Question have allied with threatening outside powers.

Richard B. Elrod's "The Concert of Europe: A Fresh Look at an International System," in *World Politics* (January 1976), crisply conveys the systemic nature of nineteenth-century European international politics, with passing attention to how that system affected the Middle East.

A thorough and up-to-date study that integrates most of the prevailing social science theories and methodologies on international reactions is *Conflict Among Nations*, by Glenn H. Snyder and Paul Diesing. This is a solid work, but it is rather ponderous.

The best recent general collection on diplomatic history and international relations (and one conceived as an effort to better integrate these two approachs to the same subject) is *Diplomacy: New Approaches in History, Theory, and Policy*, edited by Paul Gordon Lauren.

A good book with which to end this bibliographical essay is *The Last Crusade: A Negotiator's Middle Eastern Handbook*, by William R. Brown. Written by an "old Middle Eastern hand" who is a trained social scientist, *The Last Crusade* concentrates on Kissinger the diplomat and on the period when Kissinger conducted American diplomatic efforts to resolve the Arab-Israeli confrontation. Brown provides a sensitive and clear interpretation of both Arab and Israeli (as well as American) perceptions and operating style. This finely honed case study says much about both diplomacy and Middle Eastern political culture.

BIBLIOGRAPHY

THIS bibliography lists all works cited in the book, including the bibliographical essay, plus a few others deemed relevant to the subject of the Eastern Question system. Those works mentioned in the bibliographical essay are marked by an asterisk.

Abdul Nasser, Gamal, *Egypt's Liberation: The Philosophy of the Revolution*. Washington, 1955.

*Abu-Lughod, Ibrahim, *Arab Rediscovery of Europe: A Study in Cultural Encounters*. Princeton University Press, 1963.

*Abun-Nasr, Jamil M., *A History of the Maghrib* (second edition). Cambridge University Press, 1975.

*Adomeit, Hannes, "Soviet Policy in the Middle East: Problems of Analysis," *Soviet Studies* (April 1975).

*Ahmed, Jamal Mohammed, *The Intellectual Origins of Egyptian Nationalism*. Oxford University Press, 1960.

*Ajami, Fouad, "The Middle East: Important for the Wrong Reasons," *Journal of International Affairs* 29, no. 1 (spring 1975). A short, biting review of Ismael, "The Middle East: A Subordinate System in Global Politics" (q.v.).

*Albrecht-Carre, Rene, *A Diplomatic History of Europe Since the Congress of Vienna*. New York, 1958.

*Allen, Richard, *Imperialism and Nationalism in the Fertile Crescent: Sources and Prospects of the Arab-Israeli Conflict*. Oxford University Press, 1974.

Almond, Gabriel, "Comparative Political Systems," *The Journal of Politics* 18 (August 1956), reprinted in Almond, *Political Development: Essays in Heuristic Theory*. Boston, 1970.

———— and Verba, Sidney, *The Civic Culture*. Princeton University Press, 1963.

*Anderson, M. S., *The Eastern Question, 1774-1923: A Study in International Relations*. London, 1966.

*———— (ed.), *The Great Powers and the Near East*. New York, 1970.

*Andrew, Christopher M., and Kanya-Forstner, A. S., *The Climax of French Imperial Expansion, 1914-1924*. Stanford University Press, 1981.

*Andrić, Ivo, *The Bridge on the Drina* (translated from the Serbo-Croat). New York, 1967.

Antonius, George, *The Arab Awakening*. London, 1938 (reprinted several times).

Aronson, Shlomo, *Conflict and Bargaining in the Middle East: An Israeli Perspective*. Johns Hopkins University Press, 1978.

*Badeau, John S., *The American Approach to the Arab World*. New York, 1968.

*Balta, Paul, and Rulleau, Claudine, *La Politique Arabe de la France: De Gaulle à Pompidou*. Paris, 1973.

Bar-Simon-Tov, Yaacov, *The Israeli-Egyptian War of Attrition, 1969-1970: A Case Study of Limited Local War*. Columbia University Press, 1980.

*Bell, Coral, *The Conventions of Crisis: A Study of Diplomatic Management*. Oxford University Press, 1971.

*Berkes, Niyazi, *The Development of Secularism in Turkey*. McGill University Press, 1964.

*Binder, Leonard, "The Middle East as a Subordinate International System," *World Politics* (April 1958). Reprinted in Leonard Binder, *The Ideological Revolution in the Middle East*. New York, 1964.

Bolsover, G. H., "Nicholas I and the Partition of Turkey," *The Slavonic and Eastern European Review*. 28, 68 (December 1948).

Bourne, Kenneth, *The Foreign Policy of Victorian England*. Oxford University Press, 1970.

*Brecher, Michael, with Benjamin Geist, *Decisions in Crisis: Israel, 1967 and 1973*. University of California Press, 1980.

*———, *Decisions in Israel's Foreign Policy*. Yale University Press, 1975.

*Brecher, Michael, *The Foreign Policy System of Israel: Setting, Images, Process*. Yale University Press, 1972.

*Brown L. Carl, "Tunisia," in James S. Coleman (ed.), *Education and Political Development*. Princeton University Press, 1965.

*———, *The Tunisia of Ahmad Bey, 1837-1855*. Princeton University Press, 1974.

*———, "The Tunisian Path to Modernization," in Menahem Milson (ed.), *Society and Political Structure in the Arab World*. New York, 1973.

*Brown, William R., *The Last Crusade: A Negotiator's Middle East Handbook*. Chicago, 1980.

*Brunschwig, Henri, *Mythes et Réalités de l'Impérialisme Colonial*

Français, 1871-1914. Paris, 1960. English translation—*French Colonialism, 1871-1914: Myths and Realities* (revised edition). New York, 1966.

*Bullard, Sir Reader, *Britain and the Middle East: From the Earliest Times to 1963* (3rd revised edition). London, 1963.

Bulloch, John, *The Making of a War: The Middle East from 1967 to 1973*. London, 1974. Good, informed account of these years emphasizing inter-Arab developments by a British journalist.

*Bury, J.P.T., "Diplomatic History 1900-1912," in *New Cambridge Modern History* (vol. 12).

*Busch, Briton Cooper, *Britain and the Persian Gulf, 1894-1914*. University of California Press, 1967.

*———, *Britain, India, and the Arabs, 1914-1921*. University of California Press, 1971.

———, *Mudros to Lausanne: Britain's Frontier in West Asia*. State University of New York Press, 1976.

*Campbell, John C., "The Soviet Union in the Middle East," *Middle East Journal*. 32, 1 (winter 1978).

*Cantori, Louis J., and Spiegel, Steven, *The International Politics of Regions: A Comparative Approach*. Englewood Cliffs, N.J., 1970.

*Carrère d'Encausse, Hélène, *La Politique Soviétique au Moyen-Orient, 1955-1975*. Paris, 1975.

Case, Lynn M., "A Duel of Giants in Old Stamboul: Stratford v. Thouvenal," *Journal of Modern History*. 21 (1963).

Cecil, Lady Gwendolen, *Life of Robert, Marquis of Salisbury* (4 vols.). London, 1921-1932.

Centre National de la Recherche Scientifique, *La Guerre en Méditerranée, 1939-1945*. Paris, 1971. Proceedings of an international colloquium held in 1969 with a number of relevant articles, including a special section of over 100 pages devoted to "Les Nationalismes en Afrique du Nord et au Levant."

Chapman, Maybelle Kennedy, *Great Britain and the Baghdad Railway, 1881-1914*. Smith College Studies in History. 31 (1948).

*Chastenet, Jacques, *Histoire de la Troisième République* (7 vols.) Paris, 1952-1963.

*Clayton, G. D., *Britain and the Eastern Question: From Missolonghi to Gallipoli*. University of London Press, 1971.

*Cleveland, William L., *The Making of an Arab Nationalist: Ottomanism and Arabism in the Life and Thought of Sati' Al-Husri*. Princeton University Press, 1971.

313

*Confine, Michael & Shamir, Shimon (eds.), *The USSR and the Middle East*, New York, 1973.

Copeland, Miles, *The Game of Nations*. New York, 1970. Titillating account of U.S. relations with Egypt during early Nasser years by former CIA official. The main revelation is one that perhaps author did not intend: When policy is fixed and executed by intelligence agencies, confusion follows.

Craig, Gordon, "Dulles and American Statecraft," in Craig, *War, Politics, and Diplomacy*. New York, 1966.

*————, "The System of Alliances and the Balance of Power," in *New Cambridge Modern History* (vol. 10).

*Crawley, C. W., "International Relations, 1815-1830," in *New Cambridge Modern History* (vol. 9).

*————, "The Mediterranean," in *New Cambridge Modern History* (vol. 10).

*————, "The Near East and the Ottoman Empire, 1798-1830," in *New Cambridge Modern History* (vol. 9).

————, *The Question of Greek Independence, 1821-1833*. Cambridge University Press, 1930 (reprinted 1973).

*Cumming, Henry H., *Franco-British Rivalry in the Post-War Near East: The Decline of French Influence*. Oxford University Press, 1938.

Cunningham, Allan, "Stratford Canning and the *Tanzimat*" in William R. Polk and Richard L. Chambers, *Beginnings of Modernization in the Middle East: The Nineteenth Century*. University of Chicago Press, 1968. Stresses the need to better blend Ottoman domestic issues and foreign policy considerations, both British and Ottoman.

————, "The Wrong Horse: A Study of Anglo-Turkish Relations before the First World War," in *St. Anthony's Papers: Middle Eastern Affairs* (1965). Good review of changing British policy toward the Ottomans by a scholar who knows the Ottoman side of the story as well.

Davison, Roderic H., *Reform in the Ottoman Empire, 1856-1876*. Princeton University Press, 1963. The best study of this critical period in late Ottoman history. Although the book concentrates on Ottoman domestic developments, the great power role is well presented. An excellent monograph detailed enough to satisfy the specialist but so readable as to please the layman.

————, "Turkish Diplomacy from Mudros to Lausanne," in Gordon

A. Craig and Felix Gilbert (eds.), *The Diplomats, 1919-1939*. Princeton University Press, 1953. Finely drawn case study of tenacious, and effective, Turkish diplomacy.

*Dawisha, A. I., *Egypt in the Arab World: The Elements of Foreign Policy*. New York, 1976.

*Dawisha, Karen, *Soviet Foreign Policy Towards Egypt*. New York, 1979.

Dawn, C. Ernest, *From Ottomanism to Arabism: Essays on the Origins of Arab Nationalism*. University of Illinois Press, 1973. These excellent short studies based on a thorough examination of Arabic sources as well as European materials constitute a major contribution to our knowledge both of early Arab nationalism and Middle Eastern diplomatic maneuverings during the First World War.

*DeNovo, John A., *American Interests and Policies in the Middle East, 1900-1939*. University of Minnesota Press, 1963.

*DeVore, Ronald M., *The Arab-Israeli Conflict: A Historical, Political, Social, and Military Bibliography*. Santa Barbara & Oxford, Clio Books, 1976.

Dodwell, Henry H., *The Founder of Modern Egypt: A Study of Muhammad Ali*. Cambridge University Press, 1931.

*Drabek, Anne Gordon, and Knapp, Wilfrid, *The Politics of African and Middle Eastern States: An Annotated Bibliography*. Oxford and New York, Pergammon Press, 1976.

*Driault, E., *La Question d'Orient*. Paris, 8 editions between 1898 and 1920.

Eddy, William A., *F.D.R. Meets Ibn Saud*. New York, 1954.

Eden, Anthony, *The Suez Crisis of 1956* (reprinted from *Full Circle: The Memoirs of Anthony Eden*). Boston, 1960.

Eisenhower, Dwight D., *Mandate for Change*. New York, 1963.

*Elon, Amos, *Herzl*. New York, 1975.

*———, *The Israelis: Founders and Sons*. New York, 1971.

*Elrod, Richard B., "The Concert of Europe: A Fresh Look at an International System," *World Politics* (January 1976).

Evans, Lawrence, *United States Policy and the Partition of Turkey, 1914-1924*. Johns Hopkins University Press, 1965. A useful presentation of U.S. perceptions and policies for this important decade. The viewpoint of an important outside power, the United States, which almost became a major participant in Middle Eastern politics under Wilson but then lapsed into isolationism is well delineated.

*Evron, Yair, *The Middle East: Nations, Superpowers, and Wars*. New York, 1973.

*Field, Jr., James A., *America and the Mediterranean World, 1776-1882*. Princeton University Press, 1969.

*Findley, Carter V., *Bureaucratic Reform in the Ottoman Empire: The Sublime Porte, 1789-1922*. Princeton University Press, 1980.

*————, "The Foundation of the Ottoman Foreign Ministry: The Beginnings of Bureaucratic Reform under Selim III and Mahmud II," *International Journal of Middle Eastern Studies*. 3, no. 4 (October 1972).

*————, "The Legacy of Tradition to Reform: Origins of the Ottoman Foreign Ministry," *International Journal of Middle Eastern Studies*. 1, no. 4 (October 1970).

*Fisher, Roger, *International Conflict for Beginners*. New York, 1969.

*Fitzsimons, M. A., *Empire by Treaty: Britain and the Middle East in the Twentieth Century*. University of Notre Dame Press, 1964.

Fox, Annette Baker, *The Power of Small States: Diplomacy in World War II*. University of Chicago Press, 1959. A classic study of small-state diplomacy. Republican Turkey is one of the five states treated in this book.

*Freedman, Robert O., *Soviet Policy Toward the Middle East Since 1970* (revised edition). New York, 1978.

———— (ed.), *World Politics and the Arab-Israeli Conflict*. New York, 1979. Well-organized book growing out of 1978 conference with chapters on "Superpower Perspectives," "Regional Perspectives," and "Domestic Perspectives" (the latter having separate contributions on Israeli, Palestinian, Egyptian, and Syrian policies and viewpoints).

Fromkin, David, "The Great Game in Asia," *Foreign Affairs* (spring 1980). Sees the parallels between nineteenth- and twentieth-century Eastern Question history. Notes the tendency of great powers to assume the worst about rivals. Fromkin, however, completely misunderstands Middle Eastern perceptions and actions, then and now. Note the following: "The sultans of Turkey, in particular, knowing how much the British needed to prop them up, exploited that need in such a way as to avoid making the needed reforms. They felt free to resist the demands of foreign creditors and of foreign powers because they felt that Britain would be obliged to defend them aginst any attempt at enforcement. How to deal with this sort of blackmail by a weak client

316

state is a problem that Britain was not able to solve in the nineteenth century any more than the United States has been able to do so in the twentieth century" (p. 943). It is distressing to read such outmoded, one-sided "lessons from history" written in a major journal as late as 1980.

Galbraith, John S., and Lutfi al-Sayyid-Marsot, Afaf, "The British Occupation of Egypt: Another View," *International Journal of Middle East Studies* 9, no. 4 (November 1978). Argues that an uncoordinated combination of British officials "on the spot" in Egypt and cabinet ministers in Britain managed to move a weakly led and divided government into occupying Egypt. A disturbing case study of how members of a basically liberal and democratic government can provoke avoidable Middle Eastern crises, covering up their misdeeds after the fact in a rationalizing rhetoric that they, themselves, come to believe.

*Gallagher, Charles F., *The United States and North Africa*. Harvard University Press, 1963.

*Ganiage, Jean, *Les Origines du Protectorat Français en Tunisie (1861-1881)*. Presses Universitaires de France, 1959.

Gellner, Ernest, *Saints of the Atlas*. University of Chicago Press, 1969.

*Gibb, H.A.R., and Bowen, Harold, *Islamic Society and the West* (Vol. I in two parts). Oxford University Press, 1950 and 1957.

*Gillard, David, *The Struggle for Asia, 1828-1914: A Study in British and Russian Imperialism*. London, 1977.

Glassman, Jon D., *Arms for the Arabs: The Soviet Union and War in the Middle East*. Johns Hopkins University Press, 1975. A good collection of available data. Limited interpretation or analysis.

Gleason, J. H., *The Genesis of Russophobia in Great Britain*. Harvard University Press, 1950 (reprinted 1972).

*Golan, Galia, *Yom Kippur and After: The Soviet Union and the Middle East Crisis*. Cambridge University Press, 1977.

Gordon, David C., *North Africa's French Legacy, 1954-1962*. (Harvard Middle Eastern Monograph Series. 9) Harvard University Press, 1962.

———, *The Passing of French Algeria*. Oxford University Press, 1966.

*Grafftey-Smith, Lawrence, *Bright Levant*. London, 1970.

Grenville, J.A.S., *Lord Salisbury and Foreign Policy*. London, 1964.

*Haim, Sylvia G. (ed.), *Arab Nationalism: An Anthology*. University of California Press, 1962 (paperback edition 1976).

Halle, Louis, *The Cold War as History*. New York, 1967. Nothing on the Eastern Question system, but interesting for comparative purposes. Halle emphasizes the role of the prevailing international relations system in shaping the Cold War.

*Harris, George S., *Troubled Alliance: Turkish-American Problems in Historical Perspective, 1945-1971*. American Enterprise Institute/ Hoover Institution, 1972.

Hassouna, Hussein A., *The League of Arab States and Regional Disputes: A Study of Middle East Conflicts*. New York and Leiden, 1975. Thorough and well-organized. Mainly legal in approach. Weak on the political background.

Heikal, Mohamed, *The Sphinx and the Commissar: The Rise and Fall of Soviet Influence in the Middle East*. New York, 1978.

*Henry, Clement M., with Jeffrey Wolff and Steven Heydemann, *Politics and International Relations in the Middle East: An Annotated Bibliography*. Center for Near Eastern and North African Studies, University of Michigan, 1980.

Hermassi, Elbaki, *Leadership and National Development in North Africa*. University of California Press, 1972.

*Higgins, Rosalyn, *United Nations Peacekeeping: Documents and Commentary* (Vol. I, "The Middle East"). New York, 1969.

*Hirszowicz, Lukasz, *The Third Reich and the Arab East*. London, 1966.

Hopwood, Derek, *The Russian Presence in Syria and Palestine, 1843-1914: Church and Politics in the Near East*. Oxford University Press, 1969.

*Hourani, Albert, *Arabic Thought in the Liberal Age, 1798-1939*. Oxford University Press, 1962.

*———, "Ottoman Reform and the Politics of Notables," in William R. Polk and Richard L. Chambers (eds.), *Beginnings of Modernization in the Middle East*. University of Chicago Press, 1968.

Howard, Harry N., *The King-Crane Commission: An American Inquiry into the Middle East*. Beirut, 1963.

———, *Turkey, The Straits, and U.S. Policy*. Johns Hopkins University Press, 1974. A solid historical study from the early nineteenth century to the 1970s. Contains a thorough and useful annotated bibliography.

*Hurewitz, J. C. (ed.), *The Middle East and North Africa in World Politics: A Documentary Record*. Vol. I, European Expansion, 1535-1914. Vol. II, British-French Supremacy, 1914-1945. Vol. III (in preparation). Yale University Press, 1975 and 1979.

al-Husri, Khaldun S., "The Assyrian Affair of 1933," *International Journal of Middle Eastern Studies*. Part I in 5, 2 (April 1974), Part II in 5, 3 (June 1974).

al-Husri, Sati', *Al-Bilad al-ʿArabiyya wa al-Dawla al-Uthmaniyya* (The Arab Countries and the Ottoman State). Beirut, 1957 (and many later editions).

International Institute of Strategic Studies, *The Military Balance* (annual).

*Ismael, Tareq Y., "The Middle East: A Subordinate System in Global Politics," in Ismael (ed.), *The Middle East in World Politics*. Syracuse University Press, 1974.

*Issawi, Charles (ed.), *The Economic History of the Middle East, 1800-1914*. University of Chicago Press, 1966.

———, *An Economic History of the Middle East and North Africa*. Columbia University Press, 1982.

*Itzkowitz, Norman, and Mote, Max, *Mubadele: An Ottoman-Russian Exchange of Ambassadors*. University of Chicago Press, 1970.

*Itzkowitz, Norman, *Ottoman Empire and Islamic Tradition*. New York, 1972.

Jabber, Paul, *Not by War Alone: Security and Arms Control in the Middle East*. University of California Press, 1981. Thorough study of this important subject within the context of the Arab-Israeli conflict (on arms control and arms sales, see also Andrew Pierre).

*Jelavich, Barbara, *A Century of Russian Foreign Policy, 1814-1914*. New York, 1964.

———, *The Ottoman Empire, The Great Powers and the Straits Question*, 1870-1887. Indiana University Press, 1973. Especially strong in presenting the Ottoman perspective. First part of the book does a good job in setting the general context for events of these years.

Johnson, Lyndon, *Vantage Point*. New York, 1971.

Kadi, Leila S., *Arab Summit Conferences and the Palestine Problem (1936-1950), (1964-1966)*. Beirut, 1966. Defines summit conferences broadly to include the major inter-Arab meetings on Palestine for the years covered. Very useful. Provides details on agendas, issues, personalities not readily to be found in other sources. A companion volume treating summit conferences since 1966 would be welcomed.

*Kedourie, Elie, *Arabic Political Memoirs and Other Studies*. London, 1974.

*Kedourie, Elie, *The Chatham House Version and Other Middle Eastern Studies*. London, 1970.

*————, *England and the Middle East: The Destruction of the Ottoman Empire, 1914-1921*. London, 1956.

*————, *In the Anglo-Arab Labyrinth: The McMahon-Husayn Correspondence and its Interpretations, 1914-1939*. Cambridge University Press, 1976.

*————, *Islam in the Modern World and Other Studies*. New York, 1980.

*————, "The Middle East, 1900-1945," in *New Cambridge Modern History* (vol. 12).

*Kelly, J. B., *Arabia, the Gulf, and the West*. New York, 1980.

*————, *Britain and the Persian Gulf, 1795-1880*. Oxford University Press, 1968.

*Keohane, Robert O., "Lilliputians' Dilemmas: Small States in International Politics," *International Organization* (spring 1969).

*Kerr, Malcolm, *The Arab Cold War: Gamal 'Abd al-Nasir and His Rivals, 1958-1970* (third edition). Oxford University Press, 1971.

*————, "Egypt" in James S. Coleman (ed.), *Education and Political Development*. Princeton University Press, 1965.

Khadduri, Majid, "Aziz Ali al-Misri and the Arab Nationalist Movement," *St. Antony's Papers*. 17 (*Middle Eastern Affairs*, 4).

————, "General Nuri's Flirtation with the Axis Powers," *Middle East Journal*. 16, 3 (summer 1962).

————, *Independent Iraq, 1932-1958*. Oxford University Press, 1951.

————, "The Scheme of Fertile Crescent Unity: A Study in Inter-Arab Relations," in Richard N. Frye (ed.), *The Near East and the Great Powers*. Harvard University Press, 1951. A good description of early Arab unity efforts.

*Khalidi, Walid, and Khadduri, Jill (eds.), *Palestine and the Arab-Israeli Conflict: An Annotated Bibliography*. Beirut, Institute for Palestine Studies, 1974.

*Khalil, Muhammad (ed.), *The Arab States and the Arab League: A Documentary Record* (2 vols.). Beirut, 1962.

Khouri, Fred J., *The Arab-Israeli Dilemma* (second edition). Syracuse University Press, 1976.

*Kirk, George, *The Middle East in the War*. Oxford University Press, 1951.

*————, *The Middle East, 1945-1950*. Oxford University Press, 1954.

Kissinger, Henry, *A World Restored: Metternich, Castlereagh, and the*

Problem of Peace, 1812-1822. Boston, 1957 (paperback edition 1973).

————, *White House Years.* Boston, 1979.

————, *Years of Upheaval.* Boston, 1982. One can disagree with the man. One can accept that these detailed volumes are, after all, the apologia of a former secretary of state. They stand out, nevertheless, as personal history in the grand style, with fascinating reflections on both how things work and how things should work in international diplomacy. A treasure trove for historians.

Klieman, Aaron S., *Foundations of British Policy in the Arab World: The Cairo Conference of 1921.* Johns Hopkins University Press, 1970. A solid, thorough account that helps explain how Britain moved from ambiguous or contradictory war-time commitments to a more coherent post-war policy for the Middle East.

Knapp, Wilfrid (ed.), *Northwest Africa: A Political and Economic Survey* (third edition). Oxford University Press, 1977. Third edition of a standard survey on modern North Africa. Reliable if very brief historical sketches, but most attention to the contemporary political and economic scene. Companion volume on the Middle East is that edited by Peter Mansfield (q.v.).

*Kuniholm, Bruce R., *The Origins of the Cold War in the Near East: Great Power Conflict and Diplomacy in Iran, Turkey, and Greece.* Princeton University Press, 1980.

Langer, William L., *The Diplomacy of Imperialism, 1890-1902* (2nd edition). New York, 1950.

————, *European Alliances and Alignments, 1871-1890* (2nd edition). New York, 1956. These two old examples of splendid narrative, interpretative diplomatic history offer much material on the Eastern Question.

*Laqueur, Walter, *A History of Zionism.* New York, 1976.

*Laroui, Abdallah, *The History of the Maghrib: An Interpretive Essay* (translated from the French). Princeton University Press, 1977.

*Lauren, Paul Gordon (ed.), *Diplomacy: New Approaches in History, Theory, and Policy.* New York, 1979.

*Lederer, Ivo (ed.), *Russian Foreign Policy: Essays in Historical Perspective.* Yale University Press, 1962.

Leitenberg, Milton, and Sheffer, Gabriel (eds.), *Great Power Intervention in the Middle East.* New York, 1979. Generally high-quality papers growing out of 1977 Cornell University conference. Limited historical perspective and major attention, in most cases, on developments of the last few years. More emphasis on U.S. than USSR policies and performance.

*Lenczowski, George, *The Middle East in World Affairs* (fourth edition). Cornell University Press, 1980.

*Lewis, Bernard, *The Emergence of Modern Turkey*. Oxford University Press, 1961 (paperback edition 1968/1979).

*——, *The Middle East and the West*. Indiana University Press, 1964.

*——, "Politics and War," in Joseph Schacht and C. E. Bosworth (eds.), *The Legacy of Islam* (second editon). Oxford University Press, 1974 (paperback edition 1979).

Love, Kennett, *Suez, The Twice Fought War: A History*. New York, 1969. A meticulously researched, detailed narrative and analysis, critical of the Western powers and sympathetic to Nasser's position. A must for those who wish to examine the important Suez crisis in detail.

Lowe, C. J., *The Reluctant Imperialists: British Foreign Policy, 1878-1902*. New York, 1969 (British edition 1967). Spirited book-length survey (c. 250 pages) followed by good collection of selected documents. Inclined to favor Salisbury and British-style realpolitik. In the old Eurocentric tradition as regards the Eastern Question.

*Lucas, Noah, *The Modern History of Israel*. London, 1974.

Lutfi al-Sayyid-Marsot, Afaf, see John S. Galbraith.

MacDonald, Robert W., *The League of Arab States*. Princeton University Press, 1965. A well-regarded standard account concentrating more on organization and structure than the historical development.

*McLaurin, R. D., Mughisuddin, Mohammed, and Wagner, Abraham R., *Foreign Policy Making in the Middle East: Domestic Influences on Policies in Egypt, Iraq, Israel, and Syria*. New York, 1977.

*——, Peretz, Don, and Snider, Lewis W., *Middle East Foreign Policy: Issues and Processes*. New York, 1982.

*——, *The Middle East in Soviet Policy*. Lexington, Mass., 1975.

*Mangold, Peter, *Superpower Intervention in the Middle East*. New York, 1978.

*Mansfield, Peter, *The Arabs*. Penguin Books, 1976.

—— (ed.), *The Middle East: A Political and Economic Survey* (fifth edition). Oxford University Press, 1980. A standard British survey. Companion volume on North Africa is that edited by Wilfrid Knapp (q.v.).

*Mardin, Şerif, *The Genesis of Young Ottoman Thought: A Study in the Modernization of Turkish Political Elites*. Princeton University Press, 1962.

*Marlowe, John, *Arab Nationalism and British Imperialism*. London, 1961.

*Marriott, J.A.R., *The Eastern Question: An Historical Study in European Diplomacy*. Oxford University Press, four editions between 1917 and 1940.

*Medlicott, W. N., "Austria-Hungary, Turkey, and the Balkans," in *New Cambridge Modern History* (vol. 11).

———, *Bismarck, Gladstone, and the Concert of Europe*. London University Press, 1956.

**Middle East Journal*. 30, 3 (summer 1976). Special issue with articles on history of American relations with the Middle East.

*Miller, William, *The Ottoman Empire and its Successors, 1801-1927*. Cambridge University Press, four editions between 1913 and 1936.

Millman, Richard, *Britain and the Eastern Question, 1875-1878*. Oxford University Press, 1979. A new work covering roughly the same subject as the older Seton-Watson, *Disraeli, Gladstone, and the Eastern Question*. More balanced in treatment of the Ottomans, incorporating findings of Ottomanists. Still, old-fashioned diplomatic history in its detailed narrative and its Eurocentrism. Favorable to Disraeli, harsh on Gladstone.

*Monroe, Elizabeth, *Britain's Moment in the Middle East, 1914-1971* (revised edition). Johns Hopkins University Press, 1981.

*———, *The Mediterranean in Politics*. London, 1938.

*Moore, Clement Henry, *Politics in North Africa*. Boston, 1970.

*Moore, John Norton (ed.), *The Arab-Israeli Conflict* (3 vols.). Princeton University Press, 1974.

Mosse, W. E., "The Return of Reschid Pasha; An Incident in the Career of Lord Stratford de Redcliffe," *English Historical Review*. 68 (1953).

———, *The Rise and Fall of the Crimean System, 1855-1871: The Story of a Peace Settlement*. London, 1963.

"Moyen-Orient et Relations Internationales aux XXe Siècle," *Relations Internationales* 19 and 20 (autumn and winter 1979). Special issues of this Swiss scholarly journal containing several useful articles, including three which touch on French policy in the Middle East since 1914.

*Naff, Thomas, "Ottoman Diplomatic Relations with Europe in the Eighteenth Century: Patterns and Trends," in Thomas Naff and Roger Owen (eds.), *Studies in Eighteenth Century Islamic History.* Southern Illinois University Press, 1977.

Neff, Donald, *Warriors at Suez: Eisenhower Takes America into the Middle East.* New York, 1981. A well-researched and readable account by a career journalist with considerable Middle Eastern experience.

*Nevakivi, Jukka, *Britain, France, and the Arab Middle East, 1914-1920.* London, 1969.

Nixon, Richard, *Memoirs.* New York, 1978.

*Nicosia, Francis, "Arab Nationalism and National Socialist Germany, 1933-1939: Ideological and Strategic Incompatibility," *International Journal of Middle East Studies* 12, no. 3 (November 1980).

Nutting, Anthony, *No End of a Lesson: The Story of Suez.* London, 1967.

*Page, Stephen, *The USSR in Arabia: The Development of Soviet Policies and Attitudes Towards the Countries of the Arabian Peninsula.* London, Central Asian Research Center, 1971.

Pierre, Andrew J., *The Global Politics of Arms Sales.* Princeton University Press, 1982. This highly acclaimed general study includes a strong chapter on the Middle East (on arms control and arms sales see also Paul Jabber).

*Pingaud, A., *Histoire Diplomatique de la France Pendant la Grande Guerre* (2 vols.). Paris, 1938.

*Polk, William R., *The Arab World* (fourth edition). Harvard University Press, 1980.

*———, *The Elusive Peace: The Middle East in the Twentieth Century.* New York, 1979.

Porath, Y., *The Emergence of the Palestinian-Arab National Movement, 1918-1929.* London, 1974.

———, *The Palestinian Arab National Movement, 1929-1939: From Riots to Rebellion.* London, 1977.

*Poulton, Helen J., *The Historian's Handbook.* University of Oklahoma Press, 1972.

*Quandt, William B., *Decade of Decisions: American Policy Toward the*

Arab-Israeli Conflict, 1967-1976. University of California Press, 1977.

*Ramm, Agatha, and Sumner, B. H., "The Crimean War," in *New Cambridge Modern History* (vol. 10).

*Rapoport, Anatol, *Strategy and Conscience*. New York, 1964.

*Roberts, Stephen H., *The History of French Colonial Policy, 1870-1925*. London, 1929 (reprinted 1963).

Robinson, Ronald, and Gallagher, John, with Alice Denny, *Africa and the Victorians: The Official Mind of Imperialism*. London, 1961 (paperback edition 1965). A stimulatingly different approach, neither traditional Eastern Question historiography nor a study directly focused on the Middle East. *Africa and the Historians* addresses the question of how and why the European "scramble for colonies" began in the late nineteenth century. The authors see the Egyptian crisis as the major catalyst.

*Ro'i, Yaacov, *From Encroachment to Involvement: A Documentary Study of Soviet Policy in the Middle East, 1945-1973*. New York and Toronto, 1974.

*——— (ed.), *The Limits to Soviet Power in the Middle East*. New York, 1979.

Rossi, E., "Il Congresso Interparlamentare Arabo E Musulmano Pro Palestina Al Cairo (7-11 Ottobre)," *Oriente Moderno* (November 1938).

*Rubinstein, Alvin, *Red Star on the Nile: The Soviet-Egyptian Influence Relationship Since the June War*. Princeton University Press, 1977.

*Rustow, Dankwart, "The Political Impact of the West," in *Cambridge History of Islam* (Vol. 1).

Saab, Ann Pottinger, *The Origins of the Crimean Alliance*. University Press of Virginia, 1977. A recent book on the subject that places the Ottoman Empire at the center of the story.

*Sachar, Howard M., *The Emergence of the Middle East: 1914-1924*. New York, 1969.

*———, *Europe Leaves the Middle East, 1936-1954*. New York, 1972.

al-Sadat, Anwar, *Revolt on the Nile*. New York, 1957.

*Safran, Nadav, *Egypt in Search of Political Community*. Harvard University Press, 1961.

*———, *From War to War: The Arab-Israeli Confrontation*. New York, 1969.

*———, *Israel the Embattled Ally: The Shaping of American-Israeli*

Relations and the Creation and Transformation of Israel Through Three Decades of Middle East Crises and Wars. Harvard University Press, 1978.

*Salibi, K. S., *The Modern History of Lebanon*. London, 1965.

Samuel, Herbert L., *Memoirs*. London, 1945.

*Schelling, Thomas C., *The Strategy of Conflict*. Harvard University Press, 1960 (Oxford University Press paperback, 1963 and 1975).

*Schroeder, Paul W., "Alliances, 1815-1945: Weapons of Power and Tools of Management," in Klaus Knorr (ed.), *Historical Dimensions of National Security Problems*. University Press of Kansas, 1976.

————, *Austria, Great Britain and the Crimean War: The Destruction of the European Concert*. Cornell University Press, 1972. Important new argument on role of nineteenth-century Britain in shaking stability of the European system. Little emphasis, however, on the Eastern Question issues.

*Schulz, Ann, *International and Regional Politics in the Middle East and North Africa: A Guide to Information Sources* (Vol. 6 in *International Relations Information Guide Series*). Detroit, Gale Research Co., 1977.

*Seale, Patrick, *The Struggle for Syria: A Study in Post-War Arab Politics, 1945-1958*. Oxford University Press, 1965.

*Seton-Watson, R. W., *Britain in Europe, 1789-1914: A Survey of Foreign Policy*. Cambridge University Press, 1937 (reprinted New York, 1968).

*————, *Disraeli, Gladstone, and the Eastern Question*. London, 1935.

Seton-Williams, M. N., *Britain and the Arab States: A Survey of Anglo-Arab Relations, 1920-1948*. London, 1948. Mainly of use now as convenient overview of establishment British thinking at that time. Several mistakes and misspellings of proper names.

*Shaked, Haim, and Rabinovich, Itamar (eds.), *The Middle East and the United States: Perceptions and Policies*. New Brunswick, N.J., 1980.

Shannon, R. T., *Gladstone and the Bulgarian Agitation, 1876*. London, 1963 (revised edition, 1975).

*Sharabi, Hisham, *Arab Intellectuals and the West: The Formative Years, 1875-1914*. Johns Hopkins University Press, 1970.

Shaw, Stanford J., *Between Old and New: The Ottoman Empire Under Selim III, 1789-1807*. Harvard University Press, 1971.

————, *History of the Ottoman Empire and Modern Turkey*. Vol. 1,

Empire of the Gazis: The Rise and Decline of the Ottoman Empire, 1280-1808. Cambridge University Press, 1976.

*———, and Shaw, Ezel Kural, *History of the Ottoman Empire and Modern Turkey*. Vol. 2, *Reform, Revolution, and Republic: The Rise of Modern Turkey, 1808-1975*. Cambridge University Press, 1977.

*———, "The Ottoman View of the Balkans," in Barbara Jelavich and Charles Jelavich (eds.), *The Balkans in Transition*. University of California Press, 1963.

*Shorrock, William I., *French Imperialism in the Middle East: The Failure of Policy in Syria and Lebanon, 1900-1914*. University of Wisconsin Press, 1976.

Slade, Adolphus, *Records of Travels in Turkey, Greece* (2 vols.). London, 1833.

*Smolansky, Oles, *The Soviet Union and the Arab East Under Khrushchev*. Bucknell University Press, 1974.

*Snyder, Glenn H., and Diesing, Paul, *Conflict Among Nations*. Princeton University Press, 1977.

*Spagnolo, John P., *France and Ottoman Lebanon, 1861-1914*. London, 1977.

*Spector, Ivar, "The Soviet Union and the Palestine Conflict," in Ibrahim Abu-Lughod (ed.), *The Transformation of Palestine*. Northwestern University Press, 1971.

Spiegel, Steven L. (ed.), *The Middle East and the Western Alliance*. London, 1982. One of the few books to address the important topic of NATO, EEC, and American-European-Japanese policies and diplomacy regarding the Middle East.

*Stavrianos, L. S., *The Balkans Since 1453*. New York, 1958.

*Stookey, Robert W., *America and the Arab States: An Uneasy Encounter*. New York, 1975.

Storrs, Sir Ronald, *The Memoirs of Sir Ronald Storrs*. New York, 1937.

Sumner, B. H., *Russia and the Balkans, 1870-1880*. Oxford University Press, 1937.

Syria. Prepared by Naval Intelligence Division (United Kingdom). Geographical Handbook Series B.R. 513, April 1943.

*Szyliowicz, Joseph S., *Education and Modernization in the Middle East*. Cornell University Press, 1973.

*Tanenbaum, Jan Karl, "France and the Arab Middle East, 1914-1920," *Transactions of the American Philosophical Society*. Vol. 68, Part 7 (October 1978).

*Taylor, A.J.P., "International Relations," in *New Cambridge Modern History* (Vol. 11).

*———, *The Struggle for Mastery in Europe*. Oxford University Press, 1954.

Temperley, H.W.V., *England and the Near East: The Crimea*. London, 1936.

Thornton, A. P., "Imperial Frontiers in the Levant, 1870-1900," in Thornton, *For the File on Empire*. London, 1968.

———, "Rivalries in the Mediterranean," in *New Cambridge Modern History* (Vol. 11).

———, "The Roots of Jingoism," in Thornton, *For the File on Empire*, London, 1968.

Tibawi, A. L., *Anglo-Arab Relations and the Question of Palestine, 1914-1921*. London, 1977.

Touval, Saadia, *The Peace Brokers: Mediators in the Arab-Israeli Conflict, 1948-1979*. Princeton University Press, 1982. Treats in depth a theme emphasized throughout *Old Rules, Dangerous Game*— the kaleidoscopic nature of Middle Eastern diplomacy and the Middle Eastern penchant for bringing in third party mediators.

*Toynbee, A. J., *The Islamic World Since the Peace Settlement: Survey of International Affairs, 1925*. Vol. 1. Oxford University Press/ Royal Institute of International Affairs, 1927.

———, *The Western Question in Greece and Turkey: A Study in the Contact of Civilizations*, Boston and New York, 1922. The book grew out of Toynbee's wartime experiences ending in a tour of the areas at war in 1921. Sensitive and perceptive. Toynbee was one of the few who in those years clearly saw the "Eastern" aspect of the Eastern Question.

Treverton, Gregory (ed.), *Crisis Management and the Super-Powers in the Middle East*. (Adelphia Library No. 5) International Institute for Strategic Studies, 1981.

*Trumpener, Ulrich, *Germany and the Ottoman Empire, 1914-1918*. Princeton University Press, 1968.

———, "Turkey's Entry into World War I: An Assessment of Responsibilities," *Journal of Modern History*. 34 (December 1962).

United States Arms Control & Disarmament Agency, *World Military Expenditures and Arms Transfers, 1970-1979*. Washington, D.C. (released March 1982).

Vali, Ferenc A., *Bridge Across the Bosphorus: The Foreign Policy of Turkey*. Johns Hopkins University Press, 1971.

————, *The Turkish Straits and Nato*. Hoover Institution Press, 1971.

Vambery, A., "Personal Recollections of Abdul Hamid and his Court," *Nineteenth Century* 66 (July 1909).

*Vatikiotis, P. J., *Conflict in the Middle East*. London, 1971.

*————, *The Modern History of Egypt*. London, 1969.

Verba, Sidney, see Gabriel Almond.

*Vyvyan, J.M.K., "The Approach of the War of 1914," in *New Cambridge Modern History* (Vol. 12).

*Weber, Frank G., *Eagles on the Crescent: Germany, Austria, and the Diplomacy of the Turkish Alliance, 1914-1918*. Cornell University Press, 1970.

*————, *The Evasive Neutral: Germany, Britain, and the Quest for a Turkish Alliance in the Second World War*. University of Missouri Press, 1979.

*Weisband, Edward, *Turkish Foreign Policy, 1943-1945: Small State Diplomacy and Great Power Politics*. Princeton University Press, 1973.

*Whetten, Lawrence L., *The Canal War: Four-Power Conflict in the Middle East*. Massachusetts Institute of Technology Press, 1974.

Wight, Martin, "World Politics," in Wight, *Power Politics*. Leicester University Press, 1978.

Williams, Ann, *Britain and France in the Middle East and North Africa, 1914-1967*. London, 1968.

Woodhouse, C. M., *The Battle of Navarino*. London, 1965.

*Yale, William, *The Near East: A Modern History*. University of Michigan Press, 1958.

*Yodfat, A., and Abir, M., *In the Direction of the Persian Gulf: The Soviet Union and the Persian Gulf*. London, 1977.

*Zartman, I. William, "North African Foreign Policy," in L. Carl Brown (ed.), *State and Society in Independent North Africa*. Washington, D.C., 1966.

Zeine, Zeine N., *The Emergence of Arab Nationalism, with a Background Study of Arab-Turkish Relations in the Near East* (revised edition). Beirut, 1966.

————, *The Stuggle for Arab Independence* (second edition). New York, 1967.

Zumwalt, Elmo R., *On Watch*. New York, 1976.

APPENDIX I. EASTERN QUESTION
CHRONOLOGY, 1774-1923

1774	Treaty of Kuçuk Kaynarca, ending the third eighteenth-century war between Russia and the Ottoman Empire
1792	Treaty of Jassy, ending the fourth and last eighteenth-century war between Russia and the Ottoman Empire (1787-1792)
1798	Napoleon's invasion of Egypt
1812	Treaty of Bucharest, ending war between Russia and the Ottoman Empire (1806-1812)
1818	Aix-la-Chapelle Conference decision on elimination of Barbary Piracy
1821-1829	Greek War of independence
1828-1829	War between Russia and the Ottoman Empire, ending in treaty of Adrianople
1830	Beginning of French occupation of Algeria
1832-1833	First Syrian crisis—war between Muhammad Ali of Egypt and Ottoman Sultan Mahmud
1833	Treaty of Hunkar Iskelesi (Unkiar Skelessi)˙ between Russia and the Ottoman Empire (high point of Russian influence in Istanbul)
1839	Britain occupies Aden
1839-1840	Second Syrian Crisis—war between Muhammad Ali of Egypt and his nominal sovereign, the Ottoman Sultan
1840	Treaty of London: four-power European agreement imposing settlement on Muhammad Ali
1841	London Convention (Austria, France, Great Britain, Prussia, Russia, and the Ottoman Empire) regarding use of the Straits
1853-1856	Crimean War: Ottoman Empire, Britain, France, and Sardinia v. Russia
1856	Treaty of Paris, ending Crimean War
1858-1861	Disturbances in Lebanon/French military intervention/Powers grant special status to Lebanon
1869	Opening of the Suez Canal

1870	Russia renounces Black Sea clauses of 1856 Treaty of Paris. Action accepted by the Powers in 1871 (Treaty of London)
1875	Insurrection in Bosnia and Herzegovina
1877-1878	War between Russia and Ottoman Empire
1878	Treaty of Berlin, growing out of Great Power Congress of Berlin, which softened Russian terms on Ottoman Empire imposed by Treaty of San Stefano earlier that year
1881	French Protectorate over Tunisia
1882	British occupation of Egypt
1896-1898	Anglo-Egyptian reconquest of Sudan
1904	Anglo-French Entente (free hand for former in Egypt, latter in Morocco)
1906	Tabah Incident: Anglo-Ottoman dispute over Egypt's eastern border
1911-1912	Italian invasion of Tripolitania. War between Italy and Ottoman Empire
1912-1913	First Balkan War: Bulgaria, Serbia, and Greece v. Ottoman Empire
1913	Second Balkan War: Ottoman Empire and Rumania v. Bulgaria
1914	Ottoman Empire enters First World War on the side of the Central Powers
1915-1916	Husayn-MacMahon Correspondence (British commitments to establishment of an Arab state)
1917	Balfour Declaration (British commitment to Jewish National Home in Palestine)
1918	(October) Truce of Mudros, ending Ottoman participation in First World War
1922	Acceptance of British mandates over Iraq, Transjordan, Palestine, and French over Syria and Lebanon
1923	Treaty of Lausanne, abolishing harsh terms Allies imposed on Ottoman Empire at Sèvres (1920), granting international recognition of what became Republic of Turkey

APPENDIX II. DISMEMBERMENT
OF THE OTTOMAN EMPIRE,
1774-1923

1774	Kuçuk Kaynarca. Ottomans lost Crimean areas to Russia, recognized independence of Crimean Tatars
1783	Catherine the Great unilaterally absorbed Crimean khanates into Russian state (accepted by Ottoman Empire at Treaty of Jassy, 1792)
1812	Treaty of Bucharest. Bessarabia separated from Moldavia and ceded to Russia
1817	Partial self-government granted Serbia after second Serbian insurrection (1815-1817)
1830	Greece granted independence by Powers following Greek insurrection (1821-1829) and Russo-Ottoman War (1828-1829)
1830	Beginning French occupation of Algeria
1839	British occupation of Aden
1840-1841	Sultan granted Muhammad Ali dynasty hereditary governorship of Egypt (as part of Great Power orchestrated settlement of the 2nd Syrian crisis)
1861	Five-power European commission obliged Ottoman Empire to implement plan for autonomous Mount Lebanon under non-Lebanese Christian governor
1878	Virtual self-government for Ottoman Crete following revolt
1878	Ottoman Empire ceded Cyprus to British. Treaty of Berlin, ending Eastern Crisis of 1875-1878 and Russo-Ottoman War (1877-1878). Independence of Serbia, Rumania, and Montenegro. Austria permitted to occupy Bosnia and Herzegovina. Russia granted Kars, Batum, and Ardahan. Creation of autonomous Bulgaria (scaled down from earlier San Stefano treaty)
1881	Greece acquired Thessaly and part of Epirus from Ottoman Empire
1881	French protectorate over Tunisia

1882	British occupation of Egypt
1898	Ottoman troops forced by powers to evacuate Crete. Europeans impose Cretan autonomy
1899	Establishment of Anglo-Egyptian Condominium over Sudan after reconquest
1899	Britain established secret protectorate over Kuwait
1908	Austria annexed Bosnia and Herzegovina. Proclamation of Bulgarian independence
1911	Italy invaded Tripolitania, proclaimed annexation
1912	Successful Albanian revolt. Ottomans obliged to grant autonomy
1914	British protectorate over Egypt
1920	Treaty of Sèvres. Ottomans renounced all claims to remaining non-Turkish territories. Losses in Anatolia redressed by Ataturk military successes and subsequent Treaty of Lausanne (1923)

APPENDIX III. MAJOR REGIONAL
POWER BIDS IN THE
GREATER OTTOMAN WORLD FROM
THE BEGINNING OF THE
EASTERN QUESTION TO THE
OUTBREAK OF THE
FIRST WORLD WAR

1788-1840	Long reign of Bashir II, amir of Mount Lebanon, devoted to establishing Lebanese autonomy (allied with Muhammad Ali from 1820s)	Warlord
1798-1822	Ali Pasha's rule in Northern Albania and surrounding areas	Warlord
1801-1805	Muhammad Ali, acting on the disorders following Napoleon's invasion of Egypt established his rule in Egypt, in substantive if not formal defiance of the Porte	Warlord
1803-1818	The Wahhabis under the political leadership of the Saudi family, having established control of central Arabia and captured Mecca, penetrated deep into Iraq	Muslim
1804-1817	Serbian revolt	Nationalist
1821-1829	Greek War of independence	Nationalist
1832-1833	Muhammad Ali conquered Syria from his nominal sovereign, the Sultan	Warlord
1839-1840	Following ill-fated attack by Sultan Mahmud II, Muhammad Ali's forces soundly defeated the Ottoman army. Days later the Ottoman fleet defected to Muhammad Ali. Only	Warlord

	Muhammad Ali's hesitation in the face of European opposition stopped a march into Anatolia and probably to Istanbul itself	
1843	The Grand Sanusi founded the first *zawiya* (Sufi brotherhood lodge) in Libya. Without directly challenging the Ottoman authorities, the Sanusiyya did manage to gain the religio-political loyalty of the majority of those living in the desert hinterland of Libya as well as vast areas of the Sahara.	Muslim
1859-1860	Druze-Christian war led to European imposition of autonomous status for Lebanon	Nationalist
1875	Insurrection in Bosnia and Herzegovina	Nationalist
1876	Peasant revolt in Bulgaria	Nationalist
1878	Revolt in Crete leading to partial self-government	Nationalist
1882-1898	Period of the Sudanese Mahdiyya driving the Egyptians out of Sudan and ending the last vestige of nominal Ottoman authority there	Muslim
1893-1896	Abortive Armenian independence activities and ensuing massacres	Nationalist
1896-1897	Insurrection in Crete leading to Ottoman-Greek war	Nationalist
1909	Further Armenian demonstrations followed by another round of massacres.	Nationalist
1910-1912	Albanian revolt ending in Ottoman grant of autonomy	Nationalist

(The Egyptian campaigns of expansion against targets beyond the range of effective Ottoman control—conquest of the Sudan beginning in 1820, the unsuccessful invasion of Ethiopia, 1875-1879—are not included since they fell outside the area in which the Eastern Question pattern prevailed.)

336

APPENDIX IV. ESTABLISHED AUTHORITY AND THE
EASTERN QUESTION: OTTOMAN EMPIRE, TUNISIA, AND EGYPT

Egypt	*Ottoman Empire*	*Tunisia*
	1792 Selim III begins western-style army units, Nizam-i Cedid	
	1793 First posting of resident ambassador abroad	
	1807 Selim III deposed by Janissaries and other conservative forces	
1811 Muhammad Ali massacres mamluks		1811 Revolt of Turkish jund (regular infantry)
1815 1st effort to create modern army		1816 Revolt of Turkish jund
1811-1818 Campaign against Wahhabis in Arabia		
1820 Conquest of Sudan begins		
1823 Military conscription of native Egyptians begins		
1826 Student missions to Paris	1826 Destruction of Janissaries and creation of western-style army	
1827 Opening of modern medical school followed in coming years by several other technical schools	1827 Medical School opened soon after that in Egypt, followed in coming years by other technical schools	
1829 1st newspaper, the official Vekayi-i Misriyye		

Appendix IV (*cont.*)

Egypt	Ottoman Empire	Tunisia
		1830 Abortive Franco-Tunisian plans for Tunisian beys to rule in Oran and Constantine following French conquest of Algeria
	1831 Official Gazette, Takvim-i Vekayi	1831 Husayn Bey organizes 1st Nizami troops
	1831 Census for tax and conscription purposes	
1832 Muhammad Ali conquers Syria from Ottomans	1833 Treaty of Hunkar Iskelesi, desperate Ottoman ploy relying on Russia against Muhammad Ali	
	1833-1839 Prussian military mission (young von Moltke)	
	1835 Re-establishment direct Ottoman control over Tripoli	1835 Increased fear of bey and court that Porte seeking direct control over Tunisia
		1837 Ill-fated plan by Ahmad Bey imposes conscription on inhabitants of Tunis. (Thereafter, conscription attempted only in sedentary areas of countryside.)
	1838 Anglo-Ottoman commercial treaty (Balta Liman), major step toward free trade	1838-1839 Unrealized British effort have Col. Considine organize and lead British military mission

1839 (April) Mahmud II moves v. Muhammad Ali in Syria with disastrous results

1839 Hatt-i Şerif of Gulhane, 1st great civil liberties rescript

1840-1846 Disturbances in Lebanon bring increasing European interference

1850 Ottoman commercial code promulgated

1853 Ottomans reject Vienna vote, last great power plan to avoid Crimean War (seeing strong likelihood great power support, Ottomans hold out against Russian demands)

1853 October: Ottoman Empire declares war on Russia. Beginning Crimean War

1840 Establishment of Bardo Military School, modeled on European schools and partly staffed with European instructors

1840-1855 French Military Advisory Mission

1841-1846 Ahmad Bey stops slave trade and then abolishes slavery

1846 Ahmad Bey's state visit to Paris. Cancels visit to London since British government insisted on receiving him in presence of Ottoman ambassador. (Ploy in continuing game to maintain de facto independence)

1840 Convention of Alexandria Muhammad Ali bows to European pressure, returns Ottoman fleet, and gives up Syria

1841 Muhammad Ali agrees to abide by the terms of the 1838 Anglo-Ottoman treaty (and the equivalent with other powers) thus setting in motion the undermining of his monopoly system

1851-1853 British firm built railroad from Cairo to Alexandria (only important concession to foreign interests during short reign of Abbas I [1849-1854], probably in part to better counter French pressures)

Appendix IV (cont.)

Egypt	Ottoman Empire	Tunisia
1854 Said grants Suez Canal concessions to Ferdinand de Lesseps	1854 1st loan raised in Europe	1854 May: Ahmad Bey brings Tunisia into Crimean War (effort enhance standing in Europe while also supporting Sultan)
	1855 Firman abolishing poll tax on non-Muslims and making them subject to conscription, with right of exemption by special tax—bedel—in amount of previous poll tax.*	
	1856 February 18: Hatt-i Humayun most comprehensive Ottoman rescript of civil liberties, just one week before opening of Paris Congress negotiating end of Crimean War.	1857 Fundamental Pact (Ahd al-Aman), charter of rights modeled on 1839 Ottoman Hatt-i Serif of Gulhane (response to European pressure following execution of Tunisian Jewish subject)
	1860-1861 Disturbances in Lebanon. Landing of French troops. Powers impose Lebanese autonomy on Ottomans	

* "In Europe, the promise and its abandonment were dismissed as just another piece of Ottoman insincerity. But in fact the Ottoman government gave long and earnest consideration to the problem of non-Muslim recruitment, which, besides appealing to Western and liberal opinion, offered the tempting bait of a new accession of manpower for the depleted Ottoman armies." (Bernard Lewis, *The Emergence of Modern Turkey*, pp. 331-332.) It was part of the long, and ultimately unsuccessful, effort to create a sense of Ottoman patriotism without destroying the one solid strength remaining to the embattled empire—the sense of Muslim solidarity.

1860 Muhammad al-Sadiq Bey gets draft constitution approved by Napoleon III

1861 Constitution (1st in Arab world) promulgated

1863 Doubling of the poll tax, leading to

1864 Revolt imperiling the regime and greatly increasing indebtedness

1869 Anglo-French-Italian Financial Commission following Tunisian bankruptcy

1867 Ottoman Sultan's state visit to Europe

1868 Opening of Imperial Ottoman Lycee at Galatasaray

1871 Death of last major reformist minister, Ali Pasha.

1862 1st foreign loan

1865 Egypt granted control of Suakin and Massawa on Red Sea by Ottoman Empire

1866 Ismail established representative assembly (Majlis Shura al-Nuwwab)

1867 Ismail secured title of khedive and other perquisites of semi-independence from Porte

1869 Opening of Suez Canal

1870-1873 Samuel Baker conquest of Upper Nile for Egypt

Appendix IV (*cont.*)

Egypt	Ottoman Empire	Tunisia
		1871 Rapprochement with Porte, at British urging, to resist Italian threat
		1873-1877 Reformist ministry of Khayr al-Din, last effort at reform-from-within
		1875 Founding of Sadiqi College, European curriculum school
	1875 State bankruptcy	
	1876 December: Constitution proclaimed during early phase of the 1875-1878 "Eastern Crisis" while European representatives were meeting in Constantinople & plans were being bruited for further division Ottoman Empire	
1871 Muqabala Law: landowners urged pay six times annual tax in advance in return for perpetual reduction ½ the tax. Ismail's ploy failed		
1872 Establishment of Dar al-ʿUlum, after Al-Azhar resists reform (another step in secularization and state control of education)		
1874-1879 Gordon governor-general of Egyptian Sudan		
1875 Mixed courts to replace consular jurisdiction (effort to mitigate rampant European interference)		
1875 Financially hard-pressed Ismail sold Egypt's shares in Suez Canal (purchased by Disraeli for Britain)		
1875-1879 Unsuccessful war against Ethiopia (final phase of Ismail's expansionist ambitions)		

1876 Bankruptcy. Establishment of European Caisse de la Dette to service the Egyptian debt

1878 Ismail obliged accept principle of ministerial responsibility with European backed Nubar Pasha as prime minister, a British minister of finance and a French minister of public works

1878 Britain given right to occupy Cyprus in return for British guarantee Ottoman Asian territories

1879 Ismail dismissed Nubar Pasha government (with its two European ministers) in name of ministerial responsibility, making last-ditch stand regain control. Outraged Britain and France get sultan to replace Ismail with son

1879 Sultan, urged by powers, dismissed Khedive Ismail

1881 European-directed Council of the Public Debt established

1881 1st German Military Advisory Mission

1881 France seizes pretext to occupy Tunisia and impose protectorate

1881 Beginning Urabi Pasha revolt

1882 Constantinople Conference to discuss possible Ottoman intervention in Egypt

1882 Increasing British and French support for khedive against nationalists

END OF PRE-COLONIAL EASTERN QUESTION PATTERN

Appendix IV (*cont.*)

Egypt	*Ottoman Empire*	*Tunisia*
1882 July: British bombing of Alexandria followed by British occupation		
END OF PRE-COLONIAL EASTERN QUESTION PATTERN		
	1887 Failure ratify Anglo-Ottoman convention on British withdrawal from Egypt (heeding French and Russian pressure, holding out, in vain, for better terms)	
	1888 Railroad concession to German interests, 1st phase of Baghdad Railroad project	
	1890s Armenian revolutionary ferment and ensuing massacres. No effective pressure on the Porte since the powers were divided.	
	1897 Successful war against Greece which spared penalty defeat by pressure from the powers on the Porte	
	1900-1908 Hijaz Railroad financed through public subscription of Muslims	
	1906 Tabah incident. Dispute concerning boundary between British-occupied Egypt and Palestine. Sultan yields to British ultimatum.	

1908 Young Turk Revolution
1909 Abdul Hamid deposed for supporting
      counter-revolution

Young Turk Period to outbreak of
First World War:
1. increasing cynicism concerning role of
   outside powers (e.g., 1908 Austrian annexation of Bosnia and Herzegovina,
   1911 Italian invasion of Libya)
2. increasing disillusion with notions of liberal Ottomanism transcending religious
   differences, leaving ideas of either an
   Arab-Turk Muslim empire or Turkification with the latter growing in strength.
3. continued effort to play off the great
   powers, but with an increasing emotional leaning toward Germany as the one
   power with no designs on Ottoman territory, resulting in the Ottoman decision
   to enter the war on the side of the Central Powers

APPENDIX V. MIDDLE EASTERN POLITICS AND INTERNATIONAL RELATIONS, 1919-1982: THE MAIN LINES

1919		Egyptian revolution against British presence
	May	— Greeks Land at Izmir (Smyrna)
	July	— Syrian National Congress demands independence
	Aug	— King-Crane Commission Report
1920	April	— Mandates assigned: Syria and Lebanon to France; Iraq, Transjordan, and Palestine to Britain (action formally approved by League of Nations in 1922)
	July	— French drive Faisal from Syria; Greeks begin military operations against Turkey
	July-Dec.	— Revolt in Iraq against British
	Aug.	— Treaty of Sèvres with Ottoman Empire signed but never ratified.
	Sept.	— French create greater Lebanon at expense of Syria and divide latter
1921	March	— Ataturk signs treaty with Soviet Union
	April	— Abdullah recognized by British as amir of Transjordan
	July	— Abd al-Krim victory against Spanish, beginning Riff War (Morocco)
	Aug.	— Faisal King of Iraq
	Aug.	— Palestine mandate revised to exclude Transjordan from Jewish National Home
	Oct.	— Franco-Turkish Treaty (leaving Britain more isolated in support of Greeks)
1922	Feb.	— British unilateral declaration of Egyptian independence with reservations
	Sept.	— Ataturk's forces rout Greeks. Lacking allies, Britain decides against intervention on side of Greeks
	Nov.	— Ataturk abolishes sultanate
	Dec.	— Najd (later Saudi Arabia) border agreement with Iraq
1923	July	— Lausanne Treaty, confirming post-war settlement former Ottoman Empire

14	Oct.	— Turkish capital moved from Istanbul to Ankara
29	Oct.	— Turkish Republic proclaimed
1924	March	— Ataturk abolishes caliphate
	Oct.	— Sharif Husayn forced to abdicate and leave Hijaz
1925	July	— Beginning Druze revolt v. French in Syria
	Oct.	— French bomb Damascus
	Dec.	— Soviet-Turkish alliance
	Dec.	— Ibn Saud completes conquest of Hijaz, driving out Hashimites
1926	Jan.	— Ibn Saud proclaimed King of Hijaz
	May	— French again bomb Damascus
	May	— Abd al-Krim surrenders to French, ending Moroccan Riff War
	June	— League decision settling Mosul border issue in favor Iraq accepted by Turkey
1927	Feb.	— Ibn Saud's title changed to King Hijaz and Najd
	May	— British recognition independence Ibn Saud's kingdom
1928		Neo-traditionalist Muslim Brethren founded by Hasan al-Banna in Egypt
1929	Aug.	— Wailing Wall incident in Palestine
1930	June	— Anglo-Iraqi treaty providing for termination mandate, Iraqi nominal independence, and British sponsoring Iraq as member League of Nations
1932		End pacification in Libya and in French Morocco
	Sept.	— Ibn Saud's kingdom renamed Saudi Arabia
	Oct.	— Iraq accepted into League of Nations
1933	May	— Oil concession agreement signed between Saudi Arabia and Standard Oil of California (later joined by other companies to form Aramco)
	Aug.	— Assyrian massacres (Iraq)
	Sept.	— King Faisal of Iraq dies, succeeded by son Ghazi
1934	March	— Creation of Tunisian Neo-Destour Party, challenging more traditional Old Destour Party
	March/June	— War between Saudi Arabia and Yemen, ended by British mediation with border changes favoring victor, Saudi Arabia
1935		Beginning of intensive Italian settler colonization in Libya (Mussolini's "demographic colonization")

1936	Feb.	— General Strike in Syria
	April	— Beginning Arab revolt in Palestine
	April	— Death of King Fuad, succeeded by son, Faruq
	July	— Montreux Convention, strengthening Turkish control of Straits
	July	— Spanish Civil War begins, with revolt Spanish troops loyal to Franco in Spanish Morocco
	Aug.	— Anglo-Egyptian Treaty
		Blum-Viollette proposal—major French effort cautiously grant political rights to Algerians (soundly rejected by French Chamber of Deputies following year)
	Oct.	— Bakr Sidqi coup in Iraq
1937	May	— Montreux Convention. Powers agree abolition capitulations in Egypt. Egypt accepted into League of Nations
	July	— Sa'dabad Pact—Turkey, Iraq, Iran, and Afghanistan
		— Report of Peel Commission proposing partition in Palestine
	Sept.	— Pan-Arab congress in Bludan, Syria
1938		Proto-nationalist Graduates Congress formed in Sudan; Franco-Turkish crisis over Alexandretta
	Oct.	— Cairo inter-parliamentary Arab-Muslim conference on Palestine
	Nov.	— Death of Ataturk, succeeded by Ismet Inonu
1939	Feb./March	London round-table talks on Palestine
	May	— Anglo-Turkish treaty
	May	— British White Paper on Palestine
	June	— Franco-Turkish treaty, including French acquiescence in Turkish annexation of Hatay (Alexandretta)
1940	March	— Rashid Ali government formed in Iraq
	Nov.	— Nazi-Soviet discussions re Middle Eastern spheres of influence
1941	May	— Foreign Secretary Eden statement favoring Arab unity
		British military intervention in Iraq, overthrowing Rashid Ali government
	June	— British and Free French oust Vichy French forms Syria and Lebanon

	Sept.	— Free French General Catroux proclaims Syrian independence
	Nov.	— Catroux proclaims Lebanese independence
1942	Feb.	— British impose Wafdist government on King Faruq
	May	— Biltmore program, Zionist rejection 1939 White Paper and demand Jewish state
	Oct.	— Battle of El Alamein. Farthest advance of Rommel's desert korps. British victory and turning of tide in favor of Allies in Middle East
	Nov.	— Operation Torch. Landing of U.S. troops in North Africa
1943	Feb.	— Eden reaffirms British support for Arab unity
	May	— Axis forces surrender to Allies in Tunisia. End North African campaign Emergence of Lebanese "National Pact," Muslim-Christian accord on Lebanese independence
	Nov.	— French attempt to dismiss Lebanese government seeking independence stopped by Anglo-American pressure
1944	Oct.	— Alexandria meeting of Arab leaders to draw up plans for Arab League
1945	March	— Soviets denounce 1925 Soviet-Turkish treaty
	March	— Arab League Pact signed in Cairo
	May	— French bomb Damascus in final effort impose treaty
	June	— Intensified Soviet pressure on Turkey re territorial adjustments, bases and Straits administration
	Aug.	— Saudi Arabia grants U.S. airbase rights in Dhahran
1946	March	— Anglo-Jordanian treaty recognizing Jordanian independence Agreement reached on withdrawal all foreign troops from Syria and Lebanon
	April	— Report of Anglo-American Committee of Inquiry on Palestine
1947	Jan.	— Egypt refers dispute with Britain to UN Security Council (discussed in August, with no decision reached)
	March	— Truman Doctrine
	April	— Britain refers Palestine problem to United Nations
	Nov.	— UN General Assembly votes Palestine partition

1948	Jan.	— Anglo-Iraqi treaty signed but not ratified, following adverse reaction Iraqi public (Treaty of Portsmouth)
	May	— End British Mandate in Palestine, creation of Israeli, beginning Arab-Israeli war.
	Sept.	— Egyptian-sponsored "all-Palestinian government" organized in Gaza
	Dec.	— Abdullah counters, accepting proposal Palestinian notables for absorption Arab Palestine into an Arab Kingdom of Jordan
1949		3 military coups in Syria (March/Aug./Dec.)
	Feb.-July	— Israel armistice agreement with Egypt, Lebanon, Jordan, and Syria
	April	— Transjordan renamed Hashimite Kingdom of Jordan
	Dec.	— Israel moves capital from Tel Aviv to Jerusalem, ignoring UN General Assembly resolution on internationalization
1950	April	— Jordanian annexation of West Bank formalized
	May	— Tripartite Declaration (Anglo-French-American) against armed aggression across existing Arab-Israeli armistice lines, pledging to maintain arms balance between the two sides.
1951	July	— King Abdullah assassinated in Jerusalem
	Oct.	— Wafdist government abrogates 1936 Anglo-Egyptian treaty and 1899 Condominium Agreement concerning Sudan
	Dec.	— Libya independent under King Idris
1952	July	— Nasser's Free Officers coup ousting King Faruq
1953	Feb.	— Anglo-Egyptian Agreement on self-determination in Sudan
1954	Feb.	— Naguib ousted by Nasserists but returned to office days later
	July	— Preliminary Anglo-Egyptian agreement on British withdrawal from Suez Canal base
	Aug.	— Israeli ship, *Bat Galim*, stopped in attempt use Suez Canal. Israeli effort provoke effective UN action fails
	Aug.	— Secret Israeli-French agreement on sale of military equipment

	Oct.	— Beginning of Algerian war of independence
	Oct.	— Anglo-Egyptian agreement on British withdrawal from Suez Canal base signed
	Nov.	— Naguib permanently ousted from power
1955	Feb.	— Turkish-Iraqi alliance (beginning of Baghdad Pact)
	Feb.	— Massive Israeli raid against Egyptian forces in Gaza
	March	— Nasser attends Bandung Conference
	April	— Britain joins Baghdad Pact (Pakistan joins in Sept., Iran in Oct.)
	May	— Nasser begins Soviet arms deal negotiations
	Sept.	— Soviet-Egyptian arms deal revealed
	Nov.	— Anglo-American-Egyptian talks on financing of High Dam
1956	Feb.	— Khrushchev speech 20th Communist Party Congress signals Soviet ideological change toward Third World with support for "national bourgeois" regimes
	Feb.	— Collapse two-months-old secret Egyptian-Israeli talks mediated by confidant of Eisenhower, Robert B. Anderson
	March	— King Husayn ousts British General Glubb. Nasser's influence seen by Britain
	May	— Egypt recognizes Communist China. Viewed as unfriendly act by U.S.
19	July	— Dulles withdraws High Dam offer
26	July	— Nasser nationalizes Suez Canal
	Oct.-Nov.	— Anglo-French-Israeli actions against Egypt (Suez Crisis)
1957	Jan.	— Eisenhower Doctrine
	Jan.	— Eden resigns, following British Suez debacle; Macmillan succeeds him
	Feb.	— Adamant Eisenhower stand on Israeli withdrawal from Sinai
	March	— Israeli troops withdraw
	March	— Anglo-Jordanian treaty abrogating 1948 treaty (last British troops leave Jordan by July)
	April	— Suez Canal reopens
	April	— Jordan crisis. Husayn reverses efforts align Jordan with Egypt and Syria
	Aug.	— Syrian crisis. Syria charges U.S.-Turkish plot to overthrow government

351

1958	Feb.	— Union of Egypt and Syria to form United Arab Republic
	Feb.	— French attack Tunisia border village of Sakiat Sidi Yusuf, claiming Tunisia harboring Algerian FLN units. Provokes Anglo-American good offices mission.
	May	— French Fourth Republic overthrown as result of continuing Algerian crisis. De Gaulle to power.
	July	— Hashimite monarchy in Iraq destroyed in military coup
	July	— U.S. marines to Lebanon, British troops to Jordan
	Dec.	— Soviet Union agrees aid Egypt in building High Dam
1959	March	— Iraq withdraws from Baghdad Pact (changed to Central Treaty Organization—CENTO)
1960	May	— Military intervention in Turkey overthrowing Menderes government
	Aug.	— Cyprus independent
	Sept.	— Organization of Petroleum Exporting Countries (OPEC) established
1961	June	— 1899 Anglo-Kuwait treaty terminated, Kuwait independence recognized
	July	— Iraqi claim to Kuwait stopped by British and, later, Arab League action
	Sept.	— Syria secedes from United Arab Republic
1962	July	— End of 8-year-old Algerian War with independence
	Sept.	— Revolution in Yemen overthrowing imam
1963	Feb.	— Ba'th coup overthrows Qasim regime in Iraq
	Mar.	— Ba'th coup overthrows government in Syria
	April	— Egyptian/Syrian/Iraqi federation plans announced
	July	— Nasser withdraws from federation plans after pro-Nasserists defeated and executed in Syria
	Fall	— Moroccan-Algerian border war
1964	May	— Egyptian-Iraqi agreement on joint political command working toward constitutional unity within two years
1965	April	— Bourguiba suggestion more flexible Arab negotiating tactics on Israel (based on 1947 UN partition plan) arouses storm of protest in Arab world

1966	Spring	— Egyptian-Saudi agreement on Yemen breaks down. Egyptian military presence continues
	Nov.	— Egyptian-Syrian defense alliance
1967	June	— Six Day War. 3rd Arab-Israeli war, leaving Israeli occupying Syria's Golan Heights, West Bank of Jordan, and Egypt's Sinai.
	Nov.	— UN Security Council Resolution 242 on settlement of Arab-Israeli conflict
1968	Jan.	— Egypt completes withdrawal from Yemen
	March	— Battle of Karameh (Jordan) PLO stand against Israeli military raid gives that organization psychological boost and increases its influence
	July	— 1st PLO hijacking diverting Israeli airliner to Algiers
	Dec.	— Israeli reprisal raid on Beirut airport
1969	April	— Beginning of Egyptian-Israeli "war of attrition"
	Sept.	— Coup by Col. Qaddafi overthrows King Idris of Libya
	Dec.	— 1st Rogers Plan on settlement Arab-Israeli conflict
1970	March	— Effective end of Yemeni civil war with informal Saudi-Yemeni agreement
	March	— Israeli deep-penetration raids against Egypt in continuing war of attrition. Nasser asks for, and receives, Soviet troops
	Aug.	— Egyptian-Israeli cease-fire based on Rogers initiative accepted
	Sept.	— "Black September" Palestinian guerrillas challenging cease-fire agreement and Husayn's regime in Jordan provoke massive Jordanian response
20	Sept.	— Nasser dies, succeeded by Sadat
	Nov.	— Federation plans Egypt/Sudan/Libya announced
1971	March	— Military intervention in Turkey forcing resignation Demirel government
	May	— Soviet-Egyptian treaty
1972	July	— Soviet military advisers expelled from Egypt
	Aug.	— Egyptian/Libyan agreement on unity announced
1973	Oct.	— Yom Kippur/Ramadan War—4th Arab-Israeli War
1974	Jan.	— Libya-Tunisia merger announced (plans allowed by Tunisia to lapse within a month)
	Jan.	— 1st Egyptian-Israeli disengagement agreement

	May	— Syria/Israel disengagement agreement
	July	— Military coup in Cyprus favoring union with Greece, followed by Turkish military intervention
	Oct.	— Rabat Arab Summit Conference designates PLO representative of Palestinians
	Nov.	— PLO leader Yasir Arafat addresses UN General Assembly
1975	March	— Iraq/Iran agreement ending Iranian support of Iraqi Kurds, resulting in collapse of Kurdish war v. Iraq
	April	— Beginning Lebanese civil war
	June	— Suez Canal reopens
	Sept.	— 2nd Egyptian/Israeli disengagement agreement (including U.S. surveillance teams in Sinai)
	Nov.	— UN General Assembly resolution labelling Zionism as a racism
	Nov.	— Morocco's King Hasan organizes "Green March" into former Spanish Sahara
1976	March	— Sadat abrogates 1971 Soviet-Egyptian treaty
	May-June	Syrian military intervention in Lebanon
1977	1 Oct.	— Joint U.S./Soviet statement on Arab-Israeli peace
	Nov.	— Sadat visit to Jerusalem
1978	March	— Israeli invasion of South Lebanon (withdrawing by mid-June)
	May	— Congress approves U.S. military sales to Egypt and Saudi Arabia
	Sept.	— Camp David accords—Begin/Sadat, with Carter as mediator
1979	Jan.	— Iran revolution overthrowing Pahlavi dynasty
	March	— Egyptian/Israeli peace treaty Egypt suspended from Arab League
	July	— Abrupt end Syrian-Iraqi unity talks
	Nov.	— Iranian militants seized U.S. diplomatic hostages
	Dec.	— Soviet invasion of Afghanistan
1980	Jan.	— Carter Doctrine: U.S. warning against attempts
1980	June	— EEC "Venice Declaration," calling for inclusion PLO in Arab-Israeli negotiations
	Sept.	— Iraq invades Iran
	Nov.	— Abortive Arab Summit Conference

1981	Mar.	— Creation Gulf Cooperation Council (GCC)—Saudi Arabia, Kuwait, Bahrain, Oman, and United Arab Emirates
	Aug.	— Saudi initiative (Fahd Plan) for Arab-Israeli settlement
	Oct.	— Assassination of President Sadat. Senate narrowly approves sale AWACs (Airborne warning & control system aircraft) to Saudi Arabia over Israeli objections. 3 ex-presidents (Carter, Ford, and Nixon) state U.S. must eventually recognize PLO
	Nov.	— Fahd Plan fails at Fez Arab Summit Conference. U.S. Israeli strategic accord announced
1982	Apr.	— Israel completes return of Sinai to Egypt
	June	— Beginning Israeli invasion of Lebanon
	July	— Iranian forces push into Iraq in war continuing since September 1980
	Sept.	— Reagan Peace Plan for Arab-Israeli settlement 13th Arab Summit Conference in Fez Christian massacres of Palestinians at Refugee camps (Sabra and Shatila)

INDEX

Abd al-Ilah, Regent of Iraq, 130
Abdul Aziz, Sultan, 227
Abdul Hamid, Sultan, 76-77, 96;
Arab policy, 142; and Britain,
231; and Pan-Islam, 77, 81, 246
Abdullah, King, Amir Transjordan,
98; and Arab nationalism, 151;
and Arab Revolt, 96, 112; at-
tends 1939 round-table talks,
155; in 1948 war, 135; and Pal-
estine, 153, 169-170, 205; tac-
tics, 122, 137
Aden, 25
Africa, imperialism in, 4
'Ahd al-Aman, 71
Ahmad Bey, Bey of Tunisia, abol-
ishes slavery, 71; arms policy,
237; centralizing effort, 68; early
westernizer, 64; and Eastern
Question system, 76
Akkerman Convention (1826), 53
Alamein, El, see under El Alamein
Alexander, Tsar, and Greek Revolt,
49, 51, 215; and plans partition
Ottoman Empire, 35
Alexandretta (Hatay), 119, 267
Algeria, 25, 63-64, 92, 176
Ali Mahir, 127
Ali Pasha of Janina, 40-42, 50-51,
261
Allenby, Edmund H.H., 1st Vis-
count, 115-116
American Civil War, impact on
Egypt, 74
Andrassy Note (1875), 227
Anglo-Egyptian Treaty (1936),
124-125, 127
Anglo-French Entente (1904), 89

Anglo-Iraqi Treaty (1948), 135
Anglo-Ottoman Treaty (1838, Balta
Liman), 219
Ankara, 85
Aqaba, Gulf of, 203
Arab Bureau, 114-115
Arab Higher Committee, 126, 157
Arabism, in the Fertile Crescent,
145-149; and Nasserism, 162-
175; in the Ottoman period,
139-142; reasons for, 142-143;
and world opinion, 244
Arab-Israeli Wars, 159n; character-
istics of, 240-243
Arab League, 134
Arab League boycott, 157
Arab Legion, 136, 238-239
Arab National Fund, 155
Arab summit conferences, 159-161
Arabs, and Zionism, 213
Arafat, Yasir, 205, 245
al-Asad, Hafiz, and 1970 Jordan cri-
sis, 209; October War diplomacy,
242
Assyrian massacres, 250, 250n
Aswan High Dam, 203
Ataturk, Mustafa Kemal, 79, 85-86,
144; and Arabs, 97, 142, 267;
and Britain, 124
Austria, 22, 24; role in Eastern
Question politics, 37
Ayan, 38
Aziz Ali al-Misri, 127, 127n

Baghdad Pact, 268
Balfour, Arthur James, 1st Earl of,
152
Balfour Declaration, 97, 123, 137

357

Library of Congress Cataloging in Publication Data
Brown, L. Carl (Leon Carl), 1928-
International politics and the Middle East.
Bibliography: p.   Includes index.
1. Near East—Politics and government. I. Title.
DS62.8.B76 1984   956   83-43063
ISBN 0-691-05410-X
ISBN 0-691-10159-0 (lim. pbk. ed.)